Rube Marquard

With compliments and best of luck to my room mate Jack Meyers.
Rube Marquard

Rube Marquard

The Life and Times of a Baseball Hall of Famer

by LARRY D. MANSCH

McFarland & Company, Inc., Publishers
Jefferson, North Carolina, and London

Frontispiece: Richard W. "Rube" Marquard at age 22, posing proudly in his New York uniform, about to begin his first full season with the Giants. This photograph was a gift to the author from Lawrence Ritter.

British Library Cataloguing-in-Publication data are available

Library of Congress Cataloguing-in-Publication Data

Mansch, Larry D., 1958–
　　Rube Marquard : the life and times of a baseball Hall of Famer / by Larry D. Mansch.
　　　　p.　cm.
　　Includes bibliographical references (p.　) and index.
　　ISBN 0-7864-0497-3 (softcover : 50# alkaline paper) ♾
　　1. Marquard, Rube, 1889–1980.　2. Pitchers (Baseball)— United States — Biography.　I. Title.
GV865.M346M36　1998
796.357'092 — dc21　　　　　　　　　　　　　　　　98-17876
[B]　　　　　　　　　　　　　　　　　　　　　　　　CIP

©1998 Larry D. Mansch. All rights reserved

No part of this book may be reproduced or transmitted in any form or by any means, electronic or mechanical, including photocopying or recording, or by any information storage and retrieval system, without permission in writing from the publisher.

Manufactured in the United States of America

McFarland & Company, Inc., Publishers
*　Box 611, Jefferson, North Carolina 28640*

For my mother
and in loving memory of my father
who let the kids play ball

Acknowledgments

People who know will tell you that Lawrence Ritter's *The Glory of Their Times* is the greatest baseball book ever written. It has been my pleasure, over the past few years, to come to know Mr. Ritter. His kind encouragement led me to research the life of Rube Marquard, and the confidence he showed in me and in this project means more to me than I could ever say.

Several other people deserve special thanks. Fred Schuld is an educator and baseball historian who spent hours tracking down newspaper accounts of Rube's early days in Ohio and Indiana. Fred graciously invited me into his home, and together we toured old and new Cleveland, argued over Joe Jackson's banishment from baseball, and embarked on a memorable journey to Cooperstown. Fred has assisted many other authors in their research, but I don't believe that he has ever received the proper credit. I hope to correct that now.

Bryan Di Salvatore offered much-needed guidance, reviewed the manuscript and offered many excellent suggestions, and managed to keep a terrific sense of humor throughout. Charles Guggenheimer and his family allowed me access to Rube's personal photo album and provided a wealth of information on the final 25 years of his life. Kay Marquard cheerfully answered my many questions about Blossom Seeley, Benny Fields and the glamorous lives they led. Kay's husband, Richard Marquard, Jr., passed away in January of 1997, but he knew of this project and approved, a fact that means a great deal to Kay, and to me. John Hooper and Marie Hooper Strain, the children of Boston Red Sox great Harry Hooper, have done much to keep alive the memory of their father and offered a special insight into the friendship between Harry and Rube.

For varying degrees of advice, assistance, and encouragement, I also thank Charles Alexander; Mark Alvarez of the Society for American Baseball Research; Don Beach; Julius, Nicolo, and Paul Beccari; Margaret Borg; Mike and Rose Boyle; Jim Breatty; Sandy Brunner; Bucky Brush; Thomas Busch; Sharlene

Clawsen; Everett Cope; Bob Feller; Joe Garagiola; Louis Gobeo; Patty Gracey; Art Graham; Barbara Gregorich; Mick Holien; Lou Jacobson, who led me to the Guggenheimers; Fletcher Jennings; Dave Kelly; Darci Kirk-Harrington, senior photo researcher at the National Baseball Library; Lynn and Bill Lamberty; John Locke; Dee Lyon; Doug Macaulay; Norman Macht; Bob Maisel; Scott Mansch; Julie McCarthy; Sydney McKenna; Mark McLaverty; Scot Mondore; Michael Moore; Dr. Anne Murphy; Jamie Nicholson; Richard Puff; Ray Robinson; Gabriel Schecter, who, along with Thomas Busch, is the reigning expert on Charles Victor Faust; Mike and Anne Sherwood; John E. Smith, who loaned me his leather-bound edition of *The Tumult and the Shouting*, a true family heirloom; Carroll Tenney; Dolores Vassallo; Elizabeth Wright; and Frank Youngwerth.

Finally, and most of all, I thank the loves of my life, my wife Kim and our kids Bethany, Lincoln, Abigail, and Madison, who encouraged and supported me above and beyond the call as I chased after the Rube.

Contents

Acknowledgments		vii
Introduction		1
1.	The Sandlot Capital of the World	5
2.	The One Best Bet	18
3.	"I Can Beat Anybody"	28
4.	McGraw, Merkle, and Mayhem	40
5.	The $11,000 Lemon	53
6.	Beauty	70
7.	Dangerous Men	84
8.	A Popular Young Man	95
9.	Climbing the Ladder of Fame	102
10.	Scandal	120
11.	The Best Left-Handed Pitcher in Baseball	129
12.	"We Were Both Pretty Mad"	143
13.	The Boys from Across the Big Bridge	161
14.	"I Guess I'm the Fall Guy"	177
15.	Baseball's Most Picturesque Figure	188
16.	Finally Cooperstown	204
Appendices		
A.	Playing Record of Richard W. (Rube) Marquard	223
B.	Rube Marquard's Nineteen Straight Victories in 1912	225
Notes		227
Bibliography		241
Index		245

The Game of Games

Baseball! The name chimes with the Liberty Bell. It is as American as Independence Day ... as the Declaration of Independence or the Constitution. It's American by birth and type and characteristics. If there ever was a game which merited the name of "national," baseball is it....

Why, baseball is the essence of America, as far as it goes — and it goes a long way.

Editorial
The Cleveland *Leader*
July 4, 1907

Introduction

On a hot August afternoon in 1971, Richard "Rube" Marquard sat on a library porch on Main Street in Cooperstown, New York, and waited for the baseball commissioner, Bowie Kuhn, to call his name. Along with Satchel Paige, Harry Hooper, and four others, Rube was about to receive baseball's highest honor: induction into the Hall of Fame. In the crowd of several thousand people taking in the festivities were various National and American League officials, team owners and presidents, the widows of Babe Ruth and Lou Gehrig, and at least 21 other Hall of Fame members. Rube looked out over the crowd, waved to his wife Jane and stepson Charles, and reflected on a record-setting career that had ended 46 years earlier, a career that had brought him tremendous fame, a certain amount of fortune, and immeasurable fan adoration. And he wondered why this moment had been so long in coming.

He had been, after all, in the early days of the twentieth century, one of the most celebrated figures in the country. His rise to the top — as improbable as it was uniquely American — had played out like a Horatio Alger success story. In defiance of a disapproving father who could not understand his son's indifference toward education or his obsession with a crude ruffian's game, the teenaged Rube stole out of the house and rode the rails hobo-style across the Midwest in hopes of a minor league tryout. Unfairly treated, yet ever proud and stubborn, he returned home to the sandlots of Cleveland, where his 6'3" frame and rapidly developing left arm overmatched the local competition. He quickly caught the attention of scouts and signed with Canton and then Indianapolis of the high minor leagues.

After a wildly successful minor league career, Rube's services were purchased by the New York Giants in 1908 for the staggering sum of $11,000 — the highest amount ever paid for a ballplayer — in a transaction that shook the baseball world. Christened the "$11,000 Beauty," he overcame two years of frustration and helped the Giants continue as baseball's most successful franchise, dominating opponents with a flair and style that rivaled even the great Christy Mathewson and pleased his manager, the gruff and rebellious John McGraw. And Rube had the knack, it seemed, of being everywhere.

With a wicked curveball complementing a blazing fastball, Rube won 73 games in the pennant-winning years of 1911, 1912, and 1913. He won an incredible 19 straight games in 1912, still the record over 85 years later. He helped give "Home Run" Baker his nickname in a memorable World Series against Philadelphia, threw a no-hitter against Brooklyn, and once pitched all 21 innings against Boston. He witnessed the Merkle bonehead play and suffered through the Snodgrass muff. All told, he won 201 big league games, to the delight of a now proud and forgiving father.

Rube had the golden touch and came to love the high life in New York City. Between seasons he forged a career in show business, appearing on the vaudeville stage with his sensational wife Blossom Seeley. He authored his own newspaper columns, became one of the first athletes to star in a motion picture, and delighted crowds by catching baseballs thrown from high buildings. Yet despite his success — both on and off the field — he never quite received from baseball's hierarchy the credit he deserved. After he retired in 1925, he lived quietly, and his story went untold, or worse, unremembered.

But in 1966 Rube's lucky star shone again. An economics and finance professor at New York University named Lawrence Ritter traveled the country and collected oral histories of old-time ballplayers. His purpose was to record, in the words and memories of the players themselves, "what it was like to be young and a big leaguer in a high-spirited country a long time ago." Rube's story was prominently featured in the leadoff position in a book called *The Glory of Their Times*. The book became an instant classic, riding a crest of nostalgic longing for, and appreciation of, a simpler, more innocent time. And it introduced Rube and other players from that era to a new generation of fans. Five years later Rube was in the Hall of Fame.

I was ten years old when my father brought home a copy of *The Glory of Their Times*. That wonderful book instilled in me an interest in old-time baseball that has, over the years, become my passion. I've read and reread the life stories of Joe Wood, Edd Roush, and Sam Crawford, men who lived and played in a time several generations removed from our own — a time that is almost unrecognizable to us. Their stories fascinated me and provided answers — at least, the closest thing to answers we will ever get — to baseball's eternal questions. How did it feel to stand in the batter's box when Walter Johnson was whipping fastballs home at 100 miles per hour? Why did crowds cheer just as loudly when Babe Ruth struck out as when he blasted towering home runs? How did John McGraw and Connie Mack inspire their players and teams with such totally opposite styles and temperaments? Did Ty Cobb truly have no friends in baseball, and how did that contribute to his greatness? And ultimately, what was it like to be a ballplayer, *to be alive*, at the turn of the century in America?

Of all the stories Ritter collected, I was always drawn most powerfully to Rube's tale. While it seemed to be the quintessential American story, I sensed that it was too fanciful, too sanitized, to be completely true. Slowly, in bits and pieces, mildly troubling discrepancies crept up. And so I set out, 30 years after Ritter began his "strange crusade," on an odyssey of my own: to set the record straight, to find out the truth, to discover the real Rube Marquard.

Encouraged by Ritter himself, for the next couple of years I intensified my research. I traveled to Cooperstown and reviewed, among many others, the Marquard file. I read every book, article, and contemporary newspaper account that mentioned his name. With the assistance of Fred Schuld, a fellow member of the Society for American Baseball Research, I pored over box scores, scanned microfilm copies of the *Sporting News*, and reviewed musty editions of *Variety* magazine. I interviewed people who knew, or knew of, Rube. Of particular assistance were Charles Guggenheimer, Rube's stepson by his third marriage, and Kay Marquard, the wife of Rube's only son. Through my research I was able to dispel certain elements of the myth that Rube generated through *The Glory of Their Times*. (He was, for example, three years older than he always let on, a fact that shatters the image of an innocent teenager riding the rails.) I discovered much, much more, however, and the Rube Marquard that emerged often surprised but never disappointed me.

Rube lived an extraordinary life. He was blessed with astounding physical talents, and was familiar with fan adulation, but he was touched also by personal scandal made painfully public. For all the success, he endured his share of failure. He failed miserably his first two years with the Giants; the peach became better known as the lemon and he was roasted in the papers. He tried to jump to the outlaw Federal League in 1914, swearing falsely that he was not under contractual obligation to the Giants. His career was resurrected at Brooklyn, but in 1920 he was convicted of scalping World Series tickets and very nearly run out of the National League.

Yet Rube never lost his enthusiasm for the game or his appreciation for all that came his way because of it. He lived 55 years after his retirement from baseball and looked back on his career with fondness and pride, but never bitterness. He was good-natured, good-hearted, good-humored. He rebounded from his failed first marriage and matured into a decent and gentle man, respected by virtually all who knew him. He did not waste a day of his 93 years: "I want to smell the flowers while I can," he told Ritter in a statement that could summarize his entire life.

Finally then, in 1971 when Commissioner Kuhn called his name and introduced him to the crowd at Cooperstown, the long wait for baseball immortality seemed worthwhile. He was once again the star attraction, just as he had been on the pitcher's mound at the Polo Grounds or in front of the footlights at the Palace Theater or posing for a *Sporting News* photographer. It was the only fitting end to a remarkable life. The story of that life in its truthful entirety — the phenomenal success, the scandalous headlines, the barely controlled mayhem that was baseball in its early days — deserves to be told and needs to be remembered.

I make no pretense about capturing the heart and soul of baseball in a "high-spirited country a long time ago." That has been done, in magnificent fashion, by Lawrence Ritter. But I hope that I have discovered, and put to paper, the truth about a fascinating and colorful character who epitomized, as perhaps no other, that long-gone era.

Larry D. Mansch
Missoula, Montana
March 1998

CHAPTER 1

The Sandlot Capital of the World

On the afternoon of February 15, 1861, an enthusiastic crowd of several thousand people stood in the drizzling rain outside the Euclid Street railroad station in Cleveland, Ohio, hoping to catch a glimpse of president-elect Abraham Lincoln as he came through town on his way to Washington, D.C. Support for Lincoln was strong in Cleveland—he had carried 9 of the city's 11 wards in the recent election—and as he and his wife Mary and his son Robert stepped from the train onto the platform they were greeted with cheers, bells, whistles, and firecrackers. Three local military units, including the prestigious Light Dragoons, secured the area, and a cannon salute sounded as the Lincolns boarded a carriage led by four white horses. The military escort and the throng of people followed the carriage through the heart of Cleveland into the Public Square, the crowd growing larger and louder along the way. Despite the rain, Lincoln rested his stovepipe hat on his lap as he smiled and waved. Upon his arrival at the square, Lincoln addressed the crowd from the balcony of the Weddell House hotel, downplaying the rumored secession of Southern states as "an artificial crisis.... Let it alone, and it will go down of itself." He encouraged respect for the Constitution and urged all citizens to "support our Federal Union." His brief remarks were met with lengthy applause.[1]

Four years later the mood in Cleveland was quite different. Exactly two weeks after Lincoln's April 14 assassination, the funeral train carrying his remains arrived in the city as part of the 1700-mile procession back to Springfield, Illinois, for burial. A 36-gun salute was fired as the coffin was lifted from the train to a waiting hearse and escorted by an honor guard back to the same Public Square. Again a steady rain fell, but despite the weather nearly 150,000 mourners filed past the open coffin which rested on a raised catafalque.[2]

The Civil War had consumed the nation for those four years, and Cleveland had suffered greatly because of it. Nearly 10,000 men from Cuyahoga County had served; of these, about 1,700 had died and another 2,000 had returned disabled.[3] Public support for the war effort, however, had never faltered, and generally Lincoln's policies — including the emotional issue of emancipation — were popular. And while the war dragged on for much longer than anyone had predicted, along with it came unprecedented economic prosperity.

Cleveland initially profited from its agricultural base. The opening of the Erie and Ohio canals 20 years earlier made the city a key transportation link between midwestern wheat and grain fields and the markets of the eastern seaboard, and commerce increased threefold during the war. Cleveland played a major role in many areas of industrial production in support of the Union Army. By 1864, fully half of the iron ore mined around Lake Superior was shipped to Cleveland's forgeries, where it was transformed into heavy iron and steel castings, rivets, steamboat engine shafts, and propellers. Eight major railroads were head-quartered in Cleveland, making it the nation's transportation hub between New York and Chicago. Leather and dry goods, hospital and surgical supplies, armaments, even tobacco — all these industries grew and prospered directly because of the war. A young local entrepreneur named John D. Rockefeller profited most of all with his consignment business, dealing grain, meat, and produce to the army. In 1863, Rockefeller, in partnership with several others, began in Cleveland his oil refining business which spawned an economic empire.[4]

This unparalleled era of war-fueled prosperity continued in Cleveland for nearly seven decades, lasting until the depression of the 1930s. Not unexpectedly, Cleveland came to be seen as a city of great social and economic opportunity, and the population increased steadily and dramatically. In 1860, Cleveland was a relatively small town of 43,000 inhabitants; by the turn of the century it had become, with a population of nearly one million people, the largest city in Ohio.[5] A large percentage of that population increase was foreign-born: immigrants who were eager to work and to make Cleveland, and America, their home.

The majority of those immigrants who settled in Cleveland came from Germany. By 1870 some 27,051 Germans lived in Cuyahoga County, a figure that exceeded half its total foreign population.[6] Germans quickly gained a reputation for being industrious, motivated, and skilled workers. Seeking freedom primarily from political oppression and religious persecution — although some no doubt were motivated by economic hard times brought about by Rhineland crop failures of the mid–19th century — the Germans were opportunistic and appreciative of the benefits to be seized in the new land. They distinguished themselves as jewelers, tailors, furniture makers, and cabinetmakers. They became prominent in the areas of grocery and baked goods and in the manufacture of musical instruments, metal products, tool and dye machinery and other light machinery.

Opposite: **Downtown Cleveland in 1890. Photo courtesy Cleveland Public Library.**

The Germans were known for their love of music and fine arts and their appreciation of education. They also brought to Cleveland and other Ohio communities their beer-brewing skills. While Germans were, for the most part, proud of their cultural heritage and determined to preserve their old-world ethnicity, they were remarkable for their eagerness to accept and embrace the trappings of new surroundings and new lifestyles. German neighborhoods, with their traditional cultural and fraternal clubs, were established, but they quickly fused with other elements of Cleveland society. The Germans, more than any other immigrant group, most successfully assimilated into their new home.

The experience of the Marquardt family offers a prime example of the German immigrant-Cleveland connection. Ferdinand Marquardt sailed to America in October 1874, bringing with him his wife Christina and 10-year-old son Ferdinand, Jr., or Fred. The elder Marquardt was a stonecutter and easily found steady employment in the booming Cleveland economy in masonry, carpentry, and light labor. He eventually learned to cut meat, finding a job in 1882 at the Kellog & Jenkins butcher shop. He alternated between masonry and meatcutting, but was always steadily employed until he retired in 1895. The Marquardt family, which came to include another son, Paul, born in 1877, lived in a German neighborhood (inexplicably called "Little Cuba") at 43 Milford Drive in west Cleveland, some two and one-half miles from the southern shore of Lake Erie. Ferdinand's brother Charles and his family lived only a few houses down at 63 Milford. The houses in the neighborhood were small and plain, but the lots on which they rested offered plenty of room for expansion, and the Marquardts settled comfortably into Cleveland's working middle class.

Young Fred took after his father in at least two ways: he appreciated the importance of family and he was a willing and capable worker. On October 4, 1884, he married Lena Heiser, a young girl his own age who also had German roots, and in January 1885 their first child was born. They named him Ferdinand but called him by the more Americanized "Freddie"; they also dropped the "t" from their last name and it became more simply "Marquard." A second son, Richard William, was born on October 9, 1886. As with her first child, Lena was attended by a midwife and the baby was born at the home at 43 Milford, where the young couple lived with Fred's parents. More children followed: a daughter, Hattie, in March 1889, and two more sons, Frank in March 1890 and Herbert in March 1894.

Richard later claimed that he was actually born in 1889. It is not known exactly when or why he came up with this idea, but his birth certificate and figures from the 1900 census provide the correct date: October 9, 1886. The shaving of three years from his actual age would play an important part much later when he rose to baseball prominence, and in fact would figure indirectly in his election to the Hall of Fame. In any event, his actual birthdate was not discovered until 1995.[7]

After some initial work as a general laborer, Fred soon landed a job with

This birth certificate, discovered by Fred Schuld of Cleveland, Ohio, establishes that Rube was actually born on October 9, 1886, not 1889.

the city fire department, which offered well-paying, if hazardous, employment. In spare moments, he studied to become an engineer and eventually through his civil service connections he was hired by the Building Inspector Department as a stationary engineer. In this capacity he gave examinations to those seeking state certification and licenses as engineers. Fred held that position for nearly 30 years. By 1895 he was doing well enough that he could move his family into their own home, just down the street from his parents and uncle at 45½ Milford.

The neighborhood proved ideal for a young and growing family. Just four blocks to the west stood the Clark Avenue Grade School. Since 1872, when the German language was introduced as part of a bilingual program, old-world parents like the Marquards had approved of Cleveland's public schools, rather than private or home schools, and Fred and Lena happily enrolled their children. Directly across from the Marquard home stood a vacant lot where the Thomas Jefferson Junior High School, complete with grass playground and indoor gymnasium, would be built. Several blocks to the north stood the Trinity Lutheran Church, to which the Marquards belonged. And for the adults, just beyond the grade school stood a bowling alley, two dance halls, and a beer garden, which featured local brew from the nearby George Muth Brewery. There were, of course, reminders that modern life had not fully arrived: the streets were dirt (and would not be paved until 1910) and there were as yet no trolleys or sidewalks in the neighborhood. Further, the Cleveland Stockyards, owned by the Ohio Provision Company, operated nearby. Several feed stores, liveries, and coal factories also were in close proximity to the Marquard home and provided the expected foul smells.

All of the Marquard children were tall. Richard would grow to the height of 6'3", and even Hattie grew to be 6' tall. His features were sharp; he had a large nose, full, round chin, and brown hair and eyes, and would come to be considered a very handsome man (though he would always be slightly self-conscious about his jug ears). He had a nervous disposition but was generally good-natured, and he smiled and laughed easily. Richard was bright enough, his parents thought, but very strong-willed, and he showed only a marginal interest in academics. He was happiest when playing ball, for despite his gangly build he displayed an unusual amount of coordination and athleticism as a youngster. A fast runner, he was highly competitive by nature. He preferred to spend his days developing a strong throwing arm — he was left-handed — instead of studying his lessons, a habit which consistently aggravated his parents. Richard liked to walk down to Fire Station Number 20 at 4314 Clark Avenue, where his father worked for several years, and sit with the firemen and listen to their stories. Years later neighbors remembered "little Ritchie" roaming the backyards and playing fields of the area, his cap perched on his head at a jaunty angle (a habit that he kept throughout his career), tossing a ball into the air and catching it again in his child-sized glove. He could sometimes convince his father to play catch with him after work, although his grandfather was often more willing. Even a fairly serious injury did not slow him down. A playground accident left him with severely strained tendons in his neck, and as a result it became more comfortable for him to carry his head shifted slightly to the right. This sometimes painful condition, called torticollis but more commonly known as "wry neck," remained throughout his life and is plainly visible in most photographs.

Tragedy struck the Marquard household in 1899. Lena, perhaps weakened by successive childbirths, began to experience severe abdominal pain and dysentery. She developed a bowel infection and passed away on July 21. The children naturally turned to their grandmother to fill the void left by their mother's passing, and Christina gladly assumed the role. Richard seldom spoke again of his mother, but quickly accepted his grandmother and looked to her for guidance. Years later he fondly recalled her as "the sweetest woman he'd ever known" and proudly noted that "she raised me."[8] Still, the events did nothing to discourage his independent streak, and in fact fostered it. There was little his father could do to stop him from quitting school after the fifth grade, for Richard simply refused to attend any longer. He continued to dream about baseball.

The last years of the century were exciting ones for young Clevelanders. Inspired by the terrific success of Brooklyn's Coney Island, several amusement parks began operations in Cleveland. The Forest City Park boasted such attractions as a merry-go-round, shooting gallery, and bowling lanes, as well as the wildly popular "switchback" roller coaster. Its convenient proximity to the Willson Avenue trolley lines ensured the park's success; in 1893 over 100,000 customers gladly paid the fifteen-cent admission charge. Soon other amusement

1. The Sandlot Capital of the World

Rube was born across the street but grew up here at 46 Milford Avenue (now 46th Avenue) in west Cleveland. Photo courtesy Fred Schuld.

parks, including Euclid Beach Park on the eastern lakefront and Puritas Springs Park to the west, sprang up and met with similar success.[9]

While Cleveland civic leaders had, as early as 1870, envisioned a chain of city parks and allocated public funds for their care, a true park system was not put into place until the mid–1890s. But the wait was worthwhile for most Clevelanders; eventually a total of 12,000 acres was purchased and improved, and the system rivaled any in the country. Cleveland's park commissioners had set out to create, in such places as Edgewater Park and Woodland Hills, "public pleasure grounds ... a harmonious development of sylvan beauty to which all are welcome, rich and poor alike, where all may find rest and inspiration and pleasure." It is questionable whether young Richard saw the parks as a place where "pleasure parties and children might spend a few hours in enjoyment of rural conditions."[10] He was interested mainly in finding the nearest ballgame, and Cleveland offered plenty of places for that.

Baseball had, by the 1880s if not before, secured its place as the country's national game, and Cleveland, along with other cities in Ohio and the Great Lakes region, was not immune from the phenomenon. By mid-century the game was played in the fields and cow pastures of Cuyahoga County as well as in city parks and vacant lots. Despite pressures to ban it, or at least restrict the times and places it could be played, baseball was "a daily spectacle at Public Square" as early as 1857.[11]

Brookside Park was the most convenient place for the five Marquard children to test their skills. Located on Fulton Road and Denison Avenue on the city's southwest side, Brookside was just a short eight-block walk from home. The park was developed from land purchased in 1894 (making it Cleveland's oldest park) and offered a variety of attractions, both natural and man-made. Built on a high bluff encompassing some 1200 acres, it provided picnic grounds, tennis courts, and several baseball diamonds where some of Cleveland's best amateur and semipro teams gathered for scheduled games, workouts, or batting practice. It was not uncommon for games between amateur teams to draw as many as 8,000 spectators at the park's immense natural amphitheater playing field; it was estimated that some championship games drew ten times that number. As he grew, Richard's throwing skills were in demand around Brookside's ball diamonds. He threw hard and fairly straight (when he wasn't trying to impress anyone), and his arm did not quickly tire. Since he had, as of yet, no curveball to speak of, the hitters liked to see him on the mound. He loved to pitch even if only in batting practice, and despite his young age he represented a formidable challenge.

And it was probably here, during Brookside Park practice sessions, that Richard discovered that in addition to a live arm he possessed the unique ability to hit from both sides of the plate. As his career progressed, he developed a trait virtually all pitchers share: he loved to hit. In his case, he got pretty good at it.

Fred Marquard had no particular objection to baseball as recreation. He had himself enjoyed athletics to some degree as a boy, but he was convinced that education was the key to his childrens' future and he was adamant about keeping sports in the proper perspective. Baseball, in particular, might be all right as exercise, but it was ludicrous to suggest that it could somehow provide a career. Richard had other ideas; all he could think of, "morning, noon, and night, was baseball."[12]

By the turn of the century, when Richard was 13, there were dozens of amateur baseball teams in Cleveland, as well as numerous semipro or company teams. These teams, often sponsored by local businesses, restaurants, or hotels, played at Brookside, Garfield, Washington, and Woodland Hills Park (which boasted eight diamonds by itself), among other places. The city's daily newspapers regularly covered the action from all of these venues, printing short summaries of games, box scores, and occasional photographs. These photos reveal as much about the crowds as the games: gentlemen in suits and top hats, accompanied by their lady friends in full dresses and bonnets, holding parasols to ward off the warm Sunday afternoon sun. There were no bleachers at these fields and often no grandstand. The spectators would view the game from a safe distance behind the outfielders or, if they dared, from along the foul lines extending out from first and third bases. Ballgames in Cleveland were true social events; there were so many teams and leagues, fan support was so strong, and the competition so intense that the city prided itself on being "the sandlot capital of the world."[13]

Because of his size and strong arm, Richard was, while still a teenager, a highly recruited ballplayer. Although he surely played earlier, the first-known newspaper accounts of his career appear in 1905 editions of the Cleveland *Plain Dealer*. That summer, when he was 18 years old, he pitched for the Colonials, a team sponsored by a hotel of the same name, in the City League, one of Cleveland's highest levels of amateur competition. While the team was a poor one — at one point it sported a record of one win against 15 losses — Richard was becoming a star. On August 6, in front of over 4,500 spectators, he struck out 16 batters in a game against Brittons Printing, and the *Plain Dealer* duly noted that the feat set a new City League record.

The Colonials, and the City League, concluded the season's schedule in early September, and Richard was free to hook up with another team. He joined the semipro Telling Strollers, an independent team sponsored by the Telling Ice Cream Company. Telling was a well-established Cleveland firm which sold and delivered milk, ice cream, and other dairy products. It also traditionally fielded one of the stronger semipro teams in the area; its players were typically a few years older and more experienced than those on amateur teams. Since its team belonged to no league, it was able to compete against local as well as regional teams. Telling was organized and managed by Cleveland city treasurer Herman Schleman, who was known for his ability to recognize superior, if raw, local talent, showcase those players for a season or two, and then convince minor league teams to try them out. Since 1900 dozens of Schleman's protégés had gone on to professional baseball careers, at least five making it all the way to the majors.

Richard's first opportunity to pitch against an out-of-town team came on September 14th when Telling traveled to Conneaut, a small town some 80 miles from Cleveland on the Pennsylvania border, to play their Red Sox. He won the game 4–3, striking out eight while walking only two and allowing seven hits. One spectator at that game was Ed Stearns, manager of Painesville, another independent team. Stearns was about to lead his club through Ohio and Pennsylvania for a series of games against top semipro teams, and he so badly wanted Richard to join him that he advertised in the *Plain Dealer*, requesting that Richard and a few other standouts "call and see him ... at the Kennard House Sunday from 3:30 to 9 P.M."[14] Richard had no hope of convincing his father, however, that the trip was a good idea, and he was not allowed to meet with Stearns.

Instead Richard continued to pitch outstanding baseball for Telling. On September 16, only two days after his victory over Conneaut, he pitched again at Salem, allowing only one hit over 13 innings in a scoreless tie. He struck out 10 in what the *Plain Dealer* called "without doubt the best game ever played in this vicinity."[15]

Back in Cleveland a week later, Richard dominated the Olmsted Falls team, striking out 13 while beating them 9–3. When not pitching, Richard played right field for Telling; at one point in late September he was hitting for a .500 average. On September 24, this time in Olmsted Falls, he was called out at third while trying to stretch a double into a triple. The call so infuriated him and his team that they walked off the field "amid hoots and jeers" of the crowd and forfeited the game 9–0.[16]

Telling continued to travel and play while decent weather held. On October 7, Richard shut out Salem 4–0; the *Plain Dealer* noted that he was "invincible" with men on base. It was not until the season finale on October 16 that he was beaten, by a group of All-Stars from Sandusky. The paper proclaimed that the biggest surprise of the day came when "Marquard was ordered to the bench."[17]

It was sometime during the 1905 season, as well, that another significant event occurred. A nickname was hung on him which stood for the rest of his life: Richard became "Rube." Much later he claimed that he was given the nickname after a 1908 pitching performance in which an impressed sportswriter noticed a resemblance to Rube Waddell, one of the great hurlers and eccentric figures, of the era. While Richard might have been likened to Waddell, as he claimed, newspaper accounts relate that on his first road trip to Conneaut in 1905 he was so eager to leave that he was the first player to arrive at the train station, carrying a "typical farmerish carpet bag," and teammate Tommy Hawkins named him Rube.[18]

Fred, however, was not impressed with a few newspaper clippings or stories about pro ballplayers, and he remained displeased with the direction his son's life was taking. Years later Richard recounted the nightly arguments he had with his father on the subject:

> "Now listen," Dad would say, "I want you to cut this out and pay attention to your studies. I want you to go to college when you're through high school, and I don't want any foolishness about it. Without an education you won't be able to get a good job, and then you'll *never* amount to anything."
>
> "I already have a job," I'd say.
>
> "You've got a job? What are you talking about?"
>
> "I'm going to be a ballplayer."
>
> "A ballplayer?" he'd say, and throw his hands up in the air. "What do you mean? How can you make a living being a ballplayer? I don't understand why a grown man would wear those funny-looking suits in the first place."
>
> "Well," I'd answer, "you see policemen with uniforms on, and other people like that. They change after they're through working. It's the same way with ballplayers."
>
> "Ha! Do ballplayers get paid?"
>
> "Yes, they get paid."
>
> "I don't believe it!"

Richard's grandfather would often take his grandson's side in the debate:

"Listen," he'd say to my father, "when you were a youngster I wanted you to be something, too. I wanted you to be a stone-cutter, same as I was when I came over from the old country. But no, you wouldn't listen. You wanted to be an engineer. So you became an engineer. Now Richard wants to be a baseball player. He's so determined that nothing is going to stop him. Let's give him a chance and see what he can do."

But Dad would never listen. "Ballplayers are no good," he'd say, "and they never will be any good."

And with that he'd slam the door and go outside and sit on the porch and not talk to either my grandfather or me for the rest of the evening.[19]

For all the arguments, Rube never altered his position, and he remained determined to forge a career in baseball. He pitched briefly for the Waterworks Construction team in early spring 1906 and then seemed to catch a big break. In March he was invited to try out for the Lancaster team of the Ohio-Pennsylvania League, a low-level minor league but still a step above the semipros. Manager Gray was delighted that his team signed the young star. "We are expecting to develop a cracking good southpaw in Marquard," he said.[20] Rube's father reluctantly agreed that he could travel the 100 miles to Lancaster but was relieved when the deal fell through. Rube became ill and pitched poorly, allowing five runs without retiring a batter, and Lancaster let him go. He returned, dejected, to Cleveland.

In May, though, Rube got another chance. He received a letter from two friends, Bill Sump and Staley Sheldon, who had caught on with the Waterloo team of the Iowa State League. The team was short on pitching, the letter read, and Rube had been recommended to the manager, Ernest Anklam, yet another Cleveland product. Could Rube come to Iowa and try out?

Rube knew that his father would never approve of a trip across country for a chance, and only half a chance at that, to play minor league baseball. He wrote to the club and asked for some travel money as an advance on the contract he felt sure he would be offered. He received a telegram from Anklam officially inviting him to try out, but there was no advance money. Rube wrote again asking for money, but this time received no reply. Finally, after three anxious weeks, he told his father that he was going on a camping trip with the Boy Scouts and made his way to the railroad station. He set out on the greatest adventure of his young life, one that would become a defining part of his legend.

Many years later he recounted the trip (misstating his actual age of 19):

> From Cleveland, Ohio, I bummed my way to Waterloo, Iowa. I was sixteen years old and I'd never been away from home before. It took me five days and five nights, riding freight trains, sleeping in open fields, hitching rides any way I could. My money ran out on the third day, and after that I ate when and how I could.
>
> Finally, though, I arrived at my destination. It was early in the evening

of the fifth day. The freight train slowly drew into the Illinois Central station at Waterloo, Iowa, and just before it stopped I jumped off and went head over heels right in front of the passenger house.[21]

Tired, hungry, and exhausted, Rube made his way to the local Smoke Shop where the Waterloo players passed the time. There he met manager Anklam, who also played second base for the team. Anklam informed Rube that he would pitch the following day against Keokuk. Rube's new "teammates" helped him get cleaned up and allowed him to sleep on a spare cot. The next morning they found a uniform for him, although it was a couple sizes too small.

Rube's professional baseball debut took place on June 15, 1906, in Keokuk, Iowa, before a crowd of about 750. Despite his adventurous hobo-style trip and the awkward circumstances of playing with a group of strangers, Rube pitched well. He won the game 6–2, allowing only five hits while striking out three. The performance merited feature coverage in the Waterloo *Daily Courier*, the article noting his apparent cocksure attitude as well as his throwing abilities:

> Big "Rube" Marquard blew in from Waterloo yesterday and announced that he intended to pitch one game against Keokuk. Sometime since Anklam had sent Marquard to the stables to rest up and when he unblanketed him yesterday and put the toe-weights on him he cavorted around the field like a sure winner, and he made good, too.
>
> The best Keokuk could do off him was five scattered hits, only one of which, Percival's two-bagger, accounted for anything. The Waterloo southpaw was the money-back goods at every stage. The winning of the game, however, must be credited to the entire Waterloo team, which, with one exception, played a faultless game behind Marquard.[22]

Five days later Rube pitched a second game for Waterloo, also against Keokuk. Again he struck out three, but allowed 11 hits and walked four in losing 6–3. His team committed three errors, however, which led to five unearned runs for Keokuk. Many years later, while not remembering that he had pitched a second time, Rube distinctly remembered the treatment he received from the Waterloo manager after the game:

> With that I felt sure I'd be offered a contract. So after the game I went to [the manager] and said, "Well, I showed you I could deliver the goods. Can we talk about a contract now?"
>
> "Oh," he said, "Keokuk is in last place. Wait until Oskaloosa comes in this weekend. They're in second place. They're a tough team, and if you beat them then we'll talk."
>
> "Can't I get any money, any advance money, on my contract?" I asked him.
>
> "You haven't got a contract," he said.
>
> "All right," I said, and I didn't say another word.[23]

That night Rube went back to the railroad station in Waterloo. He spoke to the stationmaster, who, having been to the ballgame that afternoon, was surprised to see Rube ready to leave town. When he heard about the unfair treatment Rube had received, the stationmaster helped him steal onto a freight train headed for Chicago. Rube arrived in Chicago at about three in the morning, and with several hours to kill before he could catch a train bound for Cleveland, he wandered around the city until he found a deserted fire engine house. He had visited his father's fire house many times, of course, and he felt comfortable in walking into this one. He sat down in front of a big-bellied iron stove and fell asleep.

Eventually Rube was rousted out of his nap when the firemen returned, and they threatened to have him arrested. But after hearing his story, they turned sympathetic and took a liking to him. They got up a pool of five dollars or so and helped him get started on his way home. Rube thanked them and promised, "When I get to the Big Leagues, I'm coming out to visit you when we get to Chicago."[24]

Rube's experience in Iowa left him disappointed but still determined to make baseball his life's career. He was more than a little embarrassed, as well, telling his friends and the *Plain Dealer* that he hadn't made it in Waterloo "because of a lame arm."[25] He came home, as he had left, without a contract, but he felt more certain than ever that he had the talent to compete at the professional level. He returned to his father's house and to the sandlots of Cleveland and began to hope again for another chance. He did not have to wait for long.

Chapter 2

The One Best Bet

At age 19, Rube was still welcome to live at home but was expected to help out with his family's bills, in return. He agreed to pitch again for Telling Ice Cream and took full-time employment with them, as well (although his father would argue it was actually the other way around). Rube later recalled that he was paid $25 per week by Telling: "$15 for checking the cans on the truck that would take the ice cream away, and $10 a Sunday, when I pitched for the company team."[1] And there was an important added benefit that came with the job: he could help himself to all the ice cream he could eat.

At his full height and now weighing 185 pounds, and having played in and around the sandlots of Cleveland for at least three years, Rube was seen as the best semipro pitcher in town. He favored the era's popular twice-around windmill windup, rocking back from the pitching rubber and then smoothly coming forward with an overhand delivery. He had always thrown hard and was just wild enough to concern opposing batters; now he had developed a slow-breaking curveball that kept them offstride. The Telling company team was the strongest semipro club in the Cleveland area, and with Rube on the mound it was nearly unbeatable. But Rube was constantly looking for better offers. By July he agreed to pitch for the Lincoln Park team, but before he ever appeared with them he joined Baehr's Brewery of the Twilight League (a six-team league featuring clubs sponsored by, among others, Cleveland Telegraph, the Clark Hat Company, and Glueck Cigars). Rube continued to dominate the local competition. On July 20 he beat the Medina team 8–2 while striking out nine. Three days later he overcame six errors, including four by his shortstop, and beat English Woolen Mills 10–7. "Marquard had the Woolens at his mercy, striking out 15," noted the *Plain Dealer*, "and had his team played ball behind him instead of taking things easy would have kept the Woolens from scoring in a number or instances."[2] Rube, though, was far from satisfied with his limited local notoriety, and he continued to aspire to a professional career, preferably with his hometown major league Naps.

Rube had, in recent years, caught a close glimpse of the professional game. During the summers of 1904, 1905, and 1906, he regularly acted as batboy for the Naps of the American League. He idolized such players as the legendary Napoleon Lajoie (after whom the team was named), Elmer Flick, and Bill Bradley. He eventually even pitched a game or two for Bradley's Boo Gang, a loosely organized group of big leaguers who barnstormed around Ohio in the fall after the regular season ended. Rube felt increasingly sure that he could make the jump into pro ball — perhaps even all the way to the major leagues — if he got the chance.

Efforts to organize Cleveland's better amateur and semipro players and teams into a strictly professional status had been made for many years. Generally those efforts followed, if not mirrored, what was happening in the larger metropolises of the East Coast.

It was in New York, logically, that the first truly organized baseball enterprise came about. The Knickerbockers Base Ball Club of New York was begun in 1842 by a group of socially prominent gentlemen led by Alexander Cartwright. These men enjoyed occasional afternoons of tasteful exercise and, more importantly, delighted in excluding those thought not to be sufficiently upper class. The Knickerbockers were soon joined by the equally snobbish Gothams, Eagles, and Empires baseball clubs, as well as four more from Brooklyn. These teams played a distinctive brand of ball called the "New York Game," which featured bases or posts laid out in a diamond shape. Their most radical departure from other styles was their elimination of "soaking" or putting the baserunner out by hitting him with a thrown ball. The attempts of these metropolitan social clubs, however, to monopolize the game and limit it to those of the "educated and refined classes" were futile. The popularity of the game ensured that it could never be confined or restricted to an elite few, and it soon spread. In just five years, there were over 50 organized clubs in New York alone. In January 1857 the first city-wide convention was held, resulting in the formation of the National Association of Base Ball Players, complete with constitution and by-laws, and the "organized" game moved westward with the homesteaders and pioneers.

The Civil War temporarily stalled the game's progression, but it was not forgotten. It was played by Union soldiers awaiting orders, by prisoners of war, and even by bureaucrats on the White House lawn. When the war ended the game quickly reestablished itself as the "National Game." No other sport, activity or athletic endeavor even came close to matching baseball's stronghold position as America's favorite pastime.

The Midwest, and particularly Ohio, rivaled New York in baseball popularity in those years. Led by the Live Oak club of Cincinnati, a group of Ohio teams, including one from Cleveland, organized the Ohio Baseball Federation, affiliated with yet another regional association, and sent delegates to the 1867 National Association convention in New York. Accepted guidelines and regulations of all these organizations prohibited both gambling (a policy that was routinely ignored from the beginning) and the paying of players (a policy that soon was abandoned). The Ohio organizations shared two very unique characteristics, however, which set them apart from most of their eastern counterparts. They enthusiastically played Sunday ball, and they tolerated, even encouraged, the sale and consumption of alcohol by fans during games. The established clubs in the East thought these practices were uncouth and crude and made a mockery of the social refinements upon which their game was initially founded. But the ideas were overwhelmingly popular among western fans, not to mention the numerous local breweries in places like Toledo, Cincinnati, and Cleveland.[3]

The first true organized team in Cleveland was the Forest City Baseball Club, founded in 1865. Originally an amateur team, the "Forest Citys" scheduled games against other Cleveland clubs as well as those from throughout northern Ohio. But several factors prompted the club to claim professional status only a few years later. Along with baseball's enormous popularity came financial concerns and abuses. Communities and ballclubs sought out the best players and began to pay them to perform. Gambling flourished, and concerns over thrown games increased. The Red Stockings of Cincinnati claimed the distinction of organizing the country's first true professional team, and in 1869 they toured the country, taking on all comers. They won 60 games without a defeat, playing in front of an estimated 200,000 spectators, and proved conclusively that professional players would easily outclass most amateur teams and make a nice profit, as well.[4] The Forest Citys followed suit, then, and renounced their amateur status, soliciting the best possible ballplayers through newspaper advertisement. The following year, 1870, saw the first national convention for strictly professional teams. The Cleveland Forest Citys team was a charter member of the first pro league, and pro baseball took a foothold in the city.

The Cleveland club of 1871 joined teams from Boston, Brooklyn, New York, Philadelphia, Washington, Troy, Chicago, Fort Wayne, and Rockford to form the new National League. Cleveland played its home games at a field located at Willson and Garden Streets. Reserved season tickets were sold at the club ticket office in the Rawson and Pratt clothing store on the Public Square. The purchaser could choose between two ticket options: six dollars for a single season ticket or ten dollars for two. With either plan, the holder was allowed the luxury of parking his carriage along the first or third baseline, locations which provided prime views of the action.

The club was not particularly successful on the field, finishing in sixth place with a record of 44–72, but it did figure in one notable historic event in that first year. Its game against the Fort Wayne Kekiongas was the first ever memorialized by a condensed box score, the invention of sportswriter Henry Chadwick (the Forest Citys lost 2–0).

The franchise was involved in other firsts a few years later. On June 12, 1880, Worcester's John Lee Richmond threw the first perfect game in organized baseball history, beating Cleveland 1–0. And in October the club played for the first time at New York's already famous Polo Grounds — a true palace of a structure with player clubhouses, covered benches, and an imposing grandstand. The Forest Citys lost two games to the Metropolitans.

Passion for baseball ran high in those early days. Umpires were tormented and abused by teams and fans alike, and policemen were routinely called out to keep order. Most players were obsessed with the game, as well. Forest City shortstop Al Hall broke his leg against Cincinnati and was never able to play again. He was so disconsolate that he was diagnosed with "intense melancholia" and died in an insane asylum in 1885.

For all the excitement, teams were not, for the most part, financially successful in the first years of professional baseball. In 1883, for example, every club in the league except Chicago lost money, and owners scrambled to draw fans to the parks. (They were not above outlandish promotional stunts. Philadelphia sponsored exhibition games against "all-Chinese" teams, and on occasion all-female and even all-amputee teams performed against local pros.) Civic and business leaders in Cleveland, however, remained optimistic that, despite the popularity of the city's sandlot leagues, with prudent management and consistent promotion the money-making potential of pro ball was enormous. In 1889 brothers Stanley and Frank Robinson saw the potential relationship between baseball and the horse-drawn trolley and streetcar companies they owned, the Payne and Superior Avenue lines. They fielded an American Association (and later National League) team called, by sportswriters and fans, the Spiders, because of the skinny and spindly appearance of several players. They built ballparks directly on their streetcar line, first at Payne Avenue and East 39th street and then at Lexington and East 66th, to attract paying customers.

The Spiders endured rocky times. Led by player-manager Pat TeBeau, the team challenged the infamous Baltimore Orioles of John McGraw, Ned Hanlon, and Wilbert Robinson for claim to the title of baseball's rowdiest club. They harassed opposing teams, fans, even umpires. Led by local farmboy Denton True "Cy" (for Cyrus) Young, George "Nig" Cuppy, and Louis Sockalexis (a Penobscot Indian, former Holy Cross and Notre Dame athlete, and notorious alcoholic who had to be bailed out of jail in order to join the club), the Spiders won the Temple Cup championship in 1895 and were crowned baseball's best team. But success was short-lived, for Robinson transferred several key players to St. Louis, another franchise he purchased in 1898, and angered fans. After a pathetic record of 20–134, Cleveland was dropped from the National League in 1900.

But Cleveland was far too fertile a baseball town to go without a professional franchise, and it was an Ohio native who helped bring one there to stay. Ban Johnson was born in 1864 at Norwalk and attended Marietta College, where he earned some degree of notoriety as a catcher who played fearlessly without glove, mask, or chest protector. His first job was as a sportswriter for Cleveland's *Commercial-Gazette*, but in 1894 opportunity knocked. When Cincinnati Red

Leg manager Charles Comiskey was fired, he teamed with Johnson to revive the old Western League. League franchises were located in Kansas City, Toledo, Minneapolis, Milwaukee, Indianapolis, Sioux City, Grand Rapids, and Detroit, and Johnson was named president. In 1901 he convinced two Cleveland businessmen, John Kilfoyle and Charles Somers, to finance a team in what was now renamed the American League.

Kilfoyle was the well-to-do owner of a men's furnishings store in Cleveland, but it was Somers, who was in the coal business with his father, who provided the greater amount of cash. In just two short years, Johnson had persuaded Somers to invest nearly one million dollars; he bankrolled other clubs in the league as well as his own.

The Cleveland team played in League Park on Lexington Avenue. Until 1909, when seating was expanded threefold, the wooden park could accommodate 9,000 fans. An open-air press box held sportswriters, and announcements were made by megaphone. The team was originally called the Blues and then was named the Bronchos. From 1903 through 1912, the team was affectionately called the Naps, after sensational player-manager Napoleon Lajoie. But when Lajoie was traded, the new nickname "Molly McGuires" never seemed to catch on. Via newspaper poll, the fans in 1915 voted for "Indians" after Sockalexis, their favorite player of the old National League Spiders team of the 1890s, and that name finally stuck.

While Lajoie was easily the favorite player of most Cleveland fans in the first years of the century, they also followed with great pride the careers of local boys who had become successful major league players. Young Rube admired, for example, players such as Tommy Leach, Jimmy Austin, Bill Bradley, and the Delahanty brothers, who had risen from modest, working-class neighborhoods of Cleveland to the big-time.

Leach was born in French Creek, New York, in 1879 but moved to Cleveland in the early 1880s. His father was a printer and settled his family in the city's Irish neighborhood. Tommy began his ball-playing career in 1898 with Louisville; despite his small size (5'6", 150 pounds) he lasted 19 years in the major leagues, most of them with Pittsburgh.

Jimmy Austin was born in Wales in 1879. His father was a shipbuilder who found steady employment in Cleveland in 1885. Abandoning a promising career as a machinist, Jimmy first played with the Franklin Athletic Club, a local amateur team, and then with the semipro factory team in Warren, Ohio, before breaking into organized ball with Dayton, of the Central League, in 1904. Four years later he joined the Yankees as a third baseman.

It was another hometown boy, however, who was most admired by Rube and other young Clevelanders his age. "Big Ed" Delahanty was the oldest of five brothers who made it to the major leagues, and one of the very best players of the era. He had a lifetime batting average of .346 and was still in his prime at age 35, when he died mysteriously at Niagara Falls in 1903.

In addition to his blossoming career in Cleveland's sandlot leagues, Rube served for a time as batboy for the Naps. He enjoyed hanging around the park and worked hard to impress the big leaguers. He was able to sit on the bench for games, run their errands, and sometimes, when not daydreaming about himself playing for the Naps, frequent their establishments. The most popular such place was a sporting goods store owned by Nap third baseman Bill Bradley and Charlie Carr, who managed and played first base for Indianapolis of the American Association. The store was located at 724 Prospect Avenue in downtown Cleveland in a structure which still stands. It was here that Rube's professional baseball career really began.

Rube recalled much later that he received a postcard from the Cleveland front office in early spring 1907 requesting that he come down and sign a contract to play for the Naps. Team owners Somers and Kilfoyle offered, according to Rube, a salary of $100 per month. Rube turned that offer down, noting that he already made that much money with the Telling Company, and left indignantly. In reality the Naps made no such offer. Manager Lajoie and scout Bade Myers had seen Rube pitch plenty of times around Cleveland, but both thought that he was not yet ready for big league competition. He was talented enough, but was "too awkward, and would never field his position properly."[5] Rube had little chance of beginning his career with the hometown team, but he got an unexpected boost from his friends at the sporting goods store.

Charlie Carr was interested in Rube for his Indianapolis club, but he thought that Rube needed some seasoning first. He offered Rube a contract, with the understanding that while the property of Indianapolis, he would report to Class B Canton of the Central League, a step down from the American Association, to be sure, but a shot at pro ball nonetheless. Ironically, the Canton manager was Bade Myers, who as a Naps scout had passed on Rube. While it is highly unlikely, as Rube maintained later, that he demanded and received a contract for $200 per month to play for Canton, he probably received a bit more than his salary with Telling or Baehr's. All he had to do now was break the news to his father.

Rube described that "terrible night" before he was to leave for Canton:

> Finally, Dad said, "Now listen, I've told you time and time again that I don't want you to be a professional ballplayer. But you've got your mind made up. Now I'm going to tell you something: when you cross that threshold, don't come back. I don't ever want to see you again."
>
> "You don't mean that, Dad," I said.
>
> "Yes I do."
>
> "Well, I'm going," I said, "and some day you'll be proud of me."
>
> "Proud!" he said. "You're breaking my heart, and I don't ever want to see you again."
>
> "I won't break you heart," I said. "I'll add more years to your life. You wait and see."[6]

Still stinging from the disappointment of perceived mistreatment at Waterloo and the failed tryout with Lancaster, Rube could not be sure how many more opportunities to play pro ball would come his way. With or without his father's blessing, he made the trip south to Canton. He reported, as did the other hopefuls, to manager Myers at the Barnett Hotel. He was confident, yet cautious, and would not rent space in a rooming house until he was assured of making the team. His arrival in town was noted by the Canton *Repository*, the daily paper which covered the Reds. Charlie Carr was quoted: "Marquard is a capable looking athlete, and he will be able to deliver the goods."[7]

The year 1907 was the fifth season of the "powerful and well-conducted" Central League, which consisted of the Canton and Dayton clubs in Ohio; Evansville, South Bend, and Terre Haute in Indiana; Grand Rapids in Michigan; Springfield in Illinois; and Wheeling in West Virginia. An unusually wet spring hampered the preseason training efforts of all the teams, which at this low level of the minors could not afford trips south. Canton had to postpone nine exhibition games while playing only once, but in that game Rube was featured. He pitched three innings against the Colts, a good local semipro club, and "performed brilliantly," striking out two and allowing one hit, a double.[8]

The season began on April 27 with the Springfield Babes visiting Canton. The following day saw Rube's debut. He pitched well until the eighth, when he was touched for two doubles and a triple, and two runs. The *Repository* proclaimed the Reds "hitless wonders" in the 2–0 defeat. A week later, this time in Springfield for the Babes' home opener, Rube was not as effective but had better luck. After an unauspicious start — he hit the first batter, center-fielder Collins, in the head with a fastball and knocked him unconscious, drawing heavy boos from the crowd of 1200 fans — he allowed nine hits but won the game 7–6. He showed his batting skills, and his footspeed as well, by banging out a triple which scored two runs.

Rube continued to pitch well, and win, for the Reds. On May 10 he beat South Bend 2–0, and four days later he beat them again, 3–1. Hampered by what the papers called "a sore left wing," he sat out a start or two, then on May 25 defeated the defending champion Ganders of Grand Rapids 4–3, striking out six hitters. The next day, Sunday May 26, was the series finale; the largest crowd of the season, however, was sent home just half an hour before the scheduled 2:30 start. The league directors cancelled the day's games upon learning that Mrs. William McKinley, wife of the Ohio–native president, had died. It was the first day off of the season for the Reds, who after one month had a record of 13–10, good enough for second place.

They traveled next to Wheeling, "home of the lengthy smokes," to take on the first-place Stogies. Rube lost a heartbreaker in the morning game of a doubleheader, giving up the game's only run on two errors and a sacrifice fly in the 11th inning. The Reds lost the remaining three games of the series, dropping under .500 and into fifth place.

The Reds continued to play mediocre baseball — save for the performance of manager and first baseman Myers, they were a weak-hitting ballclub — but Rube excelled. On June 8 he beat Terre Haute for his fifth victory of the season, and the *Repository* stated: "It is very clear that when in form and possessed of confidence, Pitcher Marquard is as good as any twirler in the league ... and has developed into a sight for sore optics."[9] On June 14 he beat Evansville 3–2 in a game prolonged more than two hours as "both teams wrangled with the umpire."[10] He won again on June 31, defeating Dayton 4–3, striking out eight and "mystifying the opposition with his sidewheel offerings."[11]

On July 12 he beat Evansville again in 13 innings, and on the twenty-first he won his ninth straight game, at Dayton by a score of 3–2. Rube drove in the winning run himself in the top of the 12th inning. The contest was played in front of a crowd of 4,000 "highly partisan Dayton fans," according to the *Repository*, fans that "got after the Reds at the drop of the hat."[12] Rube finally lost on July 26, 2–0 against the Springfield Babes, allowing only six hits. Four days later he got back on the winning track with a 2–1 victory over Terre Haute.

Rube's first horrible outing of the season came on August 2 in Evansville, where he was driven from the mound in the first inning after surrendering five runs. He came back the very next day, however, and pitched a six-hit shutout, beating the Knights 6–0.

Although the Reds continued to struggle — they remained at the .500 level throughout the season, never climbing higher than third place in the standings — Rube had easily become the league's premier pitcher. He continued to roll through August and September, winning regularly and striking out ten or twelve batters a game. When the season ended on September 17, Rube had won 23 of Canton's 69 victories. Only two other pitchers in the league managed as many as 20 wins, and Rube no doubt would have earned more had he had decent support from Reds hitters: the team batting average was an anemic .211.

When the season ended, Rube returned home to Cleveland, although he was still on shaky terms with his father. Rather than spend the winter in the house he had grown up in, he kept a close yet safe distance and moved in with his older brother Fred, who lived nearby at 4180 West 46th street. While close in age, the two brothers held very different outlooks on life and fostered their own ambitions. Fred was practical, already a homeowner at 23, and steadily employed as a machinist. In June he would marry and begin his family. Rube, however, was primarily interested in moving up baseball's ladder.

Rube spent most days that winter at Charlie Carr's sporting goods store on Prospect Avenue downtown. Carr was impressed by Rube's performance at Canton, and it was agreed that Rube was ready to pitch for Carr's Class AA Indianapolis Browns team in the tough American Association. Arthur "Paddy" Livingston, another Cleveland boy and a veteran of four minor league (and brief major league) seasons, would be the catcher, and, Carr hoped, a steadying influence on Rube and several other young pitchers he had signed. Rube and

Livingston lived near each other on the west side and worked out together in local gymnasiums. Livingston knew that Rube would need more than just a live arm to be successful at Indianapolis, and he spent many hours discussing the finer, mental aspects of the game. He wanted Rube to develop what he called the "hypnotic eye" and become a thinking-man's pitcher. It was from Livingston that Rube first learned of the importance of changing speeds on his pitches, of setting up hitters from pitch to pitch and from at-bat to at-bat, and of pacing himself appropriately throughout the course of a game. These concepts were all new to Rube, and it would be several years before he would master them, but he began to make real progress towards realizing his tremendous potential.

Livingston continued his dual duties as player and coach as the 1908 pre-season workouts got underway. Charlie Carr had business matters to tend to, so Livingston took charge and in mid–March greeted, at the training site in French Lick, Indiana, the 20 players who hoped to make the club. The Indianapolis *Star* reported that Livingston was pleased with the condition of the players, and was particularly impressed with the young pitching staff. He took advantage of the warm, dry weather and worked the club hard. The players were awakened at seven each morning and went on a two-mile run before breakfast. They then walked seven miles to the athletic complex and spent the morning stretching, hitting, throwing, and catching. Afternoons were reserved for intrasquad games — often in the form of "old one-cat," played with four men to a side and rapidly rotating pitchers — and regulation games against the French Lick Cadets, a local "colored" amateur team which challenged the minor league clubs that trained there. After dinner, another hike around the hills and local golf course preceded lights out at 10 o'clock.

When Carr finally arrived on March 20 and viewed his club he agreed with Livingston that the Browns would have "the best pitching staff in the circuit" and would contend for the league championship. Rube's arm felt strong, and he was impressive in spring workouts. Carr named his "promising recruit" as the starting pitcher in the first official exhibition game on March 26 against Connie Mack's Philadelphia Athletics. Rube threw the first three innings in a 5–0 loss to the A's, allowing four runs in the second. He only allowed two hits, however, but was victimized by two walks and an infield error. In his only at-bat, he managed to draw a walk and steal second base. A week later he pitched five strong innings against Boston of the American League, allowing only four hits in gaining the 4–1 victory.

Rainy weather cancelled an April 7 game against Ty Cobb and the reigning AL Champion Detroit Tigers, but the next day brought Napoleon Lajoie and his Cleveland Naps to French Lick. Rube had extra incentive to pitch well against his hometown heroes because he thought that the club had mistreated him two years earlier. His performance was such that he remembered it with great satisfaction 60 years later.[13] He overcame a shaky start, walking the first hitter on four pitches, hitting Bill Bradley on the side, and then surrendering a double to Lajoie, before settling down. He pitched five innings and gained a 4–2 victory, allowing only two hits in the process and gaining the respect of the big leaguers. He confidently waited for the regular season to begin.

The American Association of 1908 was one of the strongest of all the minor leagues and regularly fed its top players up to the majors. In its seventh year of existence, the league featured teams in Columbus, Kansas City, Louisville, Milwaukee, Toledo, Minneapolis, and St. Paul. Because there was no major league competition in any of these cities, all of the franchises enjoyed robust fan support and were financially secure. Indianapolis owner W. H. Watkins, along with manager Carr, took out quarter-page advertisements on the front page of the April 14 *Star*, promising a "brilliant season" and a Browns club that would "hustle for the championship flag."[14]

Opening Day was April 15th, and the game against the visiting Kansas City Blues followed a celebratory parade through downtown Indianapolis out to Washington Park. A huge crowd of 9,000 turned out to see the Browns win 4–2 behind the pitching of Doc Eubanks, the Browns' leading pitcher of a year ago. They dropped the second game of the season the next day, and finally Rube was given the chance to pitch on Friday, April 17. He responded well, allowing only three hits in a 2–1 victory in front of nearly 3,000 fans. The *Star* called him "the eminent southpaw" and "the one best bet" and predicted bright things for him.[15] The prediction could not have been more accurate.

Rube sizzled throughout the first three months of the season. Paddy Livingston found him to be "a joy" to catch, and Rube and Lou Durham won with amazing regularity, keeping the Browns in pennant contention. On April 21, Rube threw a four-hit shutout against the Milwaukee Brewers, driving in the only run of the game himself in the bottom of the 10th inning. Four days later he shut out Minneapolis 2–0, then beat St. Paul 8–1 on April 27. Indianapolis concluded its initial home stand with a record of 9–4; in Rube's three complete-game victories he allowed only nine hits. "You will have to take your hat off to him," said the *Star*. "It has been only a little over a year since Rube was playing on the Cleveland lots, but everything he does is a yard wide and all wool.... It looks very much like Charlie Carr has made the find of the season.... He has a natural, sweeping delivery that will not wear him out soon, has fine curves, a good head and a constitution that can stand the work."[16]

Rube continued to excel as the Browns went on the road. He beat Minneapolis and then St. Paul, both on two-hitters, before finally losing his first game of the season on May 8, 5–1 to Minneapolis. He won 12 of his next 15 games—two of those victories came in relief—beating every team in the league at least once. His reputation began to grow; not only did Indianapolis fans show up in record numbers when he pitched, but fans of opposing teams also turned out to see the phenom perform. Rube had become, in just a year and a half, the sensation of minor league baseball.

Chapter 3

"I Can Beat Anybody"

By mid-season 1908, with less than two full seasons of professional baseball behind him, Rube was firmly established as the most dominating pitcher in the minor leagues. He had blazed his way through the Central League in 1907, and Indianapolis was riding his powerful left arm toward the 1908 American Association championship. Now, with a record of 19 and 3, Rube was confident that he was ready to take his talents to the next level. And, in fact, big league scouts had closely monitored his progress and routinely filed positive reports because then, as now, tall, hard-throwing left-handed pitchers were at a premium. The question was which team would ultimately purchase his services.

At least twice before, Rube had nearly found himself in the big leagues. On June 23 the Detroit Tigers had attempted to trade pitcher Ed Siever to Indianapolis for Rube. Siever, then 31 years old, was a veteran of seven seasons with the Tigers and a consistent, if not spectacular, winner. His lifetime record was 83–83, and he had won 18 games twice: in his rookie year of 1901 and again in 1907, when he led the Tigers to the American League championship. (In baseball annals Siever is infamous for another reason. It was Siever who was savagely kicked in the head by teammate Ty Cobb in 1906 during an altercation in a Detroit hotel lobby.[1]) But Siever had balked at being traded down to the American Association and had retired instead, nullifying the deal. Later, a salary increase changed his mind about the minor leagues, and he finished the season with Indianapolis anyway, going 13–7 in 24 games and helping them finish on top of the league. The Tigers, meanwhile, ended up without Rube.

And a year before, after Rube's initial season at Canton, Boston of the American League had drafted him on the advice of scout George Huff, who had seen Rube strike out 13 while throwing a two-hitter against Terre Haute. But Rube was technically under contract with Indianapolis, which had merely "loaned" or farmed him out to Canton, and the National Commission, the three-man governing body of the major leagues, ruled that he could not report to the Boston club.

3. "I Can Beat Anybody"

In late June of 1908, rumors of Rube's acquisition by one of several interested big league teams were flying again, and Rube, after two years of media fanfare touting his exploits, was as much aware of that fact as anyone. On June 30 he was scheduled to pitch against Louisville, which trailed Indianapolis by three games in the standings, and manager Charlie Carr called him into his office before the game. Representatives from both American and National League teams would be at the game, Carr told Rube, to watch him pitch. If Rube did well, Carr would try to sell him for as much as he could get. Much was at stake, for Rube and for Carr, and Carr did not want his star pitcher to be nervous.

"Nervous?" asked Rube. "Have I ever been nervous all season?"

Carr had to admit he had not. "I've been in baseball a long time and I never saw anything like it. I never saw a kid like you, who can beat anybody and is so successful."

"Well," said Rube with typical bravado, "the reason I'm so successful is because I can beat anybody."[2]

Rube backed up his words that day in spectacular fashion, throwing a three-hit shutout against the Colonels (also known as the Night Riders), beating them 3–0. In complete command from the start as he effectively mixed his fastball with a slow-breaking curve, Rube struck out five batters and walked only one in front of over 5,500 fans at Washington Park. Only one hitter even managed to get to second base, on a two-out double in the ninth, and he was stranded there as Rube struck out the final batter to end the game. As if to show that he was the entire package, Rube also lined a single and later scored a run. Rube had made the opponents look "very limp," said the Indianapolis *Star*, and he himself "walked off the field fresh as a daisy."[3] (Rube later remembered incorrectly that he had faced Columbus that day and had tossed a perfect game for the benefit of the big league representatives. He did, in fact, pitch a no-hitter against Columbus that year, but the date of that game was September 2, over two months after the sale to the Giants.[4])

Rube's performance against Louisville was dazzling enough. And the feat, made even more impressive because of the pressure put on him by those watching in the stands, placed Rube directly in the driver's seat. He took a long shower after the game, ate dinner at the English Hotel with Charlie Carr, and readied himself for the evening's main event — the sale of his contract to a major league ballclub.

Rube joined Carr and team owner W. H. Watkins in a closed conference room off the hotel lobby, where the trio met owners and managers of at least ten major league franchises. Carr attempted to force the terms of any sale by initially setting the price at $12,000, a staggering figure that no team was willing to meet. Undaunted, Carr opened up the floor for bidding; Rube felt, he later remembered, "like a horse being auctioned off."[5] As the offers increased, teams folded, one by one, and their representatives left the hotel. In the end, only Detroit, Cincinnati, Cleveland, and the New York Giants remained in the hunt. Each club had its own particular reasons for risking a huge amount of money for a young pitcher with only one and a half minor league seasons under his belt.

The Tigers, through owner Frank Navin — and with the persistent urging of manager Hughie Jennings, who saw the purchase of Rube as vital to continuing their dominance of the American League, had been secretly negotiating with Carr and Watkins for several weeks and thought they had the inside track. (In fact, so many Indianapolis players had been purchased by Detroit in recent years that many fans regarded the Browns as an unofficial Tiger farm team.) Rube's performance for the last month had caused Watkins to drive up the price, however, much to the dismay of Navin and Jennings. They would go no higher than an offer of $9,000 and came up short. (The Tigers would go on to win the AL pennant, their second of three in a row, but would lose the World Series each year.)

The once-proud Red Legs of Cincinnati, one of the National League's original franchises in 1876, were the definition of mediocrity. After their fourth place finish in 1890, they would never get within 10 games of first until their pennant-winning season in 1919. The franchise was once owned by John T. Brush, but a group of Cincinnati political bosses bought it in 1902 and named the chief of the city water works commission, August "Garry" Herrmann, as president of the club. (Brush, in turn, bought the New York Giants franchise.) Herrmann ran the team and simultaneously chaired the National Commission until 1920, when a single individual, Kenesaw Mountain Landis, a federal judge, was named commissioner in the wake of the Black Sox scandal. Now seeing the opportunity to sign an Ohio native and boost his team back into contention, Herrmann eagerly joined in the bidding for Rube's contract.

The Indians found themselves in something of a dilemma. They had known of Rube since as far back as 1902 and 1903, when he had served as batboy for the club during home stands. They were aware, too, of Rube's phenomenal success both at Canton and at Indianapolis; the Cleveland newspapers had heralded Rube's performance in game-by-game detail. After Rube's year at Canton, they had offered $3500 for him, but Rube insisted that "he wouldn't play for Cleveland, no matter what." They had had first chance at him, he told Carr, and they wouldn't get another.[6] By June of 1908, however, the Indians were convinced that while Rube's defensive skills still needed polish, his wonderful arm made him a good risk. Sensitive to the public-relations benefits to be had by signing a hometown phenom, they decided to become active participants in the bidding for Rube's services. The Indians took a deep breath and made a final offer of $10,500, topping the Cincinnati offer by $500. But the Giants, represented by owner Brush and manager John J. McGraw, carried the day at $11,000.

Still stinging from the Ed Siever fiasco, Hughie Jennings, manager of the Tigers, was disgusted by the events in Indianapolis. "The price asked for this pitcher by the Indianapolis team is ridiculous," he complained afterward. "They wanted $12,000 for him.... Marquard would find different sledding if he came up in the American League. If we gave him $12,000, and he did not prove a sensation, we could never forget that we were bunkoed."⁷ (The strange Siever odyssey figured into Rube's sale in another way, as well. By mid–July, with the former Tiger now doing well for Indianapolis, the *Sporting News* remarked: "Wadkins would have had difficulty in marketing Marquard at $11,000, had not the sale been made before Siever showed how good he is in that company."⁸)

Whether Rube was worth it or not, the final purchase price of $11,000 was a newsworthy event that fairly rocked the baseball world because it was the highest price ever paid for a ballplayer by any team. (The previous record of $10,000 was paid by the Boston Red Stockings to the Chicago White Stockings, both major league teams, for Mike "King" Kelley in 1887. Kelley was, by that time, a ten-year veteran of the big leagues and was already acknowledged as baseball's first superstar.) The magnitude of Rube's sale for such an amount cannot be overemphasized. At that time high minor league, or Class AA players, were regularly sold for $2000 to $3000. Only three years earlier, in 1905, Detroit had paid $700 to Augusta for Sally League batting champion Ty Cobb.

The *Sporting News*, long known as the baseball bible and required reading for fans and players alike, placed Rube's story on the front page of its July 2 edition under the headline "LATE NEWS" and the misspelled subheading "Marquardt Brings Fancy Price."⁹ Two weeks later there appeared, again on the front page, a large photograph of Rube, in uniform and in a follow-through pose. The story read, in part:

> Richard Marquard, pitcher of the Indianapolis club of the American Association, which owes its leadership in its race to his splendid record, is a Cleveland boy, who has just turned his twentieth year.... He has won 20 of the 29 games he has twirled for Indianapolis and he has a no-hit, shutout and several other notable pitching feats to his credit. He has been purchased by President Brush and will join the Giants this fall, after the close of the American Association's race.¹⁰

The news was not lost on the papers of Rube's hometown of Cleveland. The *Leader* of July 5 carried a quarter-page photograph of Rube posing in an Indianapolis uniform, under the headline "Cleveland Boy Joins Majors." The story read, somewhat redundantly:

> New York has just paid the Indianapolis team $11,000 for the services of this sensational southpaw. This is the greatest price ever paid for a young player in the history of the game. In fact, it is a question whether such a price was ever paid for a player before. Manager McGraw believes that he will have the greatest sensation in organized baseball after Marquard joins the team next fall.¹¹

"Marquard is Now a Giant; New York Pays $11,000 for Cleveland Phenom" shouted the city's other major newspaper, the *Press*. "The New York Giants have purchased Pitcher 'Rube' Marquard, the Cleveland pitcher on the Indianapolis team," read the accompanying story, "and are said to have paid $11,000 for the

twirling phenomenon.... The Giants made an $11,000 offer and got their man."[12] Rube was now, depending upon which paper one was reading, either the "$11,000 Beauty" or the "$11,000 Peach."

For its part, the Indianapolis *Star* carried a quarter-page photo of Rube, informing readers that "the sensation" of the league had been sold at record price. The announcement of the sale "raised a terrible hubbub" around the country, the *Star* stated in an editorial a day later. It seemed that the owner who was most upset by the news was Charlie Murphy, whose Cubs were locked in a tight race with the Giants.

The New York newspapers were jubilant. Rube was "the twirling sensation of the year in the minor leagues," said the *Globe*, which called the signing "one of the greatest deals ever pulled off in baseball."[13]

While the purchase of Rube attracted most of the headlines, other minor league pitchers were secured by the Giants as well. Louis Durham, Rube's teammate at Indianapolis and a 19-game winner, was also purchased. Durham's season was overshadowed by Rube's success in 1908, but he had also played a key role for the Browns: five times that year he had pitched and won both games of doubleheaders. (McGraw had visions of another so-called Iron Man. Longtime Giant Joe McGinnity had himself accomplished that feat several times earlier in his career, but things never worked out for Durham. He would pitch just two innings for the Giants in 1908, and only four games for them the following year before leaving baseball.) Pete Wilson of Minneapolis, a 14-game winner in 1908, was also brought up by the Giants in September and won three of six decisions for them during the stretch drive.

Of more significance was the purchase by the Giants of a St. Paul catcher, John Tortes "Chief" Meyers, for $6,000, a significant amount which paled only in comparison to Rube's $11,000. Meyers was a Cahuilla Indian from California's San Jacinto Mountains who had, after a year at Dartmouth College, played against Rube many times in the American Association. He would go on to a stellar career with the Giants. Meyers and Rube would become lifelong friends and teammates on two different clubs.

McGraw had more than enough reasons for risking the huge amount of money on young Rube. His Giants had last won the pennant in 1905, and the demanding New York fans and the press were growing restless. While the 1908 club had not been expected to challenge the Cubs and contend for the pennant, it was surprising everyone by overachieving. By July 1 the Giants were in third place and, with a record of 37 and 27, only three games from the top. And they needed pitching in order to remain in contention.

Aside from Christy Mathewson, who was on his way to winning 37 games (and enjoying his finest season in a brilliant career), and George "Hooks" Wiltse,

Opposite: **The $11,000 Beauty, with Indianapolis of the Amerian Association just after his purchase by the New York Giants. Photo courtesy National Baseball Library.**

a consistent winner for the Giants since 1904 who would win 23 games in 1908, the Giant staff had struggled. And it was age, not talent, that was the problem.

Leon "Red" Ames, a 22-game winner in the Giants' last pennant-winning season of 1905, would be only 7–4 three years later. Joe McGinnity at age 37 was no longer the performer of his "Iron Man" days and would finish with a record of 11–7. But McGinnity was in his final major league season in 1908. (In fact, things got so bad for McGinnity that in June McGraw actually asked waivers on him, in part to relieve the club of his $5,000 salary, but no team would take him. He was kept on by the Giants for the remainder of the season anyway, but he more often manned the third base coaching box than the pitching mound.)

"McGraw has a problem on his hands to pull his shattered forces together and to get more pitchers," stated the *Sporting News*.[14] But the clubs with the most available talent, St. Louis and Washington, seemed reluctant to deal with McGraw. The "Little Napoleon," as he was known, believed that if his club could stay close until September, his new $11,000 phenom would arrive just in time to put his Giants over the top. McGraw was never one to look to future seasons; it was this year, not next, that concerned him most.

But in the meantime Rube was obligated to finish the season with Indianapolis, and McGraw continued to make moves to bolster his pitching staff. On July 8, after the Reds had battered starter McGinnity and reliever Wiltse for 12 hits and 8 runs, McGraw made a deal. He secured Robert Spade, who had won only one game for Cincinnati the year before, on waivers, and then traded him, along with $5,000 in cash, back to the Reds for pitcher Jake Wiemer, a three-time 20-game winner.

The shady implications of the deal did not go unnoticed by the *Sporting News*. "Why did [Reds manager] Ganzel ask for waivers on Spade just when the Giants were looking for a pitcher, and why did he let such a good left-hander as Weimer go to the Giants, after they had put in a claim for Spade? Brush and Herrmann always had their heads together. It looks like a case of Herrmann helping the wily Brush out in an emergency."[15]

The very partisan *New York Times* approved of the Giant's maneuvering: "Manager McGraw is beginning to realize that it requires more than a brace of pitchers to win the baseball championship, just as it needs more than two swallows to make a Summer."[16] But for all of McGraw's wheeling and in spite of the "favor" he had received, the deal went bad. Weimer demanded that Reds owner Herrmann give him half of the money involved in the deal or he would quit baseball altogether and "go into business in Chicago with his father-in-law."[17] Herrmann refused, and Weimer made good on his threat. (Coaxed by McGraw, he came out of retirement in 1909 and appeared in one game, but he then left baseball for good. Spade, meanwhile, went on to win 17 games for the Reds in 1908.)

Later that month, in another ominous occurrence, McGraw and Brush traveled back to the American Association to view the pitching staffs of Columbus and Toledo. Sitting in the grandstands prior to the game with Columbus president T. J. Bryce, McGraw turned to see Bryce suddenly collapse and die of a massive heart attack. The superstitious McGraw decided to make no further pitching transactions that year.

And there were other reasons, principally financial, which led the Giants to shell out unprecedented amounts of money on Rube (and, to lesser extent, the other players acquired). With the other New York team, the Yankees, well out of the American League race it was hoped that many local fans would turn their attentions, and their wallets, toward the Giants. "The whole National League, barring Chicago, is anxious to see New York win the championship, now that the Yankees are crippled, for it is realized that the American League has won over thousands of admirers in the Big Town," opined the *Sporting News*.[18] Fan attendance figures bore out the wisdom of this position. In 1907 the Giants drew 538,350 fans to their home at the Polo Grounds. A year later, buoyed by the publicity of Rube's purchase (and, no doubt, the pennant race), attendance soared to 910,000.

Rube was obligated to finish his Indianapolis season before he could join the Giants. (The purchase itself also had to be approved by the National Commission, something that would not take place before mid–September.) Amidst all the media attention and hoopla surrounding the purchase of Rube's contract, the second half of the season was far rockier than the first. On Saturday, July 4, in Rube's first start after the announcement of the sale to the Giants, a record crowd of over 18,500 fans turned out to see the famous local boy pitch the second game of a doubleheader against Toledo. As proof of Rube's drawing power, noted the *Star*, this was twice the number of fans as had seen the first game. Luck was not with Rube on this day, however, as he allowed 10 hits and lost, 2–1. The score seemed inconsequential, however, compared to the spectacle of the holiday celebration. The *Star* proclaimed:

> Truly every road led to Washington Park yesterday. From every ward and township of Indianapolis and Marion County and from every district and hamlet came the people of Hoosierdom to witness the struggle in the afternoon between the Browns and the Mud Hens. Thousands upon thousands of men and women, old and young, in fashionable dress and rough working clothes, with fair skins bleached by indoor work and with tans gathered from farm and lake, they came and fought their way into every nook and cranny of the baseball park.... Over 18,000 strong they swarmed over every chair and extra bit of bleacher that a thoughtful president had placed in readiness until there had assembled probably the most gigantic crowd that ever witnessed an American Association baseball game.... The Fourth of July was celebrated by a mighty crowd of people offering tribute not to the founders of our country, not to the men who have brought the Nation to a world-wide power, but a great tribute to the one and only national pastime.[19]

Rube took careful note of all the attention that came his way, of course, and moved quickly to capitalize on it, for while his sale to the Giants had been finalized, his contract had yet to be negotiated. In a July 9 interview with Sid Mercer of the New York *Globe*, Rube took a realistic, if not cautiously optimistic, approach. "There is nothing to gloat over," he told Mercer. "If I am worth that amount of money to the New York club, I should get a good salary. I tried to break into the big company with the Cleveland club, but they could not see where I came in at all. When I start in fast baseball, I want a salary that will make it worthwhile."[20]

Flushed with all the attention he was receiving, Rube saw the opportunity to market himself, a skill he would grow quite good at and practice regularly for the rest of his life. Acting upon the advice of Charlie Carr, and with the assistance of Sid Mercer, he wrote a remarkable letter to the fans of New York that was meant to introduce himself to his new public and give some assurances as to his worth. The letter, which appeared in the August 1 edition of the *World* was filled with falsehoods and wild concoctions and was designed to endear Rube to the fans:

> When the report circulated that I had been sold to the Giants for $11,000 I was the most interested person in Indianapolis in hearing about it. But at the time you couldn't prove by me that there was $11,000 in the whole world. Funny, isn't it, that a man can be worth so much money to somebody else and maybe not have a solitary sou himself!
>
> I was born in Cleveland, O., on Oct. 9, 1887. I hate to admit it, but you can see that I will not be old enough to vote until next October. Another thing the matter with me, besides my youth, is that I am 6 feet 3 inches tall. I weigh 182 pounds. Therefore I am a long, lank kid.
>
> My parents, who were French, died when I was a kid and I've practically been my own boss ever since. I attended institutions of learning in Cleveland, but I got most of my education on ball fields. If a man keeps his eyes and ears open he can pick up a lot of knowledge on the diamond — knowledge that has nothing to do with playing baseball, too.
>
> I began to grow when I was born and I've kept it up ever since. Unless I cease stretching out I guess they'll have to hoist the sky a little higher so that I can hobble along without bumping my head on it every time I step up on the gutter. I'm now so tall my friends have nicknamed me the "human lighthouse" and the "animated steeple" and I have to stoop when I consult with the umpire.
>
> I have not figured out whether my height is an advantage or a handicap. Sometimes I believe the short pitcher has the advantage because he can throw an upshoot easier than the tall pitcher, but then the tall fellow can shoot the ball downward in a straight slant that annoys batters.
>
> I remember the first big game I ever pitched. It was in Cleveland, my home town, and a great crowd turned out. I struck out 24 men and allowed only one hit, and the next day I was famous in my town. I was heralded as a second Rube Waddell.

About this time I had a big chicken farm 25 miles west of Cleveland, and when I wasn't playing ball I spent my time raising chickens for the Cleveland markets. Raising chickens paid me as well, if not better, than playing baseball, but the game had a fascination for me, and I could not keep out of it.

Unlike most athletes, I have no fixed method of training. I eat anything I want, providing I think it will agree with me. My methods of living and of diet are simple in the extreme. In fact, I have always been an exponent of the simple life. Only once did I try "living high." That was after I had begun pitching professional ball. I got the idea I ought to tog myself out in gay raiment, so I took the money I got for pitching and bought a gorgeous suit of clothes. It was of a florid cast of countenance, and it made itself heard in the dark, it was so loud. To match it I had a pair of yellow shoes that sneezed like a man with hay fever when I walked. I thought I was the best dressed man in the country till my friends saw me, and then I heard so many things about my appearance that I shook the duds forever. Since then I've lived quietly.

When I report to New York, I will do my best to help McGraw win the pennant. I shall strive to show New Yorkers they were not "gold-bricked" when they got me.[21]

Rube was always looking out for his own financial interests. He had asked, only half-kiddingly, if he could be cut in on part of the $11,000 purchase price. (Carr informed him that was against league rules.) And now, as he began to negotiate his contract with the Giants — he would be paid $300 for the month of September through the end of the season — he shrewdly inserted a provision that guaranteed him a full share of World Series money should the Giants win the pennant. In all things economic, pointed out *Sporting Life*, he was clearly no rube, but "foolish like a pawnbroker."[22]

Perhaps because of all the media attention and varied reaction to the signing, Rube's pitching performance suffered the entire month of July. After the loss on the Fourth of July in front of the record crowd, Rube lost at Columbus on July 8 by a score of 4–3, although he pitched well, giving up only six hits in another game attended by John McGraw. After a win at Louisville on July 12, he gave up three runs in the 9th inning against Toledo, losing 5–2, beat Minneapolis by the same score on July 21, and then lost five straight. His record since the signing was only 2–8, and the newspapers took notice, some beginning to speculate on the wisdom of the purchase.

The reversal of fortunes was so profound that the national publication *Sporting News* editorialized about it in its August 12 edition. "Some are of the opinion that Rube is experimenting with a slow ball when he should use his speed all the time," it stated, "and some are of the belief that he has thought so much about his promotion that he can not think of his pitching duties." Whatever the reason for the tailspin, the *News* now reported that while Rube would still go to New York at the end of the Browns' season, "he will have to make good there before the $11,000 purchase price is paid."²³ This was news that neither Rube nor his team needed to hear.

The New York papers also had been following Rube's lack of recent progress, and took a different angle on the story.

> It has leaked out that John McGraw had nothing to do with the purchase of Rube Marquard. The Giants' pitching staff looked a bit wobbly a while back, and John T. Brush thought he would surprise McGraw by digging up a new box artist. Accordingly, Mr. Brush did sneak away to look over minor leaguers. Through the Indianapolis officials Mr. Brush learned that two or three teams were bidding for Marquard, and that was enough for him. He plunked down $11,000, then told McGraw what he had done. There is no record of McGraw being tremendously enthused over the purchase.²⁴

This story ignored the fact that McGraw had seen Rube pitch on at least two occasions and had been present in Indianapolis when the deal was struck.

Even the Cleveland *Plain Dealer*, long one of Rube's most enthusiastic backers, now was predicting tough times ahead. In an August 16 article titled "Rube Marquard Will Have Hard Sledding," the paper predicted that while "Marquard's port side curves have certainly mystified the [American] Association batters, he will be up against a tougher game in the old National. All critics in the West feel certain that Rube will make good, but he will hardly cut the wide swath some of the over-enthusiastic are predicting." Adding to Rube's difficulties would be the added pressure of his being "the most discussed player before the public."²⁵

Rube righted himself somewhat as the season wound down and the Browns battled for the flag. He won six of his last nine decisions and continued his mastery over the Columbus club. He tossed a one-hitter on August 29 in a 3–0 victory at Washington Park and then, to prove it was no fluke, threw his no-hitter against them four days later in Columbus, winning this time 7–0. (This was the game Rube later incorrectly remembered as the one leading to the signing with the Giants.)

And while Rube's performance after the signing was not as dominant as before, his season on the whole was a great success. He finished with a league-high 28 wins against 19 losses and also led the league with 250 strikeouts. Others may have blamed his erratic performance in July and August on the publicity or his overreliance on curveballs, or both, but the real reason was, in all likelihood, fatigue. Rube appeared a whopping 47 times, pitching in nearly one-third of all the Browns' games, and he threw 367 innings. Both of these figures led the league. Manager Carr regularly started Rube on three days' rest, and even used him in relief several times in his efforts to bring the championship to Indianapolis.

In that bid Carr was successful. His club battled Louisville and three-time defending champion Columbus all season long and finally won the pennant on the next-to-last day of the season, when Lou Durham beat Indianapolis 4–2 before over 11,000 fans. The "glorious windup to a glorious season" was the Browns' first championship in six years, and their fans celebrated in fine style, with parades, brass bands, and bonfires scattered throughout the city that remained lighted until dawn. Team photographs were prominently featured in both the *Star* and the *Sporting News*, and the *Reach Official Baseball Guide* later called the Browns the most-deserving champions of all the nation's pennant races, adding that the 1908 season was the best ever.

The next night, September 15, the team held a celebratory banquet at the English Hotel which was attended by club officials, hundreds of fans, and even league umpires. The players received small bonuses for winning the championship and "toasted the town, their manager, and one another." Rube was singled out as "the lad who would always go in the box in an emergency and one ball player who never was beaten until the game was over."[26]

At the party it was announced that Carr would be given a new five-year contract to manage the Browns. (The *Sporting News* later disclosed that his salary would be the highest ever paid to a minor league manager.[27]) Then, noted the Indianapolis *Star*, an exhausted, exhilarated, yet confident Rube and Lou Durham "caught the first train they could to join the Giants."[28]

CHAPTER 4

McGraw, Merkle, and Mayhem

Rube and Durham arrived in New York on the morning of September 16 and reported to team offices at the Polo Grounds. Their arrival caused a stir in the press: "Both men are well built and fine looking athletes, who will make a favorable impression with the local players and Polo Grounds patrons," said the New York *World*.[1] The *Sporting News* also noted the event: "Both men have a good appearance and should greatly strengthen New York's pitching corps. They may or they may not get a try-out before the season ends. If appearances go for anything, both of them look as if they might be able to deliver the goods, if given the chance to show what they can do." But as always, the greater emphasis was placed on Rube and the circumstances of his signing. "Marquard comes with a heavy handicap. The title of an $11,000 beauty is not going to benefit him much. Too much will be expected from him and at any time he fails to win he is liable to get an awful pasting from the 'sympathetic' fans."[2]

Those fans in New York took their baseball seriously, and with only a few weeks remaining in the 1908 season, their support for the Giants and the demands and expectations they placed on them raised to fever pitch. Rube had gone from one pennant race to another, but nothing he saw in Indianapolis compared to what he was about to witness in New York.

The race had shaped up as the closest in history, with three teams — defending champion Chicago, Pittsburgh, and New York — competing for the pennant. By late August the Giants had moved into first place for the first time, and the rest of the season they stayed at the top or close to it.

The Cubs were two-time defending league champions and had swept Detroit in the 1907 World Series. (One game had ended in a tie.) A mainstay in the National League for over 20 years, the Cubs were truly a dynasty in the early days of the twentieth century. They won an astonishing 530 games and 4 pennants between 1906 and 1910. These Cubs are most often remembered for their poetry-inspiring infield, whose double-play skills were immortalized by columnist and Giant-fan Franklin P. Adams: "These are the saddest of possible words — Tinker to Evers to Chance. Trio of Bear Cubs and fleeter than birds — Tinker to Evers to Chance." It was the Cubs' pitching, however, led by the brilliant "Three Finger" Brown, that best marked their dominance.

Born in 1876 and christened Mordecai Peter Centennial Brown, he earned his crude nickname after a farming accident had mutilated two fingers of his hand. Pitching with only part of an index finger and no little finger, Brown mastered the sinker ball and had developed into one of the league's most successful pitchers. He was 29–9 in 1908 (the third year of six straight where he would win at least 20 games), and for good measure he saved a league-leading five more.

Backing up Brown was Ed Reulbach, who nearly matched him with a record of 24–7, Orval Overall at 15–11, and Jack "the Giant Killer" Pfiester (so named because of the regularity with which he beat the Giants over the years) at 12–10. Collectively, the team ERA was 2.14, impressive even by deadball standards. The Cub staff led the league in shutouts and strikeouts, while allowing the fewest hits per game.

The other contender in 1908 was the Pittsburgh Pirates, a team whose best players and owner had come from the defunct Louisville club. (Until the turn of the century, Louisville had had a major league franchise.) Barney Dreyfuss had purchased the Pirates and stocked it with stars, including pitcher Deacon Phillippe, outfielder/manager Fred Clarke, utility player Tommy Leach, and the incomparable Honus Wagner.

Wagner, known as "the Flying Dutchman," was, in the years before Ty Cobb fully developed his skills, the best ballplayer in the country. Born in Chartiers, Pennsylvania, in 1874, by the age of 12 he was working alongside his father in the coal mines; he earned 70 cents for every ton he could load. After a brief stint as an apprentice barber, Honus caught on with several minor league teams in Ohio and Michigan before landing with Louisville in 1896. Although most often remembered as a shortstop, in fact Wagner played every infield and outfield position, all with a combined lumbering, awkward-looking grace and power that was his trademark. His hands were huge, his forearms massive, and his legs were almost ridiculously bowed. He was best known for scooping up infield pebbles and dirt along with the baseball, then heaving everything toward first base with uncanny accuracy. Gentle and good-natured — the only thing he loved as much as baseball was throwing down a few beers after the game — he was the favorite of sportswriters as well as fans. The New York *American* described him this way:

> No one ever saw anything graceful or picturesque about Wagner on the diamond. His movements have been likened to the gambols of a caracoling elephant. He is ungainly and so bowlegged that when he runs his limbs seem to be moving in a circle after the fashion of a propeller. But he can run like

the wind. When he starts after a grounder every outlying portion of his anatomy apparently has ideas of its own about the proper line of direction to be taken. His position of the bat is less awkward and the muscular swing of his great arms and shoulders is strong enough to drive the ball further than most batters who hit from their toe spikes up. There is no question that Wagner is the greatest all-around ballplayer of this or any other season.[3]

Teammate Tommy Leach remarked that Wagner was "the best first baseman, the best second baseman, the best third baseman, the best shortstop, and the best outfielder. And since he led the league in batting eight times between 1900 and 1911 you know that he was the best hitter, too. As well as the best base runner."[4] After horrifying manager Fred Clarke and legions of Pirate fans by threatening briefly, before the season, to retire, Wagner in 1908 was in his prime. He dominated the game as few players have before or since, leading the league in batting average, hits, doubles, triples, total bases, RBIs, slugging percentage and stolen bases and single-handedly keeping his team in contention for the flag.

Rube joined a Giant team in transition. Several years removed from the greatness of the 1905 World's Championship team, McGraw had rebuilt his club with a combination of seasoned veterans and promising youngsters, all carefully molded in his own image. Stalwart catcher Roger Bresnahan, a converted pitcher, was in the midst of a solid 15-year major league career which ultimately took him to the Hall of Fame. Perhaps unfairly remembered only for the fact that he invented shinguards, he was the best receiver in baseball, along with Chicago's Johnny Kling, in the first decade of the century. In 1908 he hit .283 while catching a career-high 139 games, effectively handling the Giant's often erratic staff.

Second-year man "Laughing" Larry Doyle was at third base, only just beginning what would be a solid 14-year career (13 of these years were spent with the Giants; five times he would hit over .300). Shortstop Al Bridwell was in the first of four seasons with the Giants, and while never a flashy fielder, he batted a solid .285. Longtime Boston first baseman Fred Tenney was in the first of two seasons with New York in 1908; he was spelled only occasionally by a bright nineteen year old from Wisconsin named Fred Merkle.

The mainstay in the outfield was popular "Turkey" Mike Donlin, a line-drive hitter who led the Giants that year with a .334 batting average and also stole 30 bases. While 1908 would prove to be Donlin's last full season, he eventually made an impression on young Rube in ways other than on the playing field. Donlin had married vaudeville star Mabel Hite two years earlier; she had convinced him that show business, not baseball, was his true calling, and after he retired from the game he went to Hollywood, where he made a number of low-grade movies.

McGraw, known as "Mister" to his players and fans and "Muggsy" to nearly everyone else, was in his scheming, cunning, combative prime in 1908. In the

4. McGraw, Merkle, and Mayhem

sixth year of thirty as Giants manager, McGraw was perhaps the dominant personality of the game in its early days. After a successful playing career with the old Baltimore Orioles — a team known as much for its rowdyism as for its playing skills, which were considerable — McGraw had found his niche in New York, where owner Brush gave him carte blanche to run the club's operations as he saw fit.

McGraw was happy only when he won: "The man who loses gracefully loses easily," he said. "Personally I never could see this idea of taking a defeat philosophically."[5] He sought out every advantage for his club, instructing his players to "kick" balls from the gloves of their opponents, cut base corners prematurely, and give enemy base-runners "the hip" when the umpires were not looking. He regularly fought

John J. McGraw in 1911. Photo courtesy Lawrence Ritter.

with umpires, cursed opposing players, and taunted fans who railed at him, which happened in every city where his Giants played. He was contentious, profane and abusive, and he was fined and suspended by league officials on a regular basis. "McGraw," said one umpire, "eats gunpowder every morning for breakfast and washes it down with warm blood."[6] In uniform he was the "personification of meanness and howling blatancy," said the *Chicago Tribune* in what was meant as a compliment.[7] And his players, for the most part, loved him for it and adopted his ways. "The club *is* McGraw," said Christy Mathewson.[8]

Now, with only two weeks left in the season and the race coming down to the wire, McGraw formulated a strategy on how to best utilize his prize purchase Rube. He elected a psychological ploy first, immediately after Rube's arrival. On Thursday, September 17, the last-place St. Louis Cardinals were in town. McGinnity started and pitched the first four innings, leaving with the Giants ahead 3–1. McGraw called for Rube to take the mound, giving nearly 20,000 fans their first look at the heralded phenom they had been reading about. But a glimpse was all they got; McGraw never intended to let Rube pitch in the game, but only warm up and get the feel of the mound and the game atmosphere at the Polo Grounds. Rube threw six or seven balls to Bresnahan and then gave way to Dummy Taylor, who finished the game and secured the 10–5 victory.

W. W. Aulick of the *New York Times* recorded the event in the jocular style of the day: "So McGinnity is out of the game, and across the lawn lopes something about 18 feet high, or so it seems, and the aidful umpire says: 'Ladiesgmn, this is Mr. Marquard come to pitch for you. Grant him a little greet.' Mr. Marquard, who arrived in town a couple of days ago, comes high — if we win the pennant we won't have to buy a flagpole; that is, if we can get Marky to stand still long enough. But after Marquard has thrown a few practice balls to Bresnahan, along comes Taylor, and the skyscraper retires to the bench."[9]

The New York *American* agreed that "the main feature of the afternoon was the appearance of Marquard, the $11,000 peach" and reported that Rube seemed not to lack confidence. "Mr. Marquard may or may not prove to be a big league star, but if he falls a bit short, it won't be because he is lacking in genuine nerve and boyish self-confidence. He was in the pitcher's box only long enough to give the yearning fans one peek at him, but they were impressed by his pitching manners, and so was McGraw."[10]

Five days later the Giants led Chicago by 2½ games, and with the Cubs in town for an important double-header, McGraw again tried to "use" Rube to his advantage without ever letting him in the game. But the strategy backfired, as the Cubs took both games, 4–3 and 2–1. The *Chicago Tribune* happily, and sarcastically, recorded the events:

> "Muggsy" McGraw, the "Napoleon of baseball," was outgeneraled all the way yesterday, and to his bad judgment may be charged the loss of the second game.
>
> To begin with, "Muggsy" tried to be foxy and "put something over" on [Cubs player-manager] Chance, with disastrous results. Before the first game he had Marquard, his $11,000 beauty, warm up as though intending to work him. He even went so far as to let Marquard walk out on the diamond just as the game was about to start, then suddenly called him back and out came Ames, who had been warming up secretly behind the grandstand. McGraw tried this trick again in the second game, Marquard and McGinnity warming up, and at the last minute Crandall showing from behind the stand. McGraw hoped to catch Chance napping and get some other pitcher than Overall and Brown. Instead he got two beatings.[11]

But McGraw's ill-advised maneuvering was only a precursor to what happened the following day, September 23. That day saw the wildest and most controversial baseball game ever played, and not coincidentally crushed the Giants' spirits and sent them reeling down a path from which they could not recover.

The day itself began with promise. In light of the overflow crowds the pennant race had brought to the Polo Grounds, owner John Brush announced that a 7,000-seat expansion to the park would be completed in time for the World Series — an event that all Giant fans confidently expected. Further, the great Mathewson was pitching for the Giants, and the nearly 28,000 fans on hand for the game and the thousands more who were following the game via a huge electric scoreboard set up at Times Square, were wild with enthusiasm and confidence.

Matty was locked in a tight duel with Jack Pfeister, and the score stood at 1–1 in the bottom of the ninth. Moose McCormick represented the winning run when Merkle, playing first base, came to the plate. The regular first baseman, Tenney, was suffering from a variety of ailments. He had torn some skin off his back, and although a plaster had been placed on it for protection the skin was extremely tender. He had, over the course of the long season, been spiked at least once and now had a painful set of bone spurs on his heels that would require off-season surgery. Despite the discomfort, today's key game was the first, and only, game Tenney would miss all year.[12]

Merkle took two called strikes, then a ball, and then lined a long drive down the first base line, just over the outstretched glove of Frank Chance. (That pitch, Merkle admitted later, was actually outside, but he was afraid to let it go because the day before, when pinch hitting for Tenney, he had struck out; he couldn't bear to face the wrath of McGraw if he fanned again with the game on the line.) The ball landed just fair, kicking up white chalk when it landed. McCormick stopped at third and Merkle, though he probably could have made second base, wisely stopped at first since, in baseball jargon, he "didn't mean anything." But that proved to be very, very wrong.

Bridwell was next, the huge crowd yelling and cheering with all they had. As the left-handed hitter stepped in to face the southpaw Pfeister — McGraw giving no thought to pinch hitting for him — he noticed Merkle edging too far off first, as if he were going to steal. That made no sense, of course, so Bridwell stepped back and stared Merkle down until he nervously went back and stood on the bag. Pfeister finally threw a fastball over the heart of the plate, and Bridwell drilled a line past Evers into right-center field, knocking base umpire Bob Emslie "on his can."[13] McCormick jubilantly ran home with the winning run as many thousands of fans raced onto the field in celebration (and to get to the elevated train on Eighth Avenue, just beyond the left-field seats). Merkle, who was halfway to second, saw the ball fall safely and was aware of the on-rushing crowd; he broke off from the baseline and sprinted towards the Giant clubhouse past the center-field wall.

The only man in the Polo Grounds who noticed what Merkle had done — or failed to do — was second baseman Evers, who frantically signaled for centerfielder Artie Hofman to throw him the ball, the idea being to touch second and force out Merkle for the third out, nullifying McCormick's run. Amidst the confusion and with the infield now crowded with fans, third base coach Joe McGinnity realized what Evers was trying to do. He ran out and intercepted Hofman's relay and heaved the ball as far as he could into the grandstand behind third base. According to Evers, the ball was caught by "a tall, stringy middle-aged gent with a brown bowler hat on."[14] Cub players Harry Steinfeldt and Floyd Kroh chased him down and secured the ball only after knocking the man's hat down over his

Rube as a rookie with the Giants. Photo courtesy Library of Congress.

eyes, and then made their way back through the mob to second base. Bedlam reigned. Meanwhile, several Giants, suspicious to these wild proceedings, grabbed Merkle and hustled him back to the field, fighting through the crowds until he finally touched second. No one could say whether he beat the ball to the bag. By now Frank Chance had retrieved chief umpire Hank O'Day and Emslie from their dressing room behind home plate, the two having assumed, like nearly everyone else, that the game was over.

After much argument from both sides, O'Day finally ruled that the run should not count and declared the game a 1–1 tie. The decision made no one happy; Chance and the Cubs arguing that the pandemonium on the field meant the Giants must forfeit, McGraw wildly and profanely maintaining that the run must count and any other interpretation of the rule-book only robbed the Giants of what was rightfully theirs. The police had to be called, meanwhile, to clear the field of the fans, who were whipped to moblike frenzy. Sometime during the melee the Cub clubhouse was robbed of some $200 cash and $5000 in jewelry.

McGraw's appeals to the league hierarchy (which included affidavits signed by Giant players and numerous fans who insisted Merkle had touched the bag) were denied. President Harry Pulliam ruled, in fact, that a strange sort of precedent applied. Not quite three weeks earlier in Pittsburgh, the same scenario had unfolded, again with Johnny Evers arguing that a run be disallowed when a Pirate had failed to touch second base. That appeal had been denied, but the play had sparked much debate over the correct interpretation of the rule; in fact, the *Sporting News* had devoted a front-page story to it.[15] The call in New York was the correct one, and McGraw was powerless to change it. The game would be replayed later, at the end of the season, if necessary.

The Giants were still in good position to win the pennant, but the bizarre scene on September 23 clearly deflated their spirits. The press blamed Merkle ("crucified him," said Al Bridwell), branding him with the "bonehead" label he would never live down.[16] On September 24, Wiltse beat Three Finger Brown 5–4 before 25,000 angry fans, but it was the Giants last gasp. McGraw sensed the defeatism running through his club—even the sainted Matty could not get over the tie game, stating that if the decision cost the Giants the pennant, he would "never play baseball again."[17] In an attempt to rouse his team, McGraw chose this moment to call on his prize Rube. He would start his first game on September 25, against fourth-place Cincinnati, only two days removed from the most controversial game in history, and with the pennant perhaps on the line. The New York fans, who had been clamoring for Rube to make his debut, were ecstatic, and for the time being, it allowed them to take their minds off the Merkle disaster.

But Rube was not ready to be thrust into this pressure-cooker. Before another crowd in excess of 20,000, Rube was, understandably, so nervous he could hardly concentrate. In the top of the first, his first pitch to leadoff hitter Johnny Kane, a curveball, was a called strike, and the crowd roared happily. But his next pitch hit Kane in the ribs, and it all fell apart after that. He got Dick Egan to pop out to Buck Herzog, but then Kane stole second and Hans Lobert tripled. Bob Bescher also tripled but was thrown out at home trying to stretch it into a home run. At the end of the inning, Rube was behind 2–0.

Rube struggled with his control (at least five of his pitches bounced in the dirt in front of Bresnahan, who somehow lost part of a fingernail on one of the stops), but he escaped any more damage until the fifth. Two line-drive singles sandwiched around Bridwell's error, a wild pitch and another single scored three more, and Rube was done for the day. The official line in his inglorious major league debut: five innings pitched, five runs allowed on seven hits, two walks, one strikeout. He was relieved by his Indianapolis teammate Durham, who after striking out the side in the sixth was battered for three runs in the next inning and also relieved. The Giants lost 7–1; they also dropped the second game of the doubleheader 4–2 and now stood only one percentage point ahead of the Cubs.

Rube always remembered the experience as one of the worst of his life. "I'll never forget that day," he said several years later in an interview with the New York *Sun*. "[The huge crowd] had come to see the wonderful $11,000 pitcher they'd heard about. They expected him to pitch $11,000 worth — just like that. Nothing but a miracle would have satisfied 'em. I was so nervous I could scarcely stand; honest, my legs were shaking. It was awful."[18]

The New York papers were not kind. Rube had "stage fright," wrote William Kirk of the *American*:

> He did not know what to do with his hands, and he wasn't quite sure what to do with the ball. First he tucked it under his right armpit, then he slammed it into his glove, then he spat on it, then he made a wild pitch with it, and then he aimed it over in the groove, only to see it soaring safe into the outfield. Gentle Roger Bresnahan tried his derndest to hold up the young pitcher, and stopped more than one apparently wild pitch, but the kid was not quite ready for the ordeal, and after he had been clouted grievously, and had shown unmistakable signs of unsteadiness, he left the mound.[19]

W. W. Aulick of the *Times* was also not impressed:

> We trotted out the pitching gent we gave $11,000 newspaper money for and he was worse stage frightened than a school of acting young women at a professional debut, and besides this, he was wilder than a hawk and nowhere near as harmful. He had speed to spill, as Roger Bresnahan will tell you. After a few innings of ineffectual attempt to hold the Marquard delivery Bresnahan, with half or more of his hand ripped to ribbons, retired to the clubhouse veranda and gave way to pained wonder as to how long it would take this marvel to mutilate an opposing team if he could disable the star catcher of his own gang without half a try.[20]

Wrote the New York *Morning Telegraph*:

> The fans have been so insistent demanding a tryout for Marquard, the $11,000 pitcher the Giants got from Indianapolis, that McGraw yesterday decided to give them what they wanted.... Marquard, warming up, was a sight to warm the cockles of a fan's heart. The enthusiasts liked him — then. The Reds liked him when they got him in the game. They touched him up for five runs and made him look like a selling plater hobbled and lashed to a hitching post ... Marquard was all to the bad ... had blown to bits ... McGraw's $11,000 perfecto didn't burn even or smoke right.[21]

McGraw too came in for his share of criticism for the timing of Rube's appearance. It was "surprising," said the *Times*, "that Marquard should receive his major league baptism of fire under yesterday's unfavorable conditions. Cincinnati has but one left-handed batter. The Red players are partial to left-handed pitchers, and they made short work of the Western phenom."[22]

The Indianapolis *Star*, however, sarcastically noted the "bitter dose delivered by critics of Metropolis" and offered a bit of smaller-city paranoia as well: "You know anything that is not born, reared and laid away to rest in New York is a mere worthless provincial anyhow, but when you spend $11,000 to get someone from way out somewhere in Indiana or Ohio where the Indians grow, he must deliver the goods as never delivered before, according to the viewpoint of the great city."[23]

It was to be Rube's only appearance of the season for the Giants. (He did pitch a few innings on Sunday, September 27, against a group of all-stars from the New York State League.) The Giants' troubles, however, only worsened. Harry Coveleski of the Phillies, one of two Polish-American brothers (and pitchers) from the coal mines of Pennsylvania, beat them three times in the next five days, ultimately forcing a one-game playoff against the Cubs for the championship. (On October 4 the Cubs had beaten the Pirates, behind Brown, 5–2, and finally eliminated them from the race. Brown pitched in 11 of the Cubs' final 14 games.)

The deciding game was played on October 8 at the Polo Grounds. The Cubs traveled all night via the Twentieth Century Limited passenger train, arriving in Manhattan by midmorning. Greeted by hundreds of jeering Giant fans, they traveled by private cars to the ballpark and came upon a sight unmatched in sports history.

People were everywhere. By 12:30 P.M., fully 2½ hours before the 3 P.M. start, the stands were filled and the police ordered the gates closed. Another 250,000 people (more, by some estimates) gathered outside the park, on fences, roofs, smokestacks, and advertising signs. Hundreds more jammed the plateau atop Coogan's Bluff, the rocky cliffs which hovered directly behind the grandstand and offered a view of part of the outfield. One man fell to his death from a pillar; even as his body was being carried away, a scramble ensued as to who would take his place atop the pole.

Three hundred fifty policemen, some on horseback, had been called out to keep order, a nearly impossible job in view of the angry mood of the crowd. Alcohol flowed abundantly. Scalpers operated freely, selling phony tickets to unsuspecting patrons. Dozens of fights broke out, and ambulances ran between the Polo Grounds and the hospitals all day. Thousands of people congregated on the elevated tracks though they were repeatedly driven off by firemen with powerful hoses; finally the trains stopped running altogether. Some fans who did not get tickets even tried to burn their way into the park. The crowd extended for nearly a mile in several directions. Emotions ran extremely high, and many wild-eyed fans — some "raving mad" — were carted away.[24] "Never in the history of the game," wrote W. J. Lampton of the *New York Times*, "have there been so many to see a game who didn't see it."[25]

The crowd inside the park was unruly and abusive toward the hated Cub players; Evers, Chance, and Tinker were on the receiving end of most of the harangue. "I have never heard anybody or any set of men called as many foul names as the Giants fans called us that day, from the time we showed up till it was over," recalled Brown. "There was bedlam in the air.... Wild men were yelling for our blood."[26] The abuse was not always verbal; on one occasion beer bottles were thrown at Kling when he settled under a foul pop fly.

The Giants, however, were glorified. Rube was one of the first Giants to emerge from the clubhouse, and he tossed a ball with Chief Meyers in the outfield. For this, they earned mild applause. Larry Doyle was the first regular to appear, and the crowd cheered wildly. McGraw himself commanded an even louder roar and grandly doffed his cap. Mathewson, the starting Giant pitcher, made his usual "lordly entrance," as always the last player to come onto the field. "He'd always wait until about 10 minutes before game time," recalled Brown. "Then he'd come from the clubhouse across the field in a long linen duster like auto drivers wore in those days, and at every step the crowd would yell louder and louder. This day they split the air."[27] The cheering subsided only when Fred Merkle slowly walked across the field and took his place on the bench.

McGraw was behind two underhanded attempts to throw the Cubs further off their game. He kept his club on the field for over an hour before the game and only allowed the Cubs 15 minutes to loosen up. And a bizarre plot was hatched against Chance; McGraw ordered McGinnity to get into a fight with Chance before the game (an order he cheerfully accepted), so that both players would be kicked out. The Giants could do without Joe, but the Cubs sorely needed their manager/first baseman. McGinnity did his best to no avail. "He called Chance names on some pretext or other, stepped on his toes, pushed him, actually spit on him," recalled Fred Snodgrass, then a rookie Giant outfielder. "But Frank wouldn't fight. He was too smart."[28] (Umpire Bill Klem was approached at one point by a Dr. William Creamer, who was the Giants' unofficial physician, and offered a bribe to throw the game. It is unclear, but doubtful, whether McGraw knew of this scheme. Creamer was subsequently barred for life from major league ballparks.)

Not all the dirty tricks belonged to McGraw's Giants. Each Cub player was ordered to "pick out a New York player to work on.... Call 'em everything in the book."[29] The Cubs needed little encouragement, but their efforts were minuscule compared to those of the righteous Giants and their frenzied fans.

In fact the game was very nearly not played at all. The Giants were still incensed at the ruling over the Merkle game, and McGraw left it up to the players to decide whether they would or would not play. Finally John Brush offered the players a bonus of $10,000, win or lose, to be split among them. Mathewson,

Bresnahan, and Donlin led a committee of player representatives that finally voted to play.

But for all the drama, it was not the Giants' day. Helped by some poor judgment by outfielder Cy Seymour (who refused to budge when Matty waved him back and then saw Joe Tinker's fly ball sail over his head), the Cubs erupted for four runs in the third, Frank Chance slamming a double to drive in the Cubs final run. Three Finger Brown, ignoring the death threats against him should he dare pitch—"black-hand letters," he called them—came on in relief of Pfeister and snuffed a rally by striking out Art Devlin with two men on.[30] From there on out he was magnificent, holding the Giants in check and silencing the crowd. In the end the Cubs won the game 4–2, and with it the pennant.

The Giants retired disconsolately to the clubhouse, but the Cubs had a more difficult time, as hundreds of fans poured onto the field and accosted them. Despite the protective efforts of policemen, Pfeister was staggered by a blow to his jaw, then slashed on the shoulder with a knife, and Kling was thrown to the ground. The verbal abuse hurled at the Cubs from the mob continued and escalated. Even after they were inside their clubhouse they were not safe, as enraged fans threw bottles against the door and tried to break it down with bricks. After changing out of his uniform, Brown wisely rejected a police escort, figuring he would draw less attention without them, and he made it safely through the crowd to a waiting automobile. He was happy and relieved to get out of "the lunatic asylum" that the Polo Grounds had become.[31]

Frank Chance was not as lucky; he was assaulted by one drunken fan and suffered a broken cartilage in his neck. Despite the treatment he had received, Chance kept his composure, stating only that he "had no ill feelings against anyone."[32] After a celebration dinner at the Somerset Hotel late that evening, the Cubs caught a train for Detroit (they still needed a police escort to the train station), where they would face and defeat the Tigers in the 1908 World Series.

McGraw never got over the bitter end to the season. He defiantly had medallions made up for his team which read "Real Champions, 1908." No rulebook technicality, he reasoned, could take away what rightfully belonged to his club. And he never forgave the National League president, Harry Pulliam, for upholding the Merkle ruling. The next year, when Pulliam put a gun to his temple and ended his life—perhaps, in part, because of the criticism resulting from his decision after the Merkle game that so greatly impacted the 1908 season—McGraw could not bring himself to offer condolences. He crudely commented, "I didn't think a bullet to his head could hurt him."[33] (He did, however, forgive Merkle; he raised his salary by $300 and relied on him, both for his ability on the field and for strategic advice, for the next eight years.)

For his part, Rube hurried home to Cleveland immediately after the season. He had plenty of stories to tell family and friends about two spectacular pennant races, his headline-making purchase by the Giants, and the dizzying couple of weeks he had spent in New York. His father was remarried on October 29, to a neighborhood woman named Katie Lewis, and while Rube was happy about the event his thoughts were of New York. He had experienced only a glimpse of the city, its energy, motion, and bright lights and its passion for baseball, but he had seen enough to know that he could never be satisfied with life in the Midwest.

In fact, the allure of the big city probably eclipsed the first serious romance of his life. Back in Indianapolis a young lady named Clara Hazelton had caught his attention. They had met on a street car one afternoon after a ballgame, and he had offered her his seat. She became a fan, and for the rest of the summer she attended, along with her father, nearly every home game. The couple announced their engagement and were to be married at the home of Clara's parents on December 18. For reasons not clear, however, the ceremony never took place (though an erroneous account of the wedding appeared in the *Sporting News*), and Rube remained a bachelor.

Rube had the New York Giants on his mind. He had witnessed firsthand the adulation given to McGraw and Mathewson and the others; he was not ashamed to admit he craved the same attention for himself. Despite his inauspicious debut, he had every reason to believe that he fit into McGraw's plans for the future, and he was determined to prove his worth as a ballplayer — to McGraw, his teammates, the Giants fans, to his father, obviously, even to the Indians club that had, in his mind, snubbed him. And as he thought about his future, he could not have imagined that he would endure two full years of frustration and failure, experiences which, in his short career, he had only rarely known. But neither could he have guessed, when success in New York would finally come, just how high his star would rise.

CHAPTER 5

The $11,000 Lemon

For the second year in a row, John McGraw assembled his Giants for spring training in Marlin Springs, Texas, a small town about 100 miles south of Dallas. Marlin did not boast particularly extravagant baseball facilities, and the strong, dry winds blew constantly across the prairie, but neither did its remote locale offer much in the way of night-life temptations found elsewhere. Despite the close second-place finish of the year before, McGraw knew his club had some serious deficiencies to address, and he saw discipline, concentration and hard work as essential if the team was to compete again in 1909.

As practice began in late February, there were some notable absences from the squad. Christy Mathewson exercised the favored-player status reserved only for the likes of Cobb and Wagner and stayed north, coaching the Harvard baseball team and working out at his own pace. Matty, who was still grieving over the suicide of his younger brother Nicholas in January and was involved in several business ventures outside of baseball, was no fan of spring training, especially for pitchers. "We have the hardest time of any specialists who go to spring camp," he complained. "It's nothing but a daily grind."[1]

Roger Bresnahan had been traded to St. Louis, as he wished, and was now player/manager for the Cardinals. He had secured a five-year contract calling for $10,000 per year plus 10 percent of the team's profits, and McGraw could not blame him for jumping ship. (Bresnahan's younger brother Phil, however, was in Marlin trying unsuccessfully to make the Giant roster.) Art Devlin and Hooks Wiltse were holding out for more money, as was Laughing Larry Doyle. Doyle employed perhaps the most interesting strategy in negotiations: in 1908 he had been one of the few rookies who had ever received significant playing time from McGraw. Joe McGinnity had been released and, along with a Chicago millionaire named H. C. Smith, had purchased the Newark club of the Eastern Association for $50,000. And Mike Donlin had been persuaded by his wife, Mabel Hite, that his real talents lay in show business. The two were in Boston appearing in a song-and-dance show called "Stealing Home." Their 20-week theatrical contract would take them up and down the East Coast, and it was expected that "Turkey Mike" had retired from baseball for good.

But Rube arrived on schedule on February 20, fit and eager to prove himself to McGraw and his teammates. He was assigned to a room at the Arlington Hotel with Chief Meyers—"the big Indian," everyone called him—and both men were pleased with the arrangement. They quickly settled into the daily routine. The rookies, or yannigans, ate breakfast at the hotel first and then started for Emerson Field, walking two miles along railroad tracks, arriving no later than 9 A.M., an hour before the veterans. After a quick jog around the park and some extensive stretching and throwing, the players spent most mornings in the fundamental work for which McGraw's teams were famous: bunting, fielding, and baserunning drills, review of signals and signs, and sliding practice. (McGraw was the first manager to utilize sandpits and specialized hip pads, and his players worked every day on their form—especially the hook slide, which was the toughest to learn.) Batting practice was reserved for late mornings and early afternoons (interrupted by lunch, which in Texas was often the biggest meal of the day), and then the team split up for intrasquad games—usually the regulars versus the yannigans, with John Brush often in attendance and occasionally offering cigars for the winners. On weekends the club often traveled to Houston, Waco, or Dallas for exhibition games against local college or semipro teams.

Occasionally the Giants played against other National League teams training in the vicinity, although McGraw would never permit games against American League clubs. Most evenings were spent back at the hotel writing letters home, shooting pool, or playing checkers—Mathewson was renowned for playing, and beating, several men at the same time. Some of the veteran ballplayers organized duck or so-called snipe hunting excursions, and naturally some players sought out the saloons of Marlin's "downtown" section. (McGraw himself was a regular patron of several establishments where one could hear ragtime, jazz and blues music.) Rube was generally content, however, to hold back from those extracurricular activities and concentrate on playing the best ball he could.

Rube knew his defensive skills needed work, and he enthusiastically joined in the daily drills reserved for pitchers: fielding bunts, covering the bag on ground balls hit to the first baseman, and backing up throws from the outfield. Wilbert Robinson, McGraw's old friend from their Baltimore days, was on hand to coach pitchers and catchers, although he seemed to spend more time telling stories about the Orioles than instructing anybody. Charlie Carr was another interested observer in camp; he enjoyed reminding everyone of the success that Indianapolis and Rube had enjoyed the year before, and he was also on the lookout for anyone McGraw might release to his team. Carr often played a few innings in the intrasquad games, something McGraw also enjoyed, and his presence bolstered Rube's confidence.

Rube saw his first mound action on March 2 but was ineffective, giving up home runs to Merkle and Meyers in a five-inning practice game. He was not overly concerned by his poor performance, however, because he was under strict orders to limit the number of curveballs he threw and McGraw promised him plenty of future opportunities to pitch. Three days later he threw four strong innings for the regulars, holding the yannigans scoreless. Against Texas Christian University in Waco on March 10, he came on in relief with none out and the bases full, struck out two, and earned the save. (The feat might have generated more excitement, but Mathewson chose that day to arrive in camp, an event which overshadowed everything else.) On March 14 Rube threw four shutout innings against a Dallas semipro club, striking out seven, and on the eighteenth he pitched six scoreless innings against the Giant regulars. McGraw himself got into the act by playing third base and driving in six runs. After striking out eight in five innings against Fort Worth, Rube began to believe that not only would he make the team, but he might even earn a regular spot in the Giant rotation. First baseman Fred Tenney was covering spring training for the *New York Times* and noted in his daily column that "the elongated southpaw" was a "crackerjack" who had caught McGraw's attention with his preseason performances. "While he is new to major league work he has had phenomenal success in the minors," wrote Tenney. "If he can hold or improve his present form he should easily make good ... and join the best staff of pitchers ever assembled."[2]

That was clearly an overstatement, but the corps of pitchers showed promise. Mathewson looked brilliant in his first few outings, a fact which surprised no one but was noteworthy nonetheless. "It was really laughable to see some of the youngsters in their endeavors to hit Matty's famous fadeaway," Tenney wrote of the March 15 exhibition game. "They all agreed it beat anything they had ever seen."[3] Red Ames had consistent, if not overpowering stuff, and Hooks Wiltse eventually came around, as well. Arthur "Bugs" Raymond, acquired in the Bresnahan deal, possessed a wicked spitball but had a notorious reputation as one of the worst alcoholics in baseball. McGraw believed he could reform him, and as spring progressed Bugs seemed serious about staying sober. Nearly everyone else, however, expected Bugs to fall off the wagon at any moment. Should either Rube or Lou Durham fulfill their promise, the Giants had the makings of a solid staff.

As his team took shape, McGraw was pleased with most of his players. Outfielder Red Murray, also acquired in the Bresnahan trade, was fast, intelligent, and eager to play on a winning team. Devlin arrived, a little heavy around the midsection but glad to put his contract squabble behind him. But Chief Meyers was the biggest news in Marlin (and literally in the National League; at 230 pounds he was the largest player in the entire circuit). He hammered the ball all spring and conducted himself admirably behind the plate. At age 28 he was as old as or older than many veterans and had been around, playing in the semipro leagues of California and Montana and for St. Paul of the American Association. He also claimed to have played for Dartmouth College. (Years later he admitted that he had falsified his grade transcripts to enter the school and had

been asked to leave campus when discovered. Nevertheless, he proudly remained, until the day he died, a "Dartmouth man."[4]) It was initially expected that the Chief would share the catching duties with Cleveland native George Schlei, who had come over from Cincinnati, but as the season wore on Schlei faded from the picture and Meyers became a fixture in New York for seven straight seasons. He was a hit with the Texas fans, as well, and his good-natured outlook provided a pleasant contrast to the drudgery of spring training.

The city of Marlin did everything it could to make the Giants' stay pleasant, and McGraw appreciated the efforts. He persuaded Brush to donate the gate receipts of several exhibition games to charity; one game benefited the Ladies' Charitable Association and the widow and four children of a murdered Marlin man, and another assisted a black elementary school ("Quite a large and very enthusiastic crowd, numbering many colored persons, was present," wrote Tenney[5]). Near the end of March a banquet honoring the Giants was held at the Arlington, and by the time the Giants broke camp and headed north McGraw had vowed that he would bring his club back to Marlin each spring from now on.

Yet not everything went smoothly. On March 15 outfielder Cy Seymour argued with coach Arlie Latham outside his hotel room and then knocked Latham down and bit him on the cheek. The incident was no doubt brought on by something Latham had said in an attempt at humor. "The freshest man in baseball" was one of McGraw's favorites, but many Giants found him offensive and pretty tough to take. Unfortunately for Seymour, the ruckus brought McGraw out of his room down the hall; he arrived only in time to see Seymour on top of Latham administering the beating. McGraw pulled Seymour up and immediately threw him off the club, ordering him to catch the next train out of town. "Seymour is done with the club, and that goes. This is the worst thing I ever saw pulled off," said McGraw, himself a veteran of countless brawls.[6] Seymour would quickly repent and beg reinstatement. He eventually got it but never again returned to his manager's good graces. He stayed with the Giants for two more seasons but played only part-time.

At the end of the month, the Giants left Texas and began to work their way north, stopping off at Little Rock, Memphis, Louisville, and other cities for final exhibition games. Rube was impressive in Columbus on April 4, and in

Opposite: Rube, at far left, strikes a confident pose at the start of the 1909 season, his first full year with the Giants. Note the notorious Bugs Raymond kneeling in front next to John McGraw. Wilbert Robinson sports a mustache at lower right, and Art Shafer, standing third from right next to Chief Meyers, reminds the photographer that the Giants are a baseball team. Despite all the antics, it is the lordly Christy Mathewson, standing at middle, who dominates the picture. *Standing, left to right:* Rube Marquard, Doc Crandall, Red Ames, George Schlei, Red Murray, Christy Mathewson, Cy Seymour, Hooks Wiltse, Larry Doyle, Fred Snodgrass, Fred Tenney, Chief Meyers, Art Shafer, Art Devlin, Arlie Latham. *Seated, left to right:* Buck Herzog, Al Bridwell, Bugs Raymond, John McGraw, Bill O'Hara, Wilbert Robinson. Photo courtesy Lawrence Ritter.

Richmond on the sixth, giving up only five hits in eight innings of work. He showed improvement defensively, as well, starting a "lightning fast" double play on a bunt, "Marquard to Bridwell to Tenney." After more good outings in Baltimore and Newark, he had gained McGraw's confidence — "showed why he was worth all the cash paid out for him,"[7] wrote Tenney — and secured a spot in the rotation. He stands proudly next to Doc Crandall in the official team photo, chin down on Doc's shoulder and grinning. His first full big-league season was set to begin in New York on April 15.

Rube rented a small apartment on West 99th Street, just a short train ride to the Polo Grounds in north Harlem. The huge, bathtub-shaped structure had existed, in various forms and at various sites, since the original built by manufacturing magnate John B. Day in 1888. Home plate was nestled beneath the Speedway paralleling 8th and 9th avenues and Coogan's Bluff, which offered a cheap, if limited, view of the game below. Fans not inclined to purchase tickets could congregate and catch glimpses of part of the outfield action. It was also a convenient gathering spot to meet friends, guzzle a beer or two, and lay down a few dollars on the ballgame.

Because of the Giants' enormous popularity with these fans, who were clearly buoyed by the wild finish of the 1908 season, John Brush had authorized improvements to the stadium in preparation for the new season. The diamond itself had been moved outward, making room for seven new rows of box seats behind home plate and along the baselines. Additional bleacher sections had been added, connecting up the 25-cent seats with the 50-centers so that the bleachers now completely encircled the playing field. Nearly 700 prime seats had been hung, in units of four "boxes," along the upper grandstand, as well, and the Polo Grounds could now hold nearly 40,000 fans, making it easily the largest ballpark in the country. By comparison, two brand new parks which opened in 1909, Forbes Field in Pittsburgh and Shibe Park in Philadelphia, held 25,000 and 20,000, respectively.

Brush had spruced up the place in other ways. New clubhouses with cement floors had been constructed. The Giant bench was connected by tunnel to an open area behind the grandstand, where pitchers could warm up without being seen by the opposition. Some 7,000 cartloads of dirt had been hauled in and spread around the outfield, eliminating slopes and rough spots and finally raising it to the level of the infield. Telephone booths, with operators standing by, were installed along the first level of the grandstand, and the entire facility had been painted a bright spring green. About the only thing missing at the Polo Grounds now, wisecracked one New York scribe, was an arrow to direct Merkle to second base.

When the Giants took the field at 4 P.M. on a chilly Thursday afternoon, they wore new cream-white uniforms trimmed in violet and were greeted by the cheers of some 30,000 fans, many of whom had been there since the gates opened just after noon. Two of their heroes, however, were conspicuously absent from

Opening Day festivities. McGraw suffered from an infected index finger; the infection was so severe that for a time doctors considered amputation. It required minor surgery, and his discomfort was such that he stayed home in his 11th Avenue apartment instead of venturing to the ballpark. And Mathewson had been hit on the throwing hand by a batting practice line drive off the bat of McCormick. He was in uniform, but the familiar New York cheer, "Oh you Matty!" would not be heard at the Polo Grounds until early May. (Perhaps some of the Giants were a little tired of the constant hero-worship Mathewson received. When the injury forced him to miss his final preseason start in Dallas, Fred Tenney wrote that his absence "disappointed all the ladies who had come out to see him perform.... Wasn't it just too mean for anything?"[8])

But the game against Brooklyn went on anyway, and in spectacular deadball-era fashion. Red Ames took the mound for the Giants and threw no-hit ball for 10 innings, weakening only in the 13th. Superbas right fielder/manager Harry Lumley tripled, igniting a three-run rally for the only scoring of the day. Brooklyn pitcher Irvin "Kaiser" Wilhelm gave up only three hits to the Giants and earned the victory.

Friday's game began at 2 P.M., and the earlier start and drizzling rain kept the crowd down to about 15,000. Bugs Raymond threw a four-hitter at Brooklyn, defeating them by the same 3–0 score. Aside from Bugs' strong outing, the game was notable only for the return of Larry Doyle, whose holdout lasted the entire preseason and one regular season game. Doyle had not been successful in his bid for more money but was honored when McGraw named him team captain. He would also take over as acting manager many times in future years on the regular occasions when McGraw was suspended for umpire abuse or other objectionable behavior.

Saturday, April 17, brought warmer weather and the Philadelphia team to New York. A crowd of almost 33,000 turned out to see Rube and Chief Meyers— "the Giants' much-heralded $17,500 battery"— defeat the Phillies 4–1.[9] Rube was masterful in gaining his first major league victory, allowing only three hits and striking out seven. The only run Philadelphia could manage came on a passed ball by Meyers; the ball struck umpire Jimmy Johnstone on the shoulder, and he ruled that John Titus, who had singled and worked his way around to third, could score.

The *New York Times* gushed over Rube's "dominant" performance. "The tall, left-handed Marquard did all that was expected of him ... holding the Phillies practically helpless throughout the nine innings.... He not only dished up a dazzling array of upshoots, drops and other deceptive balls, but fielded his position faultlessly, causing the downfall of several of his opponents, and helped the good cause along by rapping out a single in the fourth inning."[10]

Rube continued to pitch well in the early part of the season but met with little good luck. He lost 3–2 to Boston (called variously the Pilgrims, Orphans, or Doves by the press) on April 26, as the Giants struggled through a variety of ailments. Shortstop Bridwell was down with a sprained ankle, Doyle had tonsillitis, and Cy Seymour, in his first game back from exile since the Dallas hotel incident, collided with Murray while chasing down a fly ball in the first inning. He remained motionless on the grass for a full five minutes and then staggered to his feet gamely and refused to be taken out. The next batter lofted a fly ball to him, which he caught. But as he drew his arm back to throw the ball in, he collapsed again and this time had to be carried from the field. It would be August before he returned to the lineup. (April 26 was an unfortunate day all around the league. In Philadelphia, catcher Mike "Doc" Powers died from the effects of gangrene poisoning; he had been taken to the hospital in the seventh inning of the first game of the season and never left.)

Rube lost on April 30 to Philadelphia and on May 7 to Boston by identical 2–1 scores. He took leads into the ninth inning of both games, but the combination of bases on balls and the opposition's timely hitting cost him. The second of these defeats was particularly tough to take. He and Chief Meyers were badly fooled on a suicide squeeze play which cost them the game, and McGraw did not appreciate being outsmarted by his own brand of "inside" baseball.

May 24 brought the still-popular Roger Bresnahan and his Cardinals to the Polo Grounds, and former Giant great John Montgomery Ward and Mayor McClellan of New York welcomed him home with speeches, flowers, and a silver loving cup. Bresnahan was also presented with the "keys to the village lockup" lest his return be too triumphant. But the ceremony was, stated the *Times*, "a notable event before a very bad game of ball," the Giants committing three errors and losing 3–1.[11] Even Mathewson's return a week later did not seem to help. He was beaten badly by the Reds in Cincinnati, and when Rube lost to the Reds by a 4–2 score the Giants fell into last place.

In June, however, their prospects seemed to brighten. In St. Louis, McGraw came to the aid of Doyle, who had been called out at first on a close play. While McGraw and umpire Rigler cursed each other, Doyle took off for second base and defiantly sat on the bag. For their theatrics both Giants were ejected, "withdrawing to the more placid atmosphere of the clubhouse bungalow," but the incident seemed to spark the team, which went on to win 8–7.[12] Matty and Wiltse returned to form, the return of Bridwell solidified the infield, and the youngsters Merkle and Snodgrass showed signs of good things to come. The wildly superstitious McGraw overlooked nothing: a fan brought a chimpanzee to the Polo Grounds one day and sat him down in a box seat next to John Brush directly behind the Giant bench. "Consul the Great," as the ape was called, was trained to clap his hands and screech with delight when the home team scored. After a doubleheader sweep of Boston on June 23, Consul was named official club mascot and appeared at home games for the rest of the season, his owner ultimately securing a contract with the William Morris agency for further bookings. On June 26, Rube beat Nap Rucker and the Superbas 2–1 for the Giants' seventh straight victory. Now with a record of 31–22, they climbed back into third place behind Chicago and Pittsburgh.

Giant fans had further reason to be hopeful as rumors circulated that Mike Donlin was negotiating his return to the club. It was not that Donlin's vaudeville career was stalling; rather, he realized that his continued success on the stage depended upon continued success on the ball diamond, and he could not afford to stay away for too long. Mike and Mabel met with Brush and offered to play out the balance of the season for $4,000, a proposition that seemed reasonable to everyone but McGraw. Offended by Donlin's lack of loyalty, he instead offered to trade him to Philadelphia for Sherwood Magee and Lew Moren, a deal that would allow Donlin to play and manage the Quakers. (Moren was a 28-year-old pitcher often called "the millionaire's kid"; he received $100 from his father after each victory he threw. In 1909 he was having his best season, on his way to 16 victories. Magee was a dependable outfielder who would average .292 over 16 seasons.)

Rube's baseball card, circa 1911, issued by the Piedmont Tobacco Company. Courtesy Lawrence Ritter.

But then it was revealed that Philadelphia owner Felix Isman was also interested in Chicago catcher Johnny Kling, who was, like Donlin, a salary holdout with unique show business aspirations — Kling toured the northeast giving billiard exhibitions. When Isman tried to persuade Kling to manage his club, Donlin in turn began to negotiate with Brooklyn. He had not, of course, been given his release by the Giants, who owned his rights under the reserve clause, and ultimately all the deals fell through.

The biggest series of the season began in New York on July 9. A huge crowd of 40,000 jammed the Polo Grounds to watch a doubleheader with the first-place Pirates. This was even more fans than had seen the playoff game with the Cubs the preceding fall, but this time they were far better behaved. McGraw brought his yellow puppy "Truxton," named after his New York hometown, and allowed him to cavort on the field before the game in the hopes of disrupting the Pirate batting practice. New York merchants showed their true partisan colors, offering, as inducements for Giant home runs, pianos, phonographs, canary birds, and pairs of rubber boots. "If this trend keeps up," observed the *Times*, "a successful batter will be able to marry, retire from business, and live on the fruits of it for the rest of his life."[13] Despite all the spectacle, however, the Giants were swept by scores of 9–5 and 4–2.

Rube pitched in the opener, coming on in quick relief of starter Ames, but he was wild, issuing five walks in only three innings and taking the loss. "The Rube blew up," stated the *Times* flatly, noting that he was in for a rough time in the big leagues if he could not gain control of his pitches. The paper took a more lighthearted view of Raymond's losing effort in the second game: "It was one of the entomologist's off days. Possibly he chafed under the recollection that somewhere in Central Park there wandered at the moment a rare beetle or other insect he had neglected to capture and preserve in the interests of science. It may be his thoughts were wholly occupied by his private collection of winged things. At any rate, he was off form."[14]

The next day the Pirates beat the Giants again, 8–2, this time Wiltse taking the brunt of the beating. "30,000 dazed fans saw the slaughter," reported the *Times*. "Butchery it was, a riotous carnival of the shambles."[15] The goat of the game was third-base coach Arlie Latham, who, after Bridwell had smashed a long drive to the center-field wall, first held him up and then sent him in from third. The hesitation cost Bridwell, and he was called out at home, killing the only Giant rally of the day. This example of "really stupid coaching" was an example of why Fred Snodgrass remembered later that Latham was "probably the worst third-base coach that ever lived," a sentiment that the *Times* would later echo, as well.[16]

The Giants never recovered from this disastrous series in New York, and the club was never in serious contention for the pennant, although Mathewson won 25 games and Wiltse earned 20 wins. Mathewson's record was down 12 from 1908 but was still an admirable number; in July he missed two weeks with yet another injured finger, resulting from a smash line drive off the bat of the Cardinals' Joe Dehahanty. McGraw's temper got the better of him repeatedly as the season wound down. He fined and suspended Otis Crandall for playing dice past hours on the train, argued constantly with umpires (particularly Johnstone and O'Day), and had to fine and suspend Raymond repeatedly for breaking curfew and violating team rules. "My life is one fine after another," moaned Bugs, and McGraw could only agree and reluctantly reinstate him.[17] Even though Raymond won 18 games in 1909, his most successful season out of six in the majors, he did not come close to fulfilling his enormous potential.

Rube lost confidence after the Pirate series, continued to struggle with his control, and eventually fell out of the rotation as McGraw searched for winning combinations. He was wound too tightly, McGraw thought, and could not seem to relax and take advantage of his natural abilities. He consistently fell behind in the count and smart hitters waited for pitches they could handle. Rube was actually relieved when he didn't start a game in Chicago on September 16. President Taft and 30,000 other spectators expected Matty to take on Three Finger Brown and their expectations were realized. Always sensitive to what the newspapers had to say, Rube was wounded to read headlines like "Marquard Wild and Quakers Win," "Marquard Batted Out of Box," and "Giants Fall Down Behind Marquard." Increasingly the topic of money found its way into the accompanying articles: The emphatic headline "Marquard Fails Again" was followed by this comment: "Manager McGraw attempted to demonstrate that Marquard was worth at least part of that $11,000 alleged to have been paid for him last fall by [pitching him again] despite his poor showing in the first inning of the day before."[18] The crowds at the Polo Grounds which had cheered Rube so enthusiastically in April now began to razz him, venting their frustrations as they sensed pennant hopes fading. McGraw had no inclination to feed him to the wolves. While Rube pitched regularly in relief, he started only two games after Labor Day, and none at the Polo Grounds.

Trying to ignore speculation that he might not return to the Giants the following year, Rube managed to win his final start of the season, defeating Cincinnati 4–2 on September 26, driving in two runs himself. He finished the season with a record of 5–13. The mark was surely a disappointment after all the hype that had surrounded his purchase and in view of his promising start, but there was some cause for hope. Despite issuing 73 walks in 173 innings of work, Rube's earned-run average was a respectable 2.60, and he struck out 109 batters. And he clearly fared better than Lou Durham, who appeared in only four games in what turned out to be his only full year in the major leagues.

The season belonged to Pittsburgh. On September 23, the "Anniversary of Merkle Day" said the *Times*,[19] the Giants took two games from St. Louis and still found themselves a full 20 games behind the Pirates. Barney Dreyfuss' club won 110 games (six more than the Cubs and 18 more than New York) and clinched their fourth pennant of the decade on September 17. Honus Wagner again showed why he was the world's best ballplayer. He led the league in batting average, slugging percentage, and RBIs, and finished in the top five in virtually every other offensive category. The Bucs claimed their first world championship by defeating the Tigers, in seven games, in the Series. Rookie Babe Adams was the pitching star, winning 3 games after winning only 12 during the regular season. His performance nearly overshadowed Wagner's duel with Cobb; the Dutchman got the better of it in the last World Series either men would ever play in.

After an anxious winter in Cleveland, Rube again reported to training camp in Marlin Springs. While he was glad to see his old teammates and welcome a few new ones, he fretted that his spot on the roster was not secure. He worried about his control and the boisterous crowds in New York, and he was haunted by the constant reminder that his purchase for $11,000 had been a bust. He kept his concerns to himself, but for the first time was privately questioning his own abilities on the mound.

The development of Rube Marquard was hardly McGraw's only concern in the spring of 1910. Mike Donlin continued to keep the club guessing about his intentions. He negotiated skillfully through the press, because he knew that the public, and most of his teammates, were on his side. Even Mabel took their position to the press, writing a series of articles on the rigors of baseball life and the equally stressful show business the pair had come to know. Given a deadline of March 10 to decide whether to report or sit out another year, Donlin chose neither option, instead wiring to Brush the one-sentence telegram "Cannot determine the matter yet."[20] Fred Tenney used his daily column to urge Brush to meet Donlin's demands. "All the boys are eagerly awaiting the news whether Mike Donlin is to rejoin the team. The consensus of opinion here is that if he does we will have a winner sure. The best is none too good for us. That's why we are pulling for his return."[21] But the two sides could not reach agreement, and Donlin returned to the stage. He signed a three-year contract with the Liebler Theatrical Management Company, appearing first with Mabel in a musical called *A Certain Party*.

Fred Tenney was given an unconditional release after injuring his foot. The popular and articulate first baseman was forced to sit out the year; he then played (and managed) one more season in Boston before retiring for good. His spot in the lineup was filled by Fred Merkle, who had overcome the disgrace of his 1908 failure and settled comfortably into the role of starter. Merkle hit .292 in his first year as a full-time player, appearing in all but 10 games, although he could not reasonably be expected to provide the leadership of Tenney.

McGraw knew that the time was approaching when the younger generation of Giant players must step up and produce. Merkle and Snodgrass obviously were to be counted on. Art Fletcher and Josh Devore would also see increased playing time this season, and their successes — along with, of course, the effectiveness of the pitchers — would determine how far the team would go.

As much as McGraw liked the remote locale of Marlin, he recognized that his players, while willing to work hard on the practice field, were often bored when not in uniform. He did his best to break up the tedium. Once again exhibition games were played for the benefit of the Ladies Social Club of Marlin ("the ladies were very much pleased at the generosity of Manager McGraw, and the attendance was large and enthusiastic"[22]), the Daughters of the Confederacy, and other civic groups. One Friday the Marlin High School team took on the Giants, and most local businesses were closed as "the whole town turned out to witness the contest."[23] The team gathered for an occasional fish fry or possum feed at picnic facilities along the Brazos River, attended ice cream socials sponsored by local merchants, and enjoyed dances at the Arlington Hotel. On March 18, McGraw arranged for the club to be guests of honor at the Marlin Opera House. After the local talent had concluded its performance, a quartet of Giants, including Chief Meyers, "were pressed into service and sang several songs for the edification of the people."²⁴ McGraw's strategy seemed to be paying off. "The boys are finding their stay at Marlin much more pleasant than last year, as they have become acquainted with so many of the residents and social attentions are quite numerous."²⁵ McGraw met with city officials and negotiated a deal to construct a new practice facility. (John Brush was ill with rheumatism and spent the spring relaxing in the hot springs near San Antonio.) The new grounds would feature a water well so that the players could shower in the modern clubhouse. The complex was deeded to the Giants in exchange for their promise to continue to train in Marlin, which they would do until 1918.

Rube showed flashes of brilliance — on March 10 he struck out eight Fort Worth batters in a row — but he was hit hard by his teammates in intrasquad games. McGraw tried to boost his confidence by pitching him more often against minor league or college teams, but Rube was embarrassed when his old Indianapolis team beat him on the fifteenth, scoring nine runs in the second inning. Despite persistent rumors that Rube would be assigned, at least temporarily, to an Eastern League team (as was Lou Durham, who was optioned to New Bedford) or perhaps traded to another big league club, McGraw chose to keep Rube on the squad as the Giants prepared to head north. As in prior years, the Giants played games in various cities en route to New York; Rube saw limited mop-up duty in Shreveport, Greenville, and Baltimore. In its preseason issue, the *Sporting News* evidently did not think Rube fit into the Giants plans; besides noting that he "lacked control," there was no other mention of him.

The season began in Boston on April 14. The Pilgrims beat Red Ames 3–2 in 11 innings, then defeated Raymond the following day 5–4. Striking out eight in a 3–1 game, Mathewson gained the first Giant victory of the year on Saturday the sixteenth. (Matty was often reserved for Saturday games when crowds were likely to be larger; many big league clubs, including the Giants, did not yet play Sunday baseball.) After several days of rain, the Giants held their home opener on April 20, Hooks Wiltse shutting out Boston 4–0. The crowd of 25,000 included such dignitaries as Mayor Gaynor of New York, who threw out the first ball (days earlier President Taft had done the same thing in Washington, starting a presidential tradition), and Lord Kitchenor of Khartoum, who was seeing his first American baseball game. When the Giants rallied, noted the *Times*, the Lord heard from the crowd something "that has not jarred his ears since the Boers were whooping it up in South Africa."²⁶

Finally on Thursday, April 21, Rube was given the chance to pitch, against weak Boston and before only 7,000 fans at the Polo Grounds. He started well, allowing only two hits in five innings. He struck out seven and, reported the *Times*, "had them dazzled with the bewildering jumps of his shoots."²⁷ But disaster struck in the bottom of the sixth. Leading off against Buster Brown, Rube slammed a low liner into the left-center-field gap. He slid hard into second base, safe with a double, but jammed his right ankle and had to be carried from the

Rube with teammates Ned Washburn, and "Turkey" Mike Donlin at the Polo Grounds, circa 1911. Photo courtesy Library of Congress.

field. Crandall came on in relief and secured the 3–2 victory, but Rube now had a physical injury to deal with, along with an already fragile psyche.

After their sluggish start, the Giants righted themselves. On May 2 against Brooklyn, Mathewson was perfect for six innings and finished with a no-hitter. With Rube scheduled to pitch four days later against Philadelphia, the Giants had the chance to take over first place. They did just that, but with little credit to Rube. Staked to a 7–0 lead in the fourth inning, he surrendered five hits and two walks and had to be relieved by Wiltse, who finished the game. McGraw was not pleased that he had to "waste" regular starter Wiltse, and he was concerned that even with a big lead Rube could not be counted on to throw strikes. Although Rube was credited with his second win of the season, and the Giants were on top of the league with a record of 13–5, Rube's descent had begun.

The Giants began their first western swing of the season. In Chicago on May 14, Rube was pounded for eight hits and four runs in only 4⅔ innings, and McGraw removed him from the starting rotation. Rube fared no better in relief, getting blasted for five runs in St. Louis (and blowing a save in support of Raymond), then allowing three runs in just an inning of work against Cincinnati. In both games wildness was the problem. Rube now was known for walking the bases full at least once in every outing.

The *Sporting News* took the problem to its readers. "Marquard is still a mystery," wrote Ernest Lanigan. "He seems to have everything a pitcher needs in his line, except control of the ball. He certainly has had ample time to get control of his curves, if he ever expects to do so."[28] Perhaps he should give up on the idea of becoming a pitcher, speculated Lanigen; he could hit and maybe he could make it as an outfielder.

The debacle in Cincinnati was Rube's last appearance on the mound for six weeks. When he did return on July 2, it was inconsequential. He relieved Ames in a 6–3 loss to Brooklyn, then sat out another month. He worked hard on the sidelines, however, in hopes of regaining his control and his confidence. It was McGraw's habit to announce his starting pitcher either the day before or the day of the game, but as each day came and went the call was for someone else. Would Rube "ever present his act?" wondered the *Sporting News*.[29] The Giants, as they had the year before, played decent baseball but were not the class of the league. No team could catch the Cubs in 1910, and finally, with his club clearly out of contention for the flag, McGraw began to allow Rube to pitch, but the results were disastrous.

September was easily the worst month of Rube's life. On the fifth he pitched in an exhibition game. Players from the Giants, Yankees, and Superbas split into two squads and played for the benefit of 20,000 "newsies," young boys who hawked papers on street corners. Rube threw four innings and gave up two runs. To make matters worse, most of the damage came off the bats of his Giant teammates.

On September 15, with his club fully 12 games behind the Cubs, McGraw called on Rube to pitch against Pittsburgh. "Pirates Feast on Marquard" blared the headline, and it was not an overstatement. Rube was touched four hits, allowed six walks, and surrendered five runs in seven innings. The sportswriter did not spare the sarcasm:

> That six-foot instance of the high cost of living, Rube Marquard, who has warmed up more and pitched less than any two pitchers in the major leagues this year, was trotted out for a trial mid thunderous applause. A lot of people still believe Rube will yet make good, because he cost so much. He hasn't been on slab in so long that it was just like breaking into the big leagues all over again for him. Rube still has those beautiful curves which dance in all the available space around the plate. He can put the ball nearer the pan without getting it over than any man that ever wore a toe plate.
>
> How reminiscent it all seemed, how outrageously familiar, to see Rube pass Byrne, the first man who faced him. Yes, Geraldine, and even more familiar when he passed Leach with just as much ease. But now listen to the clamor and the noise. He fanned Campbell, and Rube's admirers confided to themselves that the human beanpole had at last found the platter and there was nothing more to it. Wagner spilled a grounder at Bridwell, who forced Leach at second.... Ha,Ha, Marquard is right on the job again and Miller walks.... All together now, three long groans and a hard luck chirp for ol' Rube.[30]

A few days later, with the Giants ahead 11–3 in the 8th against St. Louis, McGraw "took a long chance and put Marquard in to pitch," acccording to the Times.[31] Rube took after the sportswriter the next day, cursing him, crushing the man's bowler hat, and yanking him by the necktie. He was fined $25 for the outburst.

Rube was given one final chance to start, in New York on September 22, again against the Cardinals. He gave up three triples in the first two innings, beaned Steve Evans with a fastball, and lost 5–4. He was loudly booed as he walked to the clubhouse; his nickname of "the $11,000 lemon" was used as commonly in New York as McGraw's "Muggsy," Mathewson's "Big Six," or Merkle's "Bonehead." Rube finished the year with a miserable record of four wins and four losses. He walked 40 batters in only 71 innings, and his ERA was an astronomical 4.46.

Years later Rube recalled how devastated he was by his pitching failure and the treatment he received because of it. He told the *Sporting News* in an interview:

> I think I've got the words "eleven thousand dollar lemon" memorized better than any other four words in the language. If I'd open a paper the first few words I'd see on the sporting page were those.... If some kid saw me on the street he'd call out, "There goes the eleven thousand dollar lemon."

I'd get it in the baseball grounds whenever I'd show my face. I'd get it in the hotel when I'd catch little scraps of conversation. If I went to a show some comedian would be sure to have something about it. The fans were full of it. Why, I stopped reading the newspapers and got so I even hated to show myself on the street for fear I'd be recognized. It was awful.

The one thing I couldn't sidestep was my mail. I'd get 12 or 15 letters a day. I'd call 'em "big-stiff" letters because they always commenced, "You big stiff, go back to the plow."[32]

For the rest of his life, Rube maintained that the press had at least something to do with his failures. In an article he wrote for *Baseball* magazine, he complained that the newspapers "set a standard for me (after his purchase from Indianapolis) that I could not possibly attain; it roused the expectations of the fans to a high pitch, and when these expectations failed to be realized the public was naturally disappointed.... They called me a big league failure and ... I was."[33]

It was widely speculated in the press that Rube would not return to the Giants in 1911 and might not be able to catch on with any other major league team. "If McGraw were to ask waivers on Marquard now they would be granted by the other seven managers in the league," stated the *Sporting News*. "His showing has been horrible to behold."[34]

Chapter 6

Beauty

Wilbert Robinson was born in 1864 in Hudson, Massachusetts, the son of the village butcher. He quit school at age sixteen to pursue a career in baseball. Working his way up the ranks through town ball, various New England minor leagues, and Philadelphia, which was in the original American Association, he ultimately landed with Baltimore of the 12-club National League in 1892. He was the star catcher for Ned Hanlon's Orioles for the rest of the decade, playing alongside Wee Willie Keeler, Joe Corbett (brother of heavyweight champion Gentleman Jim), and John J. McGraw. At 5'8" and 170 pounds, Robbie was fast. (He once stole 40 bases in a single season), and he was a good hitter (he hit as high as .354 in 1896 and set the record of seven hits in seven at bats, with 11 RBI, in one game in 1892.) With Robbie behind the plate, the old Orioles won three straight pennants before the turn of the century.

Robbie also teamed with McGraw in business ventures, operating for several years the Blue Diamond cafe in Baltimore, a sporting establishment of some renown. After several coaching stints, Robbie was out of baseball by 1904. He had met a young lady from Ireland, whom he married — he convinced her to tear up her return ticket home — and they had a young son. In 1911 he was back in Maryland, managing a prosperous meat market but hankering to get back into the game. He had, for several years, traveled to Marlin Springs to spend spring training with the Giants, where he offered advice to pitchers and catchers, managed the yannigans in exhibition games, and generally tried to make himself useful. But now in 1911 McGraw had a special project in mind for his old friend: he wanted Robbie to resurrect Rube Marquard's career. And when Rube stepped off the 4:20 P.M. train from San Antonio on February 28th, Robbie was waiting at the station to greet him.

Robbie believed that what Rube needed above all else was a massive boost of self-confidence, and Rube clearly was relieved to learn that McGraw had not given up on him. As camp progressed, Rube and Robbie became constant companions on the field and off. Robbie stressed the importance of getting ahead in the count, challenging the hitter, and forcing him to swing at Rube's best pitch, not the hitter's. More importantly, if he did fall behind, he could not afford to let up but had to continue to throw hard and take advantage of his natural "stuff." Rube had to learn to conquer his fear of being wild, to ignore the crowd and worry less about the reports in the press. (One persistent rumor that spring was that Joe McGinnity, who had broken his wrist, needed pitching help at Newark and McGraw would send Rube there.) But Robbie massaged Rube's ego and assured him that McGraw believed that, along with Mathewson, Rube would become a mainstay of the staff.

In fact Matty was to play a vital role in Rube's development, as well. McGraw assigned Matty to room with Rube, both at the Arlington and on the road once the season began. It proved to be a smart move, for Rube, as nearly everyone else, revered the "Big Six." Mathewson was unquestionably the leader of the club. A product of Bucknell University, he was widely credited with single-handedly bringing a new level of sophistication to baseball. While he was hardly the only college man to make the major leagues, his good looks, demeanor, and sterling record made him the most popular player in the game. He was truly a hero of the age.

Mathewson was clearly admired by his teammates. Chief Meyers held him in the highest esteem. "How we loved to play for him!" the Chief reflected 50 years later. "We'd break our necks for that guy. If you made an error behind him, he'd never get mad or sulk. He'd come over and pat you on the back. He had the sweetest, most gentle nature. Gentle in every way."[1]

Fred Snodgrass was equally laudatory. "Matty was the greatest pitcher who ever lived, in my opinion. He was a wonderful, wonderful man too, a reserved sort of fellow, a little hard to get close to. But once you got to know him, he was a wonderful friend."[2] To Rube, Mathewson was a "grand guy," and 50 years later he proudly recalled that they had been roommates. "At eleven o'clock we all had to be in our rooms and the trainer would come around and check us off. We'd usually have a whole floor in a hotel and we'd be two in a room.... The door would be wide open at eleven o'clock and the trainer would come by with a board with all the names on it. He'd poke his head in:

Mathewson, Marquard, check. And lock the door. Next room, check, lock the door."[3]

So while Robbie focused on improving Rube's mental toughness, Matty worked on his physical makeup: his control, mechanics, and assortment of pitches. Under Matty's tutelage, Rube simplified his windup and dropped his throwing arm down from an overhand style delivery to three-quarters. He learned the basics of Mathewson's most powerful weapon, the "fadeaway," now more commonly called the screwball. The pitch was thrown with an inward snap of the wrist and elbow and broke in the opposite direction of the curveball. Hence Rube's left-handed fadeaway broke down and away from right-handed hitters.

And it was more than just mastering the mechanics of this pitch, Matty advised. It was knowing when to throw it, and to whom. Although he would never utilize it primarily as his "out" pitch, in time Rube was able to throw the pitch nearly as effectively as his famous mentor.

And Rube also finally began to master the change of pace — a pitch thrown with the same motion as the fastball but with the ball tucked deeper into the grip, so that it traveled at a deceptively slower speed. Rube referred to his changeup as his "turkey trot" pitch, and in just a few short weeks of spring training he had added two new, effective pitches to his arsenal.

Sensing that perhaps Rube had been brought along too quickly in past years, McGraw and Robinson proceeded more cautiously in 1911. In his first few outings, Rube threw for the yannigans, and only against area college or semipro competition. He was in fine physical shape, and his arm felt strong and loose; with each successful outing his confidence grew. On March 12 he pitched six innings against Fort Worth, allowing only two scratch singles and striking out four, and four days later against Houston he "held the locals in the hollow of his hand,"[4] again striking out four and facing only 30 batters over the full nine innings. After a strong performance against Dallas on March 26 (six strikeouts and one walk in four innings), he began to pitch for the regulars. By the end of the month when the Giants left Texas, his place in the rotation seemed once again secure.

McGraw stubbornly resisted suggestions that he trade Rube or ship him to the minors. "I'll stick with Marquard because he has shown me that he has something," he told one reporter. "A young fellow with 'stuff,' even if he cannot get it over, needs time. He's as valuable an asset as an old fellow who goes along delivering with a cheap arm and a good head. You never can tell when a youngster is going to cut loose and make good."[5]

The early *New York Times* reports were characteristically positive: "Rube Marquard is working ... showing lots of speed ... has regained form, showing excellent control.... His work has been the feature of several games."[6] But *Sporting Life*, a national magazine published in Philadelphia, noted that Rube had been impressive in previous spring training camps. "As usual every spring, the reports of Mr. Marquard's good work comes to us. It is said that never has he given such promise as this year...If Marquard could only realize some of these brilliant hopes upon his return that he inspires every spring in the training camp it would, of course, mean a vast deal for the Giants, but he has disappointed us all so many times in this way that we don't dare hope too much for fear of being once more disappointed. Still, there is always the chance that Marquard will finally make good."[7] The *Sporting News* was even less enthusiastic; its only mention of Rube in preseason publications was the observation that he would probably be assigned to Newark of the Eastern League. But Rube was more confident than at any time since leaving Indianapolis. He was going to "put the knockers" to his detractors this year, he predicted, "and make good with the Giants."[9]

For the most part, it was a quiet spring. The only hint of sensation in Marlin was the rumored appearance of star Japanese player Togo Hammanoto, who had been negotiating with McGraw over the winter months. But Hammanoto did not show up and offered no explanation, disappointing McGraw and the newspapermen, as well. In one of the final exhibition games, both Devlin and Merkle were tossed out of a ballgame for brawling, and Rube was also ejected for arguing over an umpire's call. McGraw was convinced his club was in fighting shape and ready to start the season.

On Saturday, April 7, the Giants played their annual preseason finale against Yale, at the Polo Grounds. Just over 2,000 shivering fans turned out to see Rube baffle the collegians 4–0, allowing only one hit in the first game of a doubleheader. The *Times* took notice of Rube's new and improved presence on the mound. "Right up there in the top of the story the glad tidings ought to be spread that the lanky Marquard wasn't knocked out of the box nor did he blow up like a keg of dynamite, nor did he get wild or savage.... His control was a work of art. He fielded his position with the speed of a sprinter, and whipped the ball over so fast that it looked foggy shooting past the young Yale batsmen."[9]

Four days later Red Ames lost his third consecutive Opening Day game, this time to Philadelphia, giving up two runs in the ninth for the only scoring of the day. Mathewson was rocked by the Phillies 6–1 a day later, with Rube coming on in relief to pitch a scoreless inning. The highlight of the game came in the eighth, when Snodgrass smashed a towering drive to deep center field. Phillies outfielder Dode Paskert made "one of the most remarkable catches that has ever been seen at the Polo Grounds,"[10] running at top speed and somehow grabbing the ball with his bare hand just before crashing into the wall. Poor Snodgrass, who had run all the way around the bases with what he thought was a sure home run, could only shake his head in bewilderment.

That night and on into the early morning of April 15 the north Harlem sky was lit up in a spectacular blaze of orange and red when the Polo Grounds burned to the ground. The entire grandstand, clubhouse, and most of the bleachers were destroyed, and it was not until late afternoon that New York's entire fire fighting force, finally assisted by a steady rain, got the blaze under control. It was conservatively estimated that damages would reach a quarter of a million dollars; included was the destruction of the Interborough Railway Company's elevated terminal and repair shops which abutted the north end of the grounds, and the entire season's stock of park concessionaire Harry M. Stevens. And of no small significance to the players was the fact that, along with everything else, the fire consumed over 100 baseball bats.

New York fire officials could not agree as to the cause of the disaster. Retired fire captain and current ballpark custodian John F. Higgins was certain it was arson. "There is no other explanation," he said. "There isn't a drop of oil or gasoline or any other inflammable material on the ground."[11] But Deputy Fire Marshall F.E. McGregory opined that a smoldering fire "among the peanut shells and

other debris, fanned by the brisk southeasterly wind, was responsible for the fire."[12] Young New York *Press* sportswriter Fred Lieb had his own version of the fire's origin: it was probably caused by Paskert's "sizzling and electrifying catch" the day before.[13]

John Brush swiftly made plans to rebuild the Polo Grounds, securing a 25-year lease at the same location. In the meantime, he swallowed his pride and accepted the offer of Yankee owners Frank Farrell and William Devery to allow the Giants to use Hilltop Park in Manhattan. The arrangement required the consent of a majority of other National League owners, which was easily obtained. Brush, still seriously ill with the affects of rheumatism, was naturally dismayed at the loss of his park. Brooklyn president Charles Ebbets reacted eloquently to the situation. "I am confident you will rise, Phoenix-like, above your great loss," he wired Brush.[14] Other club owners were getting used to fires. The Polo Grounds, along with other stadiums at St. Louis and Washington, was the third park to burn in the last year.

The Giants won their first game at Hilltop the very next day, defeating Brooklyn 6–3 behind Doc Crandall. On Tuesday, April 17, Rube took the mound against the Superbas and was dominant, allowing only four hits and striking out nine, winning 7–1. "After all these long, long years of watching and waiting, Richard Marquard did his noblest to measure up to his $11,000 reputation," wrote W. W. Aulick of the *Times*, "and gave a cheerful, expectant gathering of 7,000 persons a joyful surprise.... Marquard is a new pitcher. He has laid aside that pretzel wind-up that tied him into a sailor knot every time he tossed the ball. Instead of pegging the sphere over toward the stand Rube now looks the batsman square in the face and sticks the ball right over the plate. His assortment had variety and much mystery. His drop ball rode right up to the platter and dropped two feet into the catcher's mitt as if dragged down by a magnet. The Brooklyn team, startled beyond expression, looked on in amazement and fell victim to the long, lanky pitcher's barrel-hoop tangents."[15] Rube was in serious trouble only once, in the ninth inning. With the bases loaded and slugger Tex Ervin at bat, the crowd waited, wrote Aulick, "in silent judgment. If Tex jolts it, good night Marquard! A smile spreads over the pitcher's face. He winds up and shoots the ball across and one, two, three, Ervin whiffs the Hilltop ozone and is out. A great shout goes up as the Rube — yes, he cost $11,000 — sneers triumphantly at the three runners waiting on the bases and walks to the bench. It was his hour."[16]

The "Society Editor" of the New York *Globe* (actually sportswriter Sid Mercer) celebrated Rube's victory in a humorous column headlined "Select Society Welcomes Debutante Marquard":

Opposite: Opening Day at the Polo Grounds, April 14, 1911. The happy Giants fans include women, children, an usher and at least one man (lower left) who does not want to be photographed. The next night the stadium burned to the ground. Photo from author's collection.

> One of the most brilliant affairs of the post–Lenten season took place yesterday afternoon at the beautiful country place of Frank Farrell on Washington Heights. The sole topic of conversation this morning in select baseball circles is the successful debut of Richard Marquard, the famous $11,000 beauty. John McGraw and family, who are temporarily entertaining at "The Hilltop," Mr. Farrell's picturesque country estate, sent out 7,000 invitations for the coming out party, and society flocked up in automobiles and on the subway, primarily the latter.
>
> Mr. Marquard is one of the younger set of whom much has been heard. For three years the fame of this fair debutante has been heralded in the society columns, and the presentation of such a popular and promising candidate for a high place in exclusive circles has been impatiently awaited. Fandom at large, after yesterday's triumph, admits that Mr. Marquard has "arrived."
>
> With the assistance of Mr. McGraw and his veterans of the social whirl the entertainment progressed smoothly, and applause was frequent and tumultuous. It was feared Mr. Marquard might become nervous and spoil everything, but he bore up grandly, and in his boudoir after the excitement had subsided accepted numerous congratulations.... Now that Mr. Marquard has flashed on the social horizon he no doubt will be ardently wooed by good fortune. He made such a pleasing appearance that society hopes to see him frequently hereafter.[17]

It was of course only one game, and against lowly Brooklyn at that. McGraw continued to proceed cautiously with Rube, pitching him in relief, twice against Boston and again against Chicago. On May 6, he was particularly effective, coming in for Matty in the eighth inning against Cincinnati and striking out the side. For Rube the turning point of his season, and his career, came on May 13 against St. Louis. Mathewson started the game, and by the end of the first inning the Giants had battered three Cardinal pitchers for 13 runs. McGraw gave Matty the rest of the day off and summoned Rube; all he had to do was throw strikes and certain victory was his. Rube pitched with no fear against Roger Bresnahan's team, allowing 5 runs but striking out 13. In an article he later wrote for *Baseball* magazine, Rube called it "the true beginning of my big league experience.... My old-time confidence was restored. I went back to my curves. I used full speed. I pitched as I had in the old days in Indianapolis."[18]

On May 25, Rube gave up only two hits to the Reds and banged out two hits himself in a 3–1 victory; the Giants moved into first place for the first time since May of the previous year. It was a day of great rejoicing in New York; even McGraw's puppy Truxton celebrated and delighted the crowd by performing double back-flips in front of the Giant bench. The club continued to win consistently despite some unforeseen problems. Mathewson struggled for the first two months of the season, and Wiltse was lost for six weeks when a vicious line drive off the bat of Pirate Fred Clarke lacerated his pitching hand. Then, just as Wiltse came back, Crandall was nailed on the forehead by another Pittsburgh line drive and missed several starts because of the concussion. But Rube picked up the slack. After losing to the Cubs on June 3 (giving up a ninth inning grand slam to Wildfire Schulte) and dropping a tough 5–2 game to the Reds when a sinking liner got by Murray for an inside-the-park homer, Rube hit his stride. He beat Boston 2–1 on June 20, Brooklyn 3–1 on June 27, and Boston again 3–1 on July 1, assisted by Devore's two home runs. He began to feel virtually unbeatable.

On Saturday, July 8, 25,000 fans turned out to see Rube defeat Chicago 5–2 at the new Polo Grounds. (Work on the steel and concrete structure would continue all summer, but Brush allowed games to begin there as quickly as possible to accommodate the larger crowds.) The *Times* noted the increasing popularity of "the $11,000 Beauty": "Rube had more speed yesterday than he has shown all year, and the cheers and applause that greeted him after each inning was the greatest demonstration of approval that he has heard since the New York club cashed in $11,000 for him."[19] The game was all the sweeter for Rube for another reason: in the third inning he lifted "a monstrous smash" into the right field bleachers off Harry McIntire for what was to be his only major league home run.

The race for league honors took on a familiar look, as New York, Chicago, and Pittsburgh took turns atop the standings, struggling to stave off Philadelphia and surprising St. Louis. The defending champion Cubs were still a strong team but needed to overcome the loss of John Evers. The tightly wound second baseman — he was so unpopular with his teammates they called him "the Crab" — had suffered off-season financial difficulty. He was forced to close his shoe store and nearly went bankrupt; in May he suffered a nervous breakdown that sent him into seclusion for the bulk of the season. His replacement, Henry "Heinie" Zimmerman, was a fine player, but the Cubs missed Evers' spark. To add to manager Frank Chance's woes, Joe Tinker was suspended for two weeks in July for "indifferent play," and his absence also wounded the club. Pittsburgh, as always, depended upon the health of Honus Wagner and to a lesser degree, Tommy Leach and Fred Clarke. After a slow start in April and May the Pirates battled back into contention in late summer.

In Boston, Fred Tenney had problems of his own. Moody infielder Buck Herzog sulked over his contract and in July was fined, then suspended, for insubordination. Four days later McGraw reacquired Herzog, willing to put aside personal differences if it would improve his club. He reluctantly sent Al Bridwell to the Pilgrims and then moved Art Fletcher to short and inserted Herzog at third. The move immediately paid dividends as Herzog, happy to be back with a contending team, doubled twice in his first game back with the Giants.

It began to seem that it might be the Giants' year. The nucleus of a fine young club was now firmly established. Merkle and Doyle joined Herzog and Fletcher in the infield, while Devore, Snodgrass, and Murray formed the outfield. Chief Meyers had become perhaps the finest offensive catcher in the league; in

1911 he would hit .332 and drive in 61 runs in 133 games. The mark of the team was its speed. The Giants stole a league-record 347 bases in 1911, led by Devore with 61, followed closely by Snodgrass and Merkle with 51 and 49. McGraw enjoyed taking credit for hand-selecting and molding this team by himself, and *Sporting Life* agreed, stating that the "Little Napoleon" was the "greatest single factor" in New York's success: "The overshadowing personality of McGraw obtrudes at every point."[20]

On July 12, Rube gave up two home runs to the Pirates, including a mammoth shot by Wagner, but still gained the 4–3 victory. He struck out the side twice in winning his sixth in a row, and with Mathewson floundering, McGraw stated that Rube "was his only reliable starter."[21] But then Cincinnati touched him for 12 hits (three of them by Cuban Armando Marsans) and eight runs a week later, and Rube suffered his third loss of the year, the second to the Reds. The only bright spot of the day for Giant fans was the appearance of Turkey Mike Donlin, who had finally signed a contract and delighted the crowd of 8,000 by lifting a home run into the stands. Mike's best years were behind him now, and he had little hope of cracking McGraw's outfield, but he could prove valuable in pinch-hitting roles and was perhaps the most popular player in the clubhouse.

On July 23, this time in Cincinnati, Rube avenged his defeats to the Reds by downing them 8–2. He continued his hot hitting by slamming two triples off Bobby Keefe, accounting for four Giant runs, while Meyers contributed a single, double, and triple. The national news media began to notice Rube's turnaround. He was "a sensation" and "the class of the league"[22] said the *Sporting News*, while *Sporting Life* hailed the "$11,000 beauty ... a star of purest ray serene who has eclipsed even the great Mathewson."[23] And the Cleveland newspapers enjoyed his success as well. Rube had "accomplished the seemingly impossible," wrote Paul Bishop of the *Leader*, "when he burst upon the baseball horizon in a blaze of glory. He jarred loose the hold of the great Mathewson on the hearts of the fans in little old New York.... The fans now do homage at the feet of their new idol."[24]

The facts did not seem to matter much to some sportswriters if they got in the way of a good story. Heywood Broun, Bozeman Bulger, and Sid Mercer in particular delivered fanciful accounts of Rube's background and family history, stories which must have amused readers and perhaps endeared Rube to them. Rube's father was a French soldier, wrote Bulger in one column, who had become enamored with American baseball and trained his son to pitch with either hand. When the elder Marquard died, Rube inherited a farm in New Brunswick, Ohio, where he intended to settle down after his major league career concluded. Some writers, in homage to Rube's purported lineage, took to calling him "Richard de Marquis." Sixty years later confused fans still wrongly assumed Rube was French.

On July 29, 23,000 fans turned out in St. Louis to see if their club could handle Rube and the Giants. But they were disappointed as Rube was nearly perfect. He gave up only four singles and shut out the Cards 8–0. "No pitcher could have beaten Marquard today," said the *Times*. "His fast ball came upon batters ere they could scarcely move. His curve was as wide as the Horseshoe Bend in the Mississippi River, and his control approached perfection."[25] Then with only one day's rest, Rube threw again against the Cardinals on July 31, and this time beat them 3–2. In the two games, Rube struck out 17 hitters; to add to the embarrassment of Roger Bresnahan, the Giants stole 14 bases off seven pitchers.

For all of Rube's impressive work midway through the season, there was other pitching news around the league. Pittsburgh owner Barney Dreyfuss coolly wrote a check for $22,500 and purchased pitcher Marty O'Toole from St. Paul, establishing a new record and more than doubling Rube's price tag only three years earlier. O'Toole had also broken Rube's single game strikeout record for the American Association, fanning 17 Milwaukee hitters on July 9. And a new pitching sensation had emerged in Philadelphia. Rookie Grover Cleveland Alexander, a troubled young man from Nebraska, had arrived in spectacular fashion and would soon supplant Mathewson as the next great right-handed hurler in the National League. Rube would have encounters with both O'Toole and Alexander in the coming days of the summer.

But first the Giants completed their western swing in Chicago, humiliating the Cubs 16–5 in the finale. Rube threw the first six innings and then was rested, giving way to Crandall. The club headed back to New York locked in a furious three-way fight for the flag.

The Phillies came to town on Monday, August 14, and a boisterous crowd of over 25,000 came out to see the matchup between the circuit's two hottest pitchers: Rube and Alexander. In a well-played game, Rube defeated "Alex the Great" 3–2 in 12 innings, Devore singling home Murray with the winning run. "Sing the praises of Marquard far and near for his work in the first game," said the *Times*. "Also chant a bit for the great twirling of Alexander."[26] The New York *Tribune* ran a large photo of a smiling Rube and noted that his "fame was secure."[27] Damon Runyon of the *American* wrote that Rube and Alex, "rival claimants to the pitching crown in the National League, fought out the question of supremacy ... and at the close of twelve bitter innings "King Rube" sat on the throne alone."[28]

That evening, to celebrate, Donlin and Mabel Hite took Rube to the Broadway Theater (Rube had, with this season's success, conquered his fear of being seen in public, and in fact now craved the adulation he received when he stepped out). The show was Lew Fields' production of *The Hen Pecks*, a musical comedy featuring a pert blonde sensation from California named Blossom Seeley. After the performance Rube was allowed backstage, where he met the show's star. Blossom knew little about baseball but promised she would come out to see a game with her friend Mabel. But if she did venture to the Polo Grounds that year, she probably did so without Mabel, for within two weeks Donlin had been traded to Boston.

Finally Mathewson began to win consistently. Against Cincinnati on August 16, he needed only throw a record low 92 pitches to earn the 6–1 victory.

Incredibly, it was Matty's 22d straight career win over the Reds. That same day misfortune struck Pittsburgh when Honus Wagner tore ligaments and broke a small bone in his ankle when he stumbled on second base. "The Teuton" was forced to miss three weeks of the season, all but ending the Pirates' pennant hopes.

As August turned into September, Rube's winning streak reached 12 games. He beat every team in the league in handy fashion. In a three-week stretch, he allowed only five runs in five games and struck out 63 batters. By September 1 his record stood at 18 wins and only 4 losses and the Giants were in first place. McGraw took credit for Rube's success but also increased his salary twice for a total of $1,000 and promised him a bonus of $500 if the Giants won the pennant. A wealthy fan, unidentified in the papers, offered Rube another inducement: a new Chalmers automobile, valued at $5,000, was his if the team went on to win the World Series. Mathewson was quoted as saying that Rube was in complete command of his pitches, that "he has mastered the fadeaway pitch better than anyone I have ever seen,"[29] and Wilbert Robinson predicted that the Giants would follow Rube all the way to the championship. But there was another person, stranger and far more improbable, who figured in Rube's remarkable record. He was the simple-minded son of a German-Russian immigrant from the Kansas prairie who would stumble into the annals of baseball history. His name was Charles Victor Faust, and baseball fans across the country were cheering his every move.

In 1911, Charlie Faust was 30 years old, "a tall, (6'2"), skinny man with weak eyes that did not seem to align properly and with an ever-present, semi-toothless smile on his face."[30] In May, Charlie had left his father's Marion, Kansas, farm and visited a fortune-teller in Wichita, who took his five dollars and told him that he would become a great pitcher for the New York Giants and help them win the pennant. Further, Charlie would marry a girl named Lulu and sire several generations of baseball stars. Charlie seriously believed these predictions and set out to meet his fate. On July 28, he marched into the Planter's Hotel in St. Louis and presented himself to McGraw, who had just finished breakfast with Mathewson and Ames. Charlie related to McGraw his "fortune," and the manager laughingly agreed to play along. Charlie was to come to the ballpark later that day and show McGraw and the rest of the team what he could do. That afternoon Charlie, dressed in his finest suit of clothes and sporting a black derby hat, arrived at Robison Field just as the Giants were getting loosened up. McGraw gave him a glove and said he would warm up Charlie himself. Fred Snodgrass described what happened next:

> They got up in front of the bench and tossed a few balls back and forth. "I'd better give you my signals," Charlie said. "So they got their heads together, and he gave McGraw five or six signals. Mr. McGraw would give him a signal, and he would proceed to wind up. His windup was like

a windmill. Both arms went around in circles for quite a little while, before Charlie finally let go of the ball. Well, regardless of the sign that McGraw would give, the ball would come up just the same. There was no difference in his pitches whatsoever. And there was no speed — probably enough to break a pane of glass, but that was about all. So McGraw finally threw his glove away and caught him bare-handed, thinking to himself that this guy must be a nut and he'd have a little fun with him.

"How's your hitting?" McGraw asked him.

"Oh," he said, "pretty good."

"Well," McGraw said, "we're having batting practice now, so get a bat and go up there. I want to see you run, too, so run it out and see if you can score."

Word was quickly passed around to the fellows who were shagging balls in the infield. Charlie Faust dribbled one down to the shortstop, who juggled it a minute as Charlie was turning first, and then they slid him into second, slid him into third, and slid him into home, all in his best Sunday suit — to the obvious enjoyment of everyone.[31]

The following day, and for the rest of the Cardinal series, Charlie — now in uniform and called "Victory" by his "teammates" (and "Rube" by the press in deference to his rural background) — performed the same pitching and batting exhibition before the ballgame, to the delight of the crowd. The Cardinals by now were in on the joke as well, and before the final game the players presented Charlie with a small gag medal of appreciation, which he proudly pinned on his jersey. Rube got a kick out of Charlie and wasn't one to argue over the results of McGraw's newest good-luck charm; this was the series in which he won two games in three days.

Still, it was a surprise to nearly everyone when Charlie showed up at the train station on Monday when the Giants were about to leave for Chicago. He asked McGraw about the ticket and playing contract he had been promised. McGraw saw his chance to get away from the whole thing. "Oh, didn't you get them?" he asked. "Why, I left them at the hotel for you."[32] The Giants enjoyed a good laugh as Charlie scurried back to the hotel; minutes later, of course, the train pulled out of the station without him.

But Charlie was persistent and finally caught up with the team in Boston. As the club continued to win, McGraw decided to take no chances: Charlie could stay. And while he was never formally issued a contract, his fame spread around the league. He had become the "Kansas Jinx-Killer," and his odd pregame antics made him a popular drawing card in every city where the Giants played. In Chicago club president Charles Webb Murphy hung a banner proclaiming the appearance of "The Kansas Cyclone," and he was often allowed to throw a few batting practice pitches to star players of the opposing teams. He warmed up before every game as if he were going to play and then retired to the bullpen. Sometimes, if the Giants fell behind, McGraw would summon him to sit on the bench, where his "good-luck charms" seemed to be most effective. For his efforts McGraw gave Charlie a small stipend; he traveled with the team as well, entertaining the players during train rides with his ludicrous imitations of Mathewson, McGraw, and Rube, among others (although it was often difficult to determine just whom he was imitating).

Rube seemed to benefit from Charlie's presence more than any other Giant. When Charlie was temporarily abandoned after the St. Louis series, Rube was beaten by Pittsburgh. When Charlie returned, Rube struck out 13 in a win over Brooklyn. Charlie did not miss a game as Rube sizzled through August, including one stretch in which he threw a two-hitter and back-to-back one-hitters. Charlie caught the eye of a show business promoter, who booked him to appear at the Manhattan Theater beginning on Labor Day. Charlie's "act" consisted mainly of absurd imitations of his friends on the Giants, as well as other stars like Honus Wagner and Walter Johnson. He demonstrated Ty Cobb's hook slide into a sofa cushion tossed onto a corner of the stage; he even imitated the whistle of a train and sang the Star Spangled Banner.

With Charlie absent for his holiday start against Boston, Rube blew a five-run lead and lost in extra innings. Four days later, his engagement concluded, Charlie returned to witness Rube defeat Brooklyn by a score of 3–2. "The real reason for the Giants' success lay not in the staunch arm of Marquard, nor the ready bat of Fred Merkle, but in the presence of Charlie Faust," wrote Heywood Broun of the New York *Morning Telegraph*.[33] Rube later put it another way: "When he was with us, we won. When he wasn't, we lost."[34] For the season, Rube won 10 of 11 games when Charlie was in the ballpark.

With or without Charlie, the pressures of the pennant race started to wear on the Giants. Rube complained of a tired arm and received extra attention from the trainer, but McGraw sensed that perhaps Rube and some of the other younger players who were experiencing a pennant fight for the first time, were straining. Once again he called on his old friend Wilbert Robinson. He wired Robbie to "come on first train and be in on the big finish. Team is about to go to pieces."[35]

Robbie dutifully joined the Giants in Pittsburgh and stayed with them for the remainder of the season. Bozeman Bulger later recalled that Robbie immediately went to work to loosen the team up. He took Rube and Chief Meyers out for a night on the town, bought Snodgrass and Merkle new suits of clothes, and then organized a team pool tournament. His intent was to take the players' minds, at least temporarily, off the pennant race, and indeed the club pulled together for the stretch run. On September 16, Rube took great satisfaction in defeating Pittsburgh's new sensation Marty O'Toole by the score of 6–2. (O'Toole, for all the attention surrounding his expensive purchase, never really panned out. He managed only 27 victories in a short five-year major league career.) Rube then shut out St. Louis and Chicago for his final two wins of the regular season, finishing with a mark of 23–7. His winning percentage of .774 led the league, as did his strikeout total of 237. Umpire Billy Evans commented on Rube's "terrific speed" in a column he wrote for the *Sporting News* and quoted Joe Tinker: "How can I hit the ball when I can't see it?"[36]

Finally on October 4 in Brooklyn, the Giants clinched the pennant, with Mathewson on the mound. (Matty had rebounded from a mediocre first half of the season to finish with a record of 26–13, second in the league in wins behind Alexander's 28.) Now with nine games left to play, McGraw could afford to rest his starters, look ahead to the World Series against Connie Mack's Philadelphia Athletics, and take care of one important piece of unfinished business — get Charlie Faust into a ballgame. The long-anticipated event was realized in Boston on October 7. It was a cold, gray day, and less than one thousand spectators were present to watch the last place Pilgrims play the Giants. Rube started the game and pitched five innings, leaving with the score tied 2–2. Then in the eighth, with Boston ahead 4–2, a cheer went up as Charlie came loping in from the bullpen and began to toss warmup pitches to rookie backup catcher Slick Hartley. Charlie surrendered a leadoff double to Lefty Tyler, who was later brought home on a sacrifice fly by Mike Donlin for the only run of the inning. In the top of the ninth, Charlie was on deck when the last out was made, but the Pilgrims allowed him to bat anyway. True to form, Charlie dribbled a grounder to the pitcher and was allowed to run and slide his way around the bases.

A few days later, in the last inning of the last game of the season, Charlie made another brief appearance. This time he pitched a scoreless inning and then scored a run on Buck Herzog's fly after being hit by a pitch and allowed to steal two bases. And then to no one's surprise, after the game Charlie boldly predicted that the Giants would easily win the upcoming World Series.

CHAPTER 7

Dangerous Men

Connie Mack was the only baseball personality in the first years of the century who commanded as much respect as John McGraw. He was born Cornelius McGillicudy in East Brookfield, Massachusetts, in 1862 and was playing minor league baseball by age 21. Baseball was quite literally his life's work; he never had a job in any other field. Only a mediocre player — he was a weak-hitting, barehanded catcher with Washington and Pittsburgh — he became manager (and part owner) of the Philadelphia Athletics in 1901, positions he would hold for the next 50 years. At 6'1" and only 150 pounds, "the Tall Tactician" provided a humorous contrast to the dumpy McGraw (photographers loved it when the two men stood next to one another), and as their physical characteristics differed, so too did their styles of managing ballplayers and handling men.

Mack was quiet, dignified, New England–refined. He avoided public appearances and preferred to move about town unrecognized. He always wore a dress suit of clothes, even during games, and on hottest days removed his coat to reveal a starched, high-collar white shirt. He rarely left his spot on the bench, content to position his ballplayers on the field with a wave of his trademark rolled-up scoreboard. He seldom showed a temper, did not use foul language, and saw little point in arguing with umpires. Neither was he a proponent of "inside" baseball, preferring to let his free swingers "bust 'em" as best they could. He was content to trust the judgments and instincts of his players, and he cared little whether they were college graduates or could barely write their own names.

Mack's A's were the defending World Champions, having defeated the Chicago Cubs in five games in 1910. The heart of the club was its infield. Jug-eared second baseman Eddie "Cocky" Collins hit .365 in 1911, his fourth year of twenty-five in the majors. Jack Barry was the quietly effective shortstop. Hard-hitting first baseman Stuffy McInnis was nursing a sore right wrist and could barely throw or swing a bat; he would be replaced in the Series by 38-year-old Harry Davis. Frank Baker at third led the American League in home runs with

11. (Speculation was rampant all summer that Baker and other sluggers had benefited from a new juiced baseball, a charge that club owners and the National Commission vehemently denied.) Together the group formed the "$100,000 infield," a moniker which reflected only their estimated worth, not their combined salaries, a figure which was considerably lower.

The underrated outfield consisted of Bristol "The Human Eyeball" Lord, who hit .300 in 1911 for the only time in his career; defensive standout Rueben Oldring; and Philly native Dan Murphy, the best hitter of the bunch, who was enjoying his finest all-around year. The pitching staff was the best in the league. Eddie Plank was in the prime years of a career which would total 326 victories; "Colby Jack" Coombs, with 28 wins, had led the league for the second year in a row; and a Chippewa Indian from Minnesota named Charles Bender — naturally called Chief— won 17 games and lost only 5 in 1911, his percentage of .773 the best in the AL.

To keep his team sharp while waiting for the Series to begin Mack scheduled several exhibition games with the Boston Red Sox in Washington, Philadelphia, and Baltimore. Because they had clinched the pennant early, the Giants were well-rested and healthy, and the experts all predicted a tight Series. A coin flip had determined that the Series would begin in New York, and the night before the opener Rube tried to relax in the Washington Heights apartment he now shared with Josh Devore. Newspaper speculation held that he would probably start on the mound for the Giants because "it is figured (he) could do better in the face of a home crowd," and the veteran Mathewson could more easily handle the pressures of a hostile environment in Philadelphia.[1] McGraw, however, would not announce his starter until just before game time, a fact that made Rube all the more nervous.

Meanwhile hundreds of Giant fans camped out all night outside the Polo Grounds box office in hopes of purchasing tickets for the game. It was widely rumored, however, that speculators had bought up blocks of tickets by the dozens, and scalpers were in fact commanding as much as $200 for box seats and $450 for sets of three. Counterfeit tickets were also circulating, and ushers were prepared to turn away fans who had been duped into buying them. The New York district attorney was investigating, and before the Series was over, 20 arrests would be made. And to make matters worse for Giant fans, the new construction at the stadium all but eliminated the view of the field from atop Coogan's Bluff. Hours before the 2 P.M. start, however, several hundred enthusiasts had gathered there anyway, to celebrate and show their support for the hometown team.

The Series began on Saturday, October 14. (The starting date was unusually late because Brooklyn's Charles Ebbetts had persuaded the National League to drag out the regular season through Columbus Day in an attempt to cash in on holiday customers.) A huge crowd of over 38,000 fans turned out on the crisp, sunny day. Hoping to repeat their success of 1905, when the Giants had defeated the A's behind three Mathewson shutouts, McGraw again dressed his team in black broadcloth uniforms. The World Series was no time to question good luck charms, believed McGraw, and so of course Charlie Faust emerged from the clubhouse with the rest of the team and warmed up to the cheers of the crowd. Naturally Charlie believed *he* would be the starting pitcher. The A's had a mascot of their own. Tiny hunchback Luis VanZelst bad been discovered by Eddie Collins, and the superstitious ballplayers rubbed his back for luck.

John Brush viewed the action from his limousine, parked in deep center field. A record 49 newspaper reporters from around the country were present, and for the first time a motion picture crew would record the events. Mathewson had arranged, for a fee of $500, to cover the Series for the New York *Herald*. (The daily columns would actually be written by John Wheeler, a sportswriter who had once ghosted for, among others, Pancho Villa). Rube would not be outdone in the writing department. He was to write short game summaries, a "critical analysis" for the *Times* (the column was also carried by the Philadelphia *Ledger*), and seeing no reason to obligate himself to one paper, he had reporter Fred Menke ghost-write another column for him in the *American*.

McGraw finally named Mathewson as his starting pitcher, to face Chief Bender in a rematch of the 1905 opener. Both pitchers were sharp. The A's got on board in the second inning when Baker singled, was sacrificed to second, and scored on Davis' line-drive single to left. The Giants got a break in the fourth. Snodgrass was hit by a pitch and went to second on a fielder's choice. Herzog scorched a grounder to Collins, who booted it. Seeing the ball carom into right field, McGraw, who was coaching third, waved Snodgrass in, and the score was tied.

In the sixth inning, Snodgrass was hit again by a Bender pitch and was sacrificed to second. When a curve ball to Merkle bounced in the dirt, "Snow" took off for third base. The Giants thought that Baker was spike-shy (and in fact had spent some pregame time sharpening their cleats with files, in full view of the A's, in hopes of intimidating them). But Baker held his ground this time, and Snodgrass slid into him hard, knocking him down and kicking the ball loose. Baker's pants were cut from knee to hip, and as was customary in those situations a new pair was brought out to third base and he changed behind the safety of a blanket. The play seemed inconsequential at the time but would loom large as the Series progressed.

The Giants got to Bender in the seventh inning. Chief Meyers smashed a long drive off the left field wall, missing a home run by less than a foot and settling for a double. Mathewson fanned, but Devore lined a double over Baker's head, easily scoring the Chief with the go-ahead run. Matty held on, and the Giants won the game 2–1.

While happy with the victory, McGraw had reason to be concerned. His club had managed only 5 hits off Bender and struck out 11 times. The A's had effectively negated the Giants speed on the bases, allowing only one stolen base (by Doyle) and twice thwarting double-steal attempts when Collins cut off Jack Lapp's throw to second and fired the ball home in time to catch the lead runner. Had it not been for the strong outing by Mathewson the Giants would have been in trouble.

That night a celebration was held in the Giants' honor at the New York Theater in Manhattan. For two hours popular vaudeville performers entertained a sellout crowd, and then the Giants took the stage. One by one the players, including Charlie Faust, were introduced. The loudest cheer of the night came for Rube, who was also the only player not formally attired. On short notice no tuxedo could be found to fit his long frame. He told the crowd what they came to hear and promised a victory the next day. Finally McGraw made a short speech, thanking the fans for their support and predicting "his boys" would bring home the championship. He was presented with a gold watch and diamond-studded watch fob, while the players received silver trophies 11 inches high. McGraw hustled his players back to their homes for a short night's rest. The next morning they caught the 9 o'clock train for Philadelphia, checked in at the Majestic Hotel, and began to prepare for Monday's game.

Shibe Park had opened in 1909, the first of the new steel and concrete baseball stadiums, starting a wave of new construction that would include Wrigley and Comiskey Parks in Chicago, Forbes Field in Pittsburgh, and Boston's Fenway Park, among others. Named after sporting goods magnate and principal club owner Ben Shibe, the park was located in a tough North Philadelphia neighborhood known as Swampoodle. Visiting teams, and their fans, were often impressed with the park but not with the surroundings. Across the street stood the dilapidated Hospital for Contagious Diseases, and for years passersby routinely covered their mouths with handkerchiefs until the city finally condemned and closed the facility.

Game two of the Series featured Rube versus Eddie Plank before 28,000 Philadelphia supporters. The A's right-hander began the game by fanning Devore on three straight pitches, the first of eight strikeouts on the day (Devore was the victim four times), and the Giants went quietly in the first inning. When Rube took the mound, he was quite nervous and got off to a rocky start. Lord hammered a fastball to right field for a single and took second when Murray misplayed it. Oldring sacrificed him to third, and then with Collins at bat Rube threw wildly to Meyers and Lord trotted home. Meyers came out to calm Rube, and they were soon joined by Herzog and Doyle. Whatever they said must have worked, for Rube collected himself and got out of the inning with no further damage.

The Giants evened the score in the top of the second when Meyers singled in Herzog, who had doubled to left-center. Rube settled down, matching Plank with scoreless innings and exhibiting nearly perfect control; for the day he threw only 17 balls out of 91 pitches. "That guy had everything on the ball," Devore said later.[2]

For Rube and the Giants, disaster struck in the sixth. The inning began well enough as both Lord and Oldring flied out. "When Collins came to bat I did not know exactly what to give him," Rube wrote in his *Times* article. "He is a batter without any decided weakness upon which a pitcher can figure. He may break up a game at any time, owing to his ability to hit at any height. I gave him a slow outcurve, waist high, and he cracked it all the way around to left field and took two bases."[3] Up to the plate stepped Frank Baker.

Baker took a curveball for strike one, then let another curve sail wide of the plate, evening the count. Meyers signaled for yet another curve, but Rube shook him off. His fastball came in nearly shoulder high but over the plate, and Baker drilled a shot high over the right-field wall for a two-run homer. Shibe Park exploded in sound, and many years later Baker recalled the moment as the greatest of his life.[4]

Plank continued to mystify the Giants, and poor baserunning cost them, as well. To McGraw's consternation, Snodgrass was thrown out by ten feet while trying to stretch a single into a double, and Merkle was picked off first base; both mistakes took the Giants out of potential rallies. With the 3–1 victory, the A's tied the Series at one game apiece. Despite the poor baserunning and lack of offensive support, Rube took full responsibility for the defeat. "Baker deserves credit for the victory, and I will bear the blame, for the fault is mine," he wrote in his column. "I gave him just the kind of pitch he was looking for.... I learned a whole lot about the Athletics today.... Collins and Baker are their most dangerous men."[5]

Rube's meekness turned to mild anger the following day when he read the blistering account of the game in the *Herald* presented by Mathewson through Wheeler: "Marquard made a poor pitch to Frank Baker on the latter's sixth-inning home run. There was no excuse for it. In a clubhouse talk with his players, Manager McGraw went over the entire Athletics' batting order, paying special attention to the left-handed hitter, Frank Baker. We had scouted Baker, knew what pitches were difficult for him to hit, and those he could hit for extra bases. Well, Rube threw him the kind of ball that Baker likes."[6]

McGraw and some of the other Giants, however, believed that there was more to it than just poor pitch selection. They were convinced that the A's batters knew what pitch was coming: someone was stealing their signs. It still bothered Chief Meyers many years later:

> "They're getting our signs from someplace," I told McGraw. "That coach on third, Harry Davis, is calling our pitches. When he yells 'It's all right,' it's a fast ball."
>
> "He must be getting them off you," McGraw said.
>
> "But they weren't getting them from me. I went to Rube and Matty and said, "Pitch whatever you want to pitch and I'll catch you without signals." And still the guy was hollering 'It's all right' for a fast ball. He knew something. I never did find out how he did it."[7]

Rube suspected that the sign-stealer was Luis VanZelst, the humpbacked mascot. His theory was that Luis, who also acted as the batboy, was somehow detecting signals from the on-deck circle. Neither Davis or VanZelst, however, ever owned up to the treachery.

The home run to Baker notwithstanding, Rube had pitched well, allowing only four hits while striking out two and giving it everything he had. "I feel pretty sore," he told some familiar sportswriters from Cleveland afterwards. "I wanted to win that game."[8] But for the second game in a row, the anemic Giant hitters could manage only five hits. Both teams took the night train back to New York for game three.

Despite a drizzling rain, the Polo Grounds was packed again on Tuesday afternoon to see Mathewson pitch, this time against Jack Coombs. It was another terrific pitchers' duel. Coombs surrendered but one run, in the third inning. Chief Meyers bounced a bad-hop single over Baker's head and advanced to third on Mathewson's base hit to right. Barry then bobbled Devore's groundball, allowing Meyers to score. Throughout the game the Giants continued to suffer on the basepaths, as would-be base stealers were thrown out five times. But they played tremendous defense behind Matty, who worked out of numerous jams, and the score stood at 1–0 in the top of the ninth. They needed only three outs to wrap up their second victory of the Series.

Collins grounded out to Herzog at third for the first out, and Giant fans watched anxiously as Baker stepped into the box. Mathewson threw two curveballs for quick strikes and then inexplicably tried to fool him, as Rube had the day before, with a fastball. "Baker leaned against the ball with the gentleness of a battering ram," wrote Harry Cross of the *Times*. "The ball went high and dry into the right wing of the new Brush stadium and Baker cantered around easily, touching each base with his spikes on his journey of joy. The score was tied."[9]

Mathewson angrily kicked the dirt while McGraw fumed in the dugout. Sixty-six years later Fred Lieb recalled the feeling in the press box, and at the stadium: "Giant fans were aghast; a Baker home run off Marquard could happen, but not off Matty! I can still remember the awesome silence that followed the crash of Baker's bat. It was so quiet that those with especially good hearing could pick up the patter of Baker's feet as he romped joyfully around the bases."[10]

The Giants were visibly shaken by the turn of events. Herzog juggled Murphy's easy grounder, then flew wildly to Merkle at first. But Mathewson steadied himself and retired Davis and Barry to end any further threat. Coombs sat the Giants down in order, and the game went into extra innings.

There were fireworks in the bottom of the tenth. Snodgrass, eager to get something going for his lethargic club, crowded the plate and stuck his elbow in the way of a pitch. But umpire Brennan ruled that Snow had failed to attempt to avoid the baseball and called it a strike. Snodgrass worked Coombs for a walk anyway and sprinted down to first base, representing the winning run. Murray sacrificed him to second, and when catcher Jack Lapp let a pitch get away from him, Snodgrass took off for third, where Baker was waiting.

Lapp recovered the ball quickly and fired it to Baker, who caught it while Snodgrass was still six feet from the bag. According to the account Cross gave in the *Times*: "Snodgrass must have seen that he was nailed by a whole city block and yet he jumped into the air and came into Baker spikes foremost. Baker saw the unnecessary leap and held his ground gamely. Snodgrass struck at him feet first, but Baker held the ball. His leg was spiked and his trousers badly ripped by the sharp steel. This is the second time in the series that Snodgrass has jumped roughly at Baker."[11] It was such an obviously dirty play that the New York crowd began to boo and hiss Snodgrass and cheered Baker when he was tended to and play resumed.

Now with two out Merkle walked and immediately tried to steal second. He was called out on a close play by umpire Connolly, and both Merkle and McGraw argued vociferously. On his way back to the dugout after losing the argument, McGraw looked to the box seats where members of the National Commission were sitting. Gesturing angrily at Ban Johnson, he yelled, "This is a sure-thing game. You've got it all framed up to rob us."[12]

Frame-up or not, the Giants collapsed in the 11th. After Oldring grounded out, Collins singled to left. Baker drilled a one-hopper to Herzog, but instead of forcing the runner at second Buck threw the ball over Merkle's head at first. Murphy chopped a ground ball to Fletcher, who booted it, allowing Collins to score. Davis then drove in Baker with a clean single, and suddenly the A's led 3–1. The Giants could manage only an unearned run in the bottom of the inning, and the game was over. They gathered their gear and walked slowly across the field to the clubhouse, unable to believe that they had managed to toss away certain victory. The scene at the A's bench, however, was one of "unrestrained happiness. They tossed their bats, gloves, and sweaters in the air. They hugged each other like long-lost brothers.... They had beaten Matty, the man who in all the world they feared most.... No, they were not afraid of the Big Six now."[13] In his *New York Times* article, Rube was sympathetic toward Mathewson's misfortune. "It was the hardest game to lose I ever saw," he wrote, "and Matty lost it the same way I lost the second game to Philadelphia. When he came to the bench I asked him what it was. 'The same thing you did, Rube,' said Matty. 'I gave him a high, fast one. I have been in the business for a long time and have no excuse.'"[14]

But Rube's ghost-written column in the *American* took a vastly different tone. "Will the great Mathewson tell us exactly what he pitched to Baker? He was present at the same clubhouse meeting at which Mr. McGraw discussed Baker's weakness. Could it be that Matty too let go a careless pitch when it meant the ballgame?"[15]

The retaliatory column created a stir in New York, and many fans were concerned that perhaps there really was bad blood between the two star pitchers. Years later ghost-writer Menke told Fred Lieb what had happened: "I guess I had a lot to do with it. Marquard was interested mostly in the money he was to get out of it. He was satisfied to have me do the writing. He *was* pretty mad at Mathewson's blast at him after Baker's first home run. So, when Baker smacked Matty, I told Rube, 'Now is our chance to get even.' He agreed, saying, 'Don't make it too easy.' So I didn't."[16]

For his part, Baker was peeved at what both men (or their ghosts) had written. "Say, ain't it a wonder I got any kind of average in the American League?" he asked sarcastically. "I'm a lucky guy to be in the league at all, after reading what they say where I hit 'em and where I miss 'em. I thought I hit for better than .300 this year, but I guess it's all a sad mistake. I've been hitting against some pretty swell pitchers in our league, and they've put all kinds of stuff on the ball, and for a blind man I guess I've done pretty well."[17] In any event, Baker had well earned his new nickname, "Home Run."

While sportswriters and fans speculated as to how real the "feud" was between Rube and Mathewson, John McGraw probably put the whole episode in proper perspective. In his autobiography, published in 1923, he downplayed the affair, noting that it was the first time the high-strung Rube had displayed a sense of humor.[18]

Rube and Matty had every opportunity to patch things up between them because for the next six straight days it rained. Game four was scheduled to be played in Philadelphia, and the Giants stayed again at the Majestic Hotel. While McGraw fretted over his team's poor hitting and pondered how to stop Baker, he had another distraction: Fred Snodgrass was a marked man. A rumor circulated that Baker had developed blood poisoning from his wound and was now in a local hospital. A boisterous group of A's fans crowded around the Majestic and "hooted and jeered" Snodgrass every time he ventured outside. Snodgrass' own safety would be endangered, it was said, if he dared play ball at Shibe Park. Snodgrass insisted that the spiking was accidental, and McGraw backed him up, stating that it was common knowledge around baseball that Baker customarily blocked the basepath, which belonged to the runner.

While Snodgrass tried to ignore the threats against him — "My goat," he said calmly, "is not for sale"[19] — the same could not be said for all of his teammates. Art Fletcher got into a shoving match with a "wild-eyed Athletic fan," and several other players had to break it up. When it was rumored that a crazed fan had broken into Snodgrass' room and shot him, McGraw finally sent him back to New York until play would resume, whenever that might be. Connie Mack remained characteristically above the entire fray. His only comment on the Baker spiking was that it was "one of the fortunes of war."[20]

As if he didn't have enough to worry about, McGraw was censured by the National Commission for his outbursts in game three; any further improprieties, the Commission warned, would result in his banishment from the rest of the

Series. Merkle was fined $100 for his abuse of the umpire, and the money would be deducted from his share of the Series proceeds.

The Giants idled their time away at billiard parlors, theaters, and smoke shops. Only once in six days did the rain let up enough for them to venture to the park for some light throwing and running. The A's, meanwhile, secured the use of a local armory, and by stringing some nets across the building's gymnasium were able to take some indoor batting practice. Aside from the inclement weather, the only inconvenience for the club occurred when Rube Oldring's sister died, in Mount Vernon, from tuberculosis. Oldring traveled home for the funeral and returned two days later.

Finally the skies cleared. Mack instructed the groundskeepers to pour gasoline on parts of the outfield and burn off some of the remaining wetness, and the National Commission ordered play to begin again on Tuesday, October 24, after a delay of exactly one week. Wilbert Robinson urged McGraw to start Rube on the mound, but McGraw named Mathewson, confident that the veteran was sufficiently rested and had overcome the disappointment of the heartbreaking loss in New York. He would oppose Chief Bender in game four.

The Giants started quickly, scoring two runs in the first inning. Devore singled, Doyle tripled, and Snodgrass, ignoring the catcalls, drove Doyle home with a long sacrifice fly. But Bender was magnificent from that point on, shutting out the Giants the rest of the way on seven hits. Mathewson started impressively, striking out the side in the first, but the A's got to him in the fourth when Baker doubled and then scored on Murphy's single. Davis then stroked a double to right, scoring Murphy, and the score was tied.

McGraw hurriedly sent Rube, Wiltse, and Ames to the bullpen to warm up, but it was too late. Barry sacrificed Davis to third, and Thomas brought him home with a fly ball. In the fifth, Baker touched Mathewson for an RBI single, and the 4–2 score held up for another Athletics victory. They now led the Series three games to one.

With his club facing elimination, Rube took the hill for game five, in New York. He was in fine form for two innings, but gave up yet another crucial home run — this time to Oldring, with two men on base — in the third, and McGraw yanked him from the game in favor of Crandall and then Ames. Rube was upset with his manager's decision because the runners had been allowed on base through Doyle's errors, but with the entire Series on the line McGraw was in no mood to argue.

With their team down 3–1 in the ninth inning with one out, Giants fans began to head for the exits. But doubles by Fletcher and Crandall and a clutch single by Devore tied the score. An inning later, with Plank now on in relief of Coombs, Doyle doubled and later scored the gamewinning run on Merkle's fly ball, and the Giants were still alive. (But just barely; umpire Klem announced after the game that Doyle had missed home plate when he slid in, but the Athletics did not notice it. If they had, Doyle would have been called out.)

"We'll be champions yet," predicted Rube in his *Times* column. "The boys have found their batting eye.... McGraw is out to win this series and we will do it for him."[21]

Rube was wrong. The next day in Philadelphia the A's battered Ames and Wiltse for 11 hits and 13 runs, and again Chief Bender stifled the Giants. He allowed only four hits and was never in serious trouble, striking out five in gaining his second win of the Series. Rube came on in the eighth inning in relief of Wiltse, but by then the score was already 11–1 and the game's outcome was not in doubt. With Barry on second and Davis on third, Rube faced his first hitter, Ira Thomas. He uncorked a wild pitch past Meyers, who stood at the plate, embarrassed and frustrated, as first Davis and then Barry scored. Rube and the Chief proceeded to yell at each other for several minutes, but by now even McGraw had no fight left in him and let the matter go. An inning later Fletcher grounded weakly to Collins for the last out of the game and the Series, and the A's were champions.

McGraw immediately walked to the A's bench, where he congratulated Connie Mack for his victory. "You have one of the greatest teams I've ever seen," he told Mack. "It must be. I have a great team, too, but you beat us."[22]

Rube agreed with that assessment. "The series has been won and by the better team," he wrote in the *Times*. "Defeat is always bitter, but we were fairly and squarely beaten and there isn't a Giant who is not willing to say so. Vain regrets and excuses won't go now. The Athletics beat us in the series in all departments of the game — pitching, batting, and fielding, and the last game was a deluge.... They are the best team in the world."[23] He had no choice but to laugh when he learned that for all the damage Baker had done in the Series, he had done so with a new bat — one that was given to him by Donie Bush, Rube's former teammate with Indianapolis and now the fine shortstop with the Detroit Tigers.

The statistics for the Series emphasized the A's supremacy. As a team, Philadelphia hit .244, nearly 50 points higher than the Giants. Bender, Coombs, and Plank — the only three pitchers to throw for the A's — gave up only 33 hits and had a combined ERA of 1.29. They held Giant cleanup batter Red Murray hitless in 21 appearances and allowed the speedy New Yorkers only four stolen bases. Connie Mack felt so good about the club's performance that he displayed an uncharacteristic bit of generosity, although not toward his players. He awarded the Boston Red Sox diamond watch fobs for the pre-Series exhibition games they had played against the A's.

But the Giants had little time to dwell on their poor performance. Ty Cobb had organized a group of all-stars and scheduled a game against most of the Giant regulars in New York on October 26. (Rube pitched a few innings of the game, but unfortunately there was no newspaper account of the contest and it is not known how he fared against the Georgia Peach.)

The National Commission announced that the Giant's share of the Series proceeds came to just over $51,000; each player's share came to $2,436.39. The Giants voted to award partial shares to Wilbert Robinson and Al Bridwell.

And then McGraw arranged for a six-week tour of Cuba, where a total of 12 games would be played against island national teams. Each player would receive $500, plus all expenses paid, but Rube was one of only a few who declined. He had received a better offer: he would spend his off-season on the vaudeville stage.

Chapter 8

A Popular Young Man

The first vaudeville house in America, Boston's Gaiety Museum, opened in 1883. By the turn of the century, vaudeville theaters were established all along the East Coast and in larger Midwest and western cities, as well. Many theaters were independently operated, though several large chains, most notably the Keith-Albee and Orpheum circuits, also existed and thrived. All vaudeville theaters had one thing in common: they featured strange combinations of novelty acts, designed to appeal to any and all conceivable tastes.

Patrons of a typical vaudeville show would, for 25 or 50 cents, be amused and entertained by comedians, jugglers, magicians, singers, dancers, psychics, and contortionists, one after another. Each act was allotted 15 or 20 minutes of stage time; bills consisted of 10 or more acts, and performances usually ran twice per day. Competition between entertainers, and between theaters, was fierce. An act's position on the bill was often critical to its success, and sustained popularity at any particular theater could mean an increase in salary and the opportunity to move to larger and more upscale venues. For the very fortunate, success in vaudeville might even mean a breakthrough into legitimate theater.

Baseball had a place in those early vaudeville days. Fans wanted to see and cheer their heroes in settings more personal than the ballpark. For their part, players were more than willing to test their talents on stage and cash in on the opportunities. World Series stars, for example, might command as much as $2,000 or $3,000 per week for stage appearances; thus a player could earn more in a month in vaudeville than he had in an entire baseball season. In an era long before sports agents, many players employed managers to negotiate their show business contracts. These individuals did more than secure appearance fees for their clients; they arranged to place them at particular theaters, hired writers, composers, and backup performers, and often organized advertising campaigns. And occasionally they were able to convince their clients to rehearse a time or two before getting up in front of a crowd.

The majority of vaudeville theaters were located in New York (perhaps 15 or 20 were scattered around the Broadway section of Manhattan and in other boroughs), a fact that delighted ballplayers who had been traveling all summer long (though a few would, for a price, take their acts on the road). Most performed monologues, offering "inside stuff" on the great plays they had made or famous games they had been in. Those with more courage did imitations of other players, a few danced, and a good many of them sang — although almost always supported by backups.

Although they also performed separately, Mike Donlin teamed up with Mabel Hite for a number of vaudeville acts over the years, including one sketch called "Stealing Home." (The titles of most ballplayer acts had a baseball connotation, none terribly clever.) Donlin also appeared with comedian Tom Lewis; Lewis sat on Mike's lap and acted as a dummy to Mike's ventriloquist. This pair first came up with the expression "twenty-three skidoo."

Joe Tinker of the Cubs began with a monologue, then expanded his act to include burlesque star Sadie Sherman in a skit called "A Great Catch." His teammate Johnny Kling performed sophisticated tricks on the billiard table. Germany Schaefer of the Tigers and Doc White of the White Sox danced and told jokes, and Phillies catcher Charles Dooin sang, though he restricted his performances to Dumont's Minstrel Theater in his hometown of Philadelphia.

After the 1910 season, Christy Mathewson and Chief Meyers had teamed up in a skit called "Curves" that was written for them by sportswriter Bozeman Bugler. In it, Matty played a cowboy who rescues a young girl (played by actress May Tulley), who has been abducted by, of course, the savage and bloodthirsty Indian Meyers. The act was popular with the public but received generally poor reviews, to the chagrin of Mathewson. The criticism bothered him so much, in fact, that he turned down all stage offers the next year.

John McGraw performed a baseball monologue, also written by Bugler, offering his views on favorite players, respected opponents, and the state of the game. McGraw commanded a top salary of $3,000 per week in 1913, touring the country for 15 weeks. But he was never comfortable on stage and in later years limited his appearances to New York's Lions Club, of which he was a member. Even Ty Cobb took a turn or two in vaudeville, although he eventually acted in legitimate theater in a play called *The College Widow* and in a movie called *Somewhere in Georgia*.

In the weeks and months after the 1911 World Series, several members of the champion Athletics were in great demand. Home Run Baker, of course, attracted several huge offers. (One potential skit, to be produced by David Gordon, was naturally called "The Home Run Kid.") Baker declined all offers, preferring instead to spend the off-season with his family on his Maryland farm. Pitchers Coombs, Bender, and Cy Morgan, however, found an offer of $1,750 a week too tempting to resist. Theatrical manager John Robinson and agent Alf Wilson teamed them with the popular singing Pearl sisters, Kathryn and Violet.

Their act, entitled "Learning the Game," was a clever mix of song, dance, and slapstick. Morgan had an exceptional voice and sang a solo, while the entire ensemble performed a number called "The Base-Ball Glide." After a week of rehearsal, the act opened to a packed house at Young's Pier in Atlantic City on October 30 and then had successful runs at New York's Academy of Music Theater and Chicago's Majestic Theater. When their tour was completed just before Christmas, the A's hurlers had earned a small fortune.

On the heels of his breakthrough season, Rube also found himself to be in a good bargaining position. He nearly overplayed his hand. He originally signed a five-week contract with agent William Fox to appear in a play called *Way Down East*. The play was to open at New York's Roof Theater, swing north through Boston and Philadelphia, and then close back in Rube's hometown of Cleveland. But Rube canceled the contract at the urging of his friend and unofficial adviser Mike Donlin. Rube was not yet ready for a serious dramatic production, cautioned Mike; better to try the lighter side of vaudeville first. (Fox immediately filed a lawsuit for breach of contract. Before the case went to trial, the parties settled, Rube agreeing to pay Fox $75 for advertising and promotional expenses.)

Rube was invited to appear with comedienne Rae Cox and her partner Charley Brown in their spoof "The Never Homes," but rejected the offer. He then engaged New York *American* writer William F. Kirk to work on a monologue, but neither man was satisfied with the results, and this idea, too, was scrapped. Finally Donlin introduced Rube to singers Annie Kent and Lillian Shaw, and it was agreed that together they would appear in a short comedy and dance skit. Utilizing Kent's manager for promotions, the new trio was quickly booked to open at Hammerstein's Theater in December.

Willie Hammerstein's Victoria Theater of Varieties was home to some of the most offbeat and colorful acts in all of vaudeville. Its owner proudly promoted the reputation, for vaudeville was, after all, just "one damn thing after another."[1] It was Willie's mission to fill the theater's 1,350 seats and provide some semblance of entertainment, in that order. Hammerstein's featured some of the most popular acts of the day. Harry Houdini performed there, as did Irving Berlin and trick-rope artist Will Rogers. A typical week's bill might also include such acts as the acrobatic team of Richards and Montrose, juggler Paul LaCroix (he juggled hats snatched from the heads of unsuspecting members of the audience), Lamont's Cockatoos (the birds answered questions), or "Sober Sue," who offered a $1,000 prize to anyone who could make her laugh.

The bill for the week of December 11 featured 12 acts, of which Rube, Kent, and Shaw were number eight. (The entire show was reviewed in the December 16 issue of *Variety* magazine). The high-wire balancing act of George Austin and Company opened the show, followed by "accordion virtuoso" Charlie Klass, and Louis Stone, "Topsy Turvy" dancer. Comedian E. F. Hawley appeared in a short sketch entitled "The Bandit," and then tenor Charles Mack sang "A Night in a Turkish Bath." After a short intermission, 85-year-old dancer George Primrose and the slapstick team of Gallagher and Sheen performed, and finally the curtain went up for Rube's ensemble. The three were on stage for a total of 14 minutes. Annie Kent began with a comedic solo, and then Rube joined her for a light duet. Rube had a pleasing voice and managed to smile throughout the number; the crowd cheered politely. Lillian Shaw then appeared alone, and the act changed direction. She sang a medley of "blue" songs that were considered so risqué that, noted *Variety*, "they should not be permitted even at Hammerstein's."[2] Rube and Annie reappeared and joined Lillian for the finale, a short song and shuffle-dance number. Then, following performances by Scottish youngster Laddie Cliff, the Six Musical Spillers, and the Baliots ("equilibrists"), the show closed.

Audiences and critics alike were less than dazzled by the performance because they were puzzled that Rube and his partners had decided to forego the sure thing — baseball-related material. Their contract at Hammerstein's was not renewed after the first week, but Rube was not discouraged. He knew from his experience with the Giants that persistence and hard work would pay off in the end, and he was not particularly interested in the short term. He believed that entertainment could play a big role in his future, and he made contact with a long-time vaudeville agent named Joe Sullivan, who helped him to put together a new act.

Sullivan hired another show business veteran named C. H. Kerr to write a short comedy playlet entitled "Baseball Mad" and booked Rube to appear for a week at the Orpheum Theater in Brooklyn at a salary of $1,500. In the skit Rube appeared in uniform in a ballpark setting and tried to explain the ins and outs of baseball to a perplexed Annie Kent (Lillian Shaw was not retained). The pair then sang a duet and danced, with Annie handling the fancier moves. With his height and good looks, Rube was a crowd pleaser, and audiences noticed the obviously genuine rapport he shared with Annie. After an encouraging week, Sullivan moved the show to the Colonial, where it was scheduled to run the first two weeks of 1912.

The bill at the Colonial, which opened New Year's Day with both matinee and evening performances, included only nine acts, though it offered some standard vaudeville fare. The dancing team of Adair and Dahn opened the show with a 12-minute routine, followed by singers Smythe and Hartman. The comedy duo of Lulu McConnell and Nate Simpson next appeared with their sketch "The Right Girl," in which Lulu performed a number of quick-change maneuvers necessary to the mistaken-identity plot. Longtime vaudevillians Jane Courthope and Company closed out the first half of the show with a dramatic piece called "Lucky Jim."

Joe Jackson — the entertainer, not the ballplayer — opened the second half with some bicycle stunts and pantomime, followed by impressionist Jarrow. Then the first of the bill's two headliners, English singer George Lashwood, took the stage. He took over 30 minutes to sing five songs, including the ballad "Sea, Sea" and the lighter number "Oh, for a Night on Broadway." When the stage manager finally appeared and replaced his card with Rube's, the audience applauded enthusiastically.

Rube and Annie performed "Baseball Mad" with very little change, though Rube seemed more comfortable with his lines. Annie had an additional solo number, and again the pair made their way through a fairly simple song-and-dance. The act, and particularly Rube's performance, received an encouraging amount of praise in *Variety*: "One point very much in the Giant pitcher's favor is that he appears to appreciate he is not a regular actor.... The 1911 phenom was most enthusiastically received, as was his card.... As an act it passes because Marquard undoubtedly is a popular young man in baseball circles, around New York, anyway." The engagement at the Colonial was touted as "a big success."[3]

Poor Charlie Faust was also back on the vaudeville stage for parts of the off-season, but the novelty of his eccentric behavior had, unfortunately, worn thin. He received negative reviews in *Variety* and the New York *Herald*, and even some of his co-performers objected to his presence on the bill. The Seven Picchianas, a tumbling act, went on strike after a matinee performance, complaining about having to follow Charlie and deal with a disappointed and surly crowd.

But Rube, it seemed, was popular everywhere. Friends, family, and the press in his hometown of Cleveland continued to follow his career and take pride in his accomplishments. In mid–January he returned home for a dinner honoring the "Twenty Greatest Ballplayers" Cleveland ever produced. The idea came from *Plain Dealer* sportswriter Henry P. Edwards, who noted that though the city was only the sixth largest in the country, "It comes mighty close to being first as far as the developer of baseball talent."[4] Rube was selected as the seventh greatest player, following his boyhood heroes Ed Delahanty, Bill Bradley, Tommy Leach, and Elmer Flick and old-timers Ed McKean and Larry Twitchell. Rube was "the greatest pitcher Cleveland has ever turned out. Possibly Rube may some day be entitled to a better ranking. But his work during the campaign of 1911 when he was the National League's best hurler certainly entitles him to consideration well up in the list."[5] Even Rube's father began to acknowledge that perhaps he had underestimated baseball's potential.

Rube reveled in the attention he received that winter, both onstage and off. He was vain about his looks and liked to shop for fine clothes. He bought a diamond ring and wore it fashionably on his little finger. When the anonymous benefactor from the previous fall did not come through, Rube bought himself a brand new Pope-Toledo. Too busy to take driving lessons, he hired a chauffeur and soon became a "familiar figure on the boulevards of New York."[6]

Rube became a regular member of Broadway's social scene. He was not much of a drinker (and never would be) but could regularly be seen at fashionable nightclubs and cabarets, and he enjoyed late-night dinners with his new show business friends. Mabel Hite had a busy season, appearing first at Hammerstein's and then at the Alhambra, and Rube attended her show whenever his schedule allowed. He admired Mabel's considerable talents — her 30-minute act included comedy, imitation, and burlesque — and he also knew that she was sure to have him stand and take a bow when he was in the audience. This became so popular that finally she displayed Rube's photograph at a certain point in her act. When she did so, noted *Variety*, "the gallery was ready to tear up the seats."[7]

And Rube renewed his acquaintance with Blossom Seeley, who was such a prominent star that her photograph adorned the cover of the January 13 issue of *Variety*. Blossom was funny, lively, and intelligent, and, with her platinum blonde hair and engaging smile, devastatingly gorgeous. She was also married to her manager Joseph Kane, a matter of no small concern to Rube. Still, the attraction between the two stars was undeniable, and they began to spend time together whenever schedules allowed.

For all his social and show business affairs, Rube did not forget about the upcoming baseball season. When he learned that Mathewson had signed a long-term contract, he demanded the same. Sid Mercer of the *Globe* scoffed at any comparison to the veteran Matty, wondering if perhaps the "footlights of the stage" had affected Rube's vision along with his judgment.[8] But Rube held fast, believing, as he had back in his minor league days, that "a pitcher will only last so long, and should get the money while he is good."[9] After a few weeks of bickering with McGraw, on February 9 Rube finally signed a three-year contract at $5,000 per year; he would also receive bonuses of $500 if he won 25 games and $1,000 if he won 30. He agreed to forego any further vaudeville appearances. (Negotiations were pending to take "Baseball Mad" on the road for a month-long tour of western cities, to include Indianapolis and Cleveland.) Instead he began to work out and prepare to report to Marlin Springs.

Rube arrived in camp happy, fit, and abundantly confident, although at 10 pounds below his normal playing weight he gave McGraw and Robbie some cause for concern. Rain and wind wiped out 14 of 17 preseason sessions in Texas, so the players frequented local gymnasiums to throw and stretch. McGraw organized an indoor tennis tournament, which was fun until several of the players, including Rube, developed blisters on their feet and gave up the game.

In mid–March the wet weather relented. Rube threw five innings against Galveston of the Texas League and was dominant, striking out ten and not allowing a hit in his first extended duty of the spring. A week later the team started north, playing in Mississippi, Kentucky, and Alabama. Rube continued to pitch impressively and was pleased when McGraw named him the Opening Day starter, against Brooklyn.

On Thursday, April 11, at Brooklyn's Washington Park, the Giants took on the Superbas (now often called the Trolley Dodgers), winning 18–3. An estimated crowd of 25,000 fans, or 8,000 more than capacity, jammed their way into the stadium, causing disruption and delay in nearly every inning. Lines of police were powerless to hold back the surging masses of people, and finally umpire Klem disgustedly called the game, after only six innings, on account of darkness.

Rube allowed seven hits and hit safely three times himself, in gaining his first win of the season. He had gained the confidence of his manager and the respect of his opponents, and he believed, as did his teammates, that the Giants would repeat as National League champions and then bring a World Series championship to New York. While he fully expected to have another outstanding season, he could not know that he would, in the process, set a record that would never be broken.

CHAPTER 9

Climbing the Ladder of Fame

The 1912 season was only three days old when John McGraw was tossed out of his first ballgame of the year, rookie umpire Ted Bush handling the honors in the fifth inning of the April 13 loss to Brooklyn. The Giants took it as a sure indication that their manager was his feisty, competitive self. They knew, too, that he had such confidence in his club that the starting lineup from the 1911 league championship team was left virtually intact. After splitting six road games against Brooklyn and Boston, including Rube's 8–2 defeat of the Braves on April 16, they returned to New York on April 18 and began a streak which saw them win 27 of their next 30 games; by the end of May they were in first place to stay. There were plenty of fireworks along the way.

The home opener was normally a festive occasion, but the atmosphere was more subdued than normal this year. Shocking news of the recent *Titanic* disaster had dazed the country, and flags around the Polo Grounds flew at half-mast. Still, the Seventh Regimental Band played, and Christy Mathewson was honored with his "day." As New York and Brooklyn players watched in amazement, the center-field gate swung open and a brand new Chalmers automobile was wheeled onto the outfield grass and presented to Matty. Too embarrassed to mention that he could not drive, he accepted the gift graciously anyway, and the ceremony seemed to perk everyone up. (It was rumored that Mathewson was in dire financial trouble and that the Giants had gone so far as to donate the day's gate receipts, some $30,000, to him. This story sounds far-fetched, but it was repeated in the *Sporting News* some 50 years later.) Since Mayor Gaynor was unavailable, Police Commissioner Waldo threw out the first ball, and the crowd of 18,000 sat back and enjoyed a few familiar sights. McGraw was tossed out of the game in the sixth inning (he received a five-game suspension from the league for his tirade against the umpire), the Giants stole three bases, and Matty won 6–2.

On April 20, rookie Jeff Tesreau started on the mound for the Giants. The big right-hander from Silver Mine, Missouri, and Toronto of the Canadian League had impressed McGraw in Texas and now impressed New York fans as well, striking out 10 hitters and allowing only five hits in eight innings. In the ninth the "Ozark Bear" weakened, allowing two walks and a single, and the score was tied at 2–2. Rube came on in relief to face Jake Daubert, the Trolley Dodger first baseman. Daubert smashed a liner toward the mound, which Rube knocked down with his glove and tossed home to nab the runner Tex Erwin. But when Erwin started back to third base, substitute catcher Art Wilson threw the ball into left field, and Brooklyn took the lead.

In the bottom of the ninth, Wilson came up with one man on base and made up for his error, hammering a drive into the corner of the right-field bleachers. He stood at home plate and watched the ball until umpire Charles Rigler finally called it fair. As Wilson ran triumphantly around the bases with the winning run, Brooklyn manager Bill Dahlen stormed from the dugout toward the plate and began to argue with Rigler over the call. When Dahlen began to "wave his arms in a wild rage, the umpire struck him full in the face. Then Dahlen punched Rigler and the umpire delivered another crack on the infuriated manager."[1] Both benches emptied, and hundreds of excited fans surrounded the two combatants, until finally Wilbert Robinson and a few others broke it up. This "outburst of rowdyism," said the *Times*, "was the worst seen at a National League game in many years."[2] Tesreau was awarded the victory, though under modern rules Rube would have been credited with the win. The ruling would bother Rube for the rest of his life.

The next day, April 21, saw the first big league game ever played at the Polo Grounds on a Sunday. The Giants and Yankees played an exhibition game for the benefit of destitute survivors of the *Titanic*, and nearly $10,000 was raised. Neither Rube nor Mathewson appeared, but Charlie Faust was on hand to entertain the crowd, McGraw having given in to Charlie's relentless badgering to rejoin the team. Aside from this game, however, Charlie never again appeared in uniform, but watched anxiously from the stands or from the end of the bench.

On April 24 the Giants traveled to Philadelphia, where Rube was matched against Alexander. "Alex the Great" had a poor day and was beaten badly, 11–4. Rube allowed seven hits, singled himself, and stole a base in the victory. A week later he beat the Phillies again by the same score, this time striking out nine for his fourth victory of the year.

Rube continued to win with ease as the Giants went on their first western tour of the year. On May 7 he beat St. Louis 6–2, then on the eleventh he bested Chicago 10–3. In Pittsburgh on the sixteenth he allowed only four hits and defeated Marty O'Toole 4–1 for his seventh straight win, then shut out the Reds 3–0 (for his only shutout victory of the season). Four days later he beat Brooklyn 6–3, and as the Giants moved to the top of the standings, the press began to

The 1912 New York Giants, champions of the National League. Rube won 19 straight games in 1912, still the record. He is seated fourth from right, surrounded by his support system—Christy Mathewson to his right, Wilbert Robinson directly behind him. *Standing, left to right:* Lore Bader, Heinie Groh, Dave Robertson, Ted Goulait, George Burns, Fred Merkle, Grover Hartley, Doc Crandall, Hooks Wiltse, Al Demaree, Wilbert Robinson, Art Wilson, Red Ames, Cy McCormick, La Rue Kirby, Art Shafer. *Seated, left to right:* Art Fletcher, Larry Doyle, Chief Meyers, Fred Snodgrass, Buck Herzog, Red Murray, John McGraw, Christy Mathewson, Rube Marquard, Jeff Tesreau, Josh Devore, Beals Becker. *Kneeling:* Dick Henessey, mascot. Photo courtesy National Baseball Library.

take notice of Rube's winning streak. "Rube is so tired of doing nothing this season except winning games that one of these days he's going to fool somebody and lose one for a change.... There is confidence and skill about his work that carry him through with flying colors," said the *Times*.[3] Back in Cleveland, sportswriter Harry Schumacher picked up on something the New York press missed: With his victory over Brooklyn, Rube had already beaten every team in the National League, and the season was barely six weeks old. His pitching was the "gossip for the Major Leagues."[4] Although no game was scheduled for Sunday, April 26, McGraw tried to capitalize financially on the Giants' early-season success and scheduled an exhibition game in Paterson, New Jersey. But at the last minute, the local semipro team backed out, and rather than disappoint a crowd of 8,000 McGraw agreed to play against the Smart Sets, a "colored" team, instead.

The decision did not sit well with Southerner Lou Drucke, who was scheduled to pitch. But Drucke was eager to work his way back into the rotation (his spot having been filled by Tesreau), and he finally consented to throw only if his name was announced as "O'Brien." In the seventh inning, Moose McCormick argued with umpire Jack Warner and was ejected from the game. McCormick refused to leave, and when Warner took off his mask it looked as if a fight would develop. Before any punches were thrown, however, Paterson chief of police Coughlin appeared and threatened to arrest McCormick if he did not relent. The crowd booed Moose as he sulkily returned to the bench.

The game went into extra innings, a fact which pleased none of the Giants. In the bottom of the tenth, Fletcher and Snodgrass complained that the Smart Set pitcher was using an old, scuffed baseball when new ones were available. When the umpire ignored the complaint, the Giants indignantly walked off the field. The crowd became hostile, and an angry mob formed as the Giants pushed their way toward the bus. As they boarded, some members of the crowd began to pelt the players with sticks and rocks and then followed the team to the train station, hooting at them the entire way. The Giants were relieved to leave New Jersey.

Undaunted, the club, behind Rube, sailed into June. On the third he defeated Slim Sallee and the Cardinals 8–3 at the Polo Grounds for his 11th straight victory. Aulick described the game in the *Times*:

> When lanky Rueben [sic] starts to uncurl the mysterious tangents, with all the serpentine motions of a Salome dancer, look out. The victory was easy for Rube ... because he had the ball surrounded completely by the hazy smoke which goes with top-notch pegging. The beanpole southpaw hurled a ball that assumed the shape of a pretzel as it dipped over the pan. Behind it was steam enough to run an engine. And Rube mixed 'em up. He lobbed over a slow one now and then, followed by a straight heave that whistled like a northeast wind. It was a strain on the back muscles of the Cardinal batsmen, for many of their terrific swings at the pill carried all the weight of their shoulders, churning the ozone about the plate into little whirlpools

of air.... Famous men have lived before Rube, that's true. Caesar once showed up Gaul; Alexander hung up a few victories; when William the Conqueror got into the fray he saw only the backs of the fleeing enemy. Napoleon raised a lot of havoc in the European League, but not one of these — no, not one — ever pitched eleven straight victories in the regular season up to the 3rd of June. It is repeated — not one.[5]

Five days later 35,000 fans crammed into the Polo Grounds — the largest crowd there since the first game of the World Series of 1911 — to see Rube win his 12th straight and to witness "Rube Marquard Day." In recent weeks some newspapers had opined that Rube had overtaken the beloved Mathewson not only on the mound, but in the hearts of most Giant fans. Rube was now arguably the most popular player on the team. Perhaps he took the stories a little too seriously, for he reasoned that if Matty deserved a "day," so did he, and he insisted that a ceremony be scheduled. Giant management agreed with him, with one stipulation: Rube had to provide his own car. So prior to the ballgame the center-field gate was swung open, and a nearly new Pope-Toledo was driven out and presented to Rube. It was, of course, the same automobile Rube had purchased last fall, but aside from a few snickering teammates, no one knew the difference.

After the ceremony the game got under way. This time Rube defeated another Rube, Rube Benton of Cincinnati, by a score of 6–2, aided by a grand slam from Chief Meyers. Speculation began about Rube's chances to set an all-time consecutive victory record, though there was some doubt as to just what the record might be. In 1904, Jack Chesbro of the Yankees had pitched 14 successive wins, a feat matched in 1909 by Chicago's Ed Reulbach. Back in 1890, John Luby of the Cubs had won 20 straight, and two years earlier Tim Keefe had won 19 straight, but those marks had both been accomplished with a shorter distance between the pitching rubber and home plate. The controversy was fueled by the circumstances surrounding Rube's very next performance.

On June 12 the Cubs came to New York. They took an early lead in the second inning when Gump Miller doubled and later scored on Jimmy Archer's home run. The Giants scored an unearned run in the sixth and might have had more, but Josh Devore was caught trying to "cut" second base, and the rally was killed. Trailing 2–1 in the bottom of the eighth, Rube was removed for pinch-hitter Art Shafer, and the winning streak was in jeopardy. But Shafer worked Three Finger Brown for a walk, and Doyle drove him in with a double to left-center. Moments later Snodgrass doubled home Doyle with the lead run. Crandall set down the Cubs in the ninth, and the debate was on: Which Giant pitcher should get credit for the victory?

The *New York Times* had a good time with the "momentous question" facing baseball authorities. "In many quarters the argument got so hot it seemed likely that the matter would have to be put up to the Supreme Court or else call in the wise men from Egypt. In other places the oratory about the same question got torrid, and the only means of deciding it was the police."[6] Official scorer Fred Lieb put the question to National League secretary John Heydler, who decreed that since Rube had done the bulk of the day's moundwork and was not withdrawn from the game for poor pitching, he should get credit for the victory. It was Rube's 13th straight win, one away from the record.

Rube's chance to tie the record of Chesbro and Reulbach came on Tuesday, June 17, against Pittsburgh. The Pirates were in second place with a record of 26–21, 11 games behind the Giants. With New York threatening to run away with the pennant, Pirate manager Fred Clarke tried a little psychological warfare in hopes of upsetting Rube's juggernaut. "The Pirates mean to put one over on Marquard," predicted Clarke. "We will be the first to get him. Marquard is a marvelous pitcher but was fortunate to beat us on May 16th. It was hard luck for Pittsburgh, dandy fortune for the New Yorks."[7]

Over 25,000 Giant fans came out to the park to attend the game. On display were the "$44,500 batteries"— Rube and Meyers, and O'Toole and Kelly. "Right here was a bunch of baseball talent that cost so much money," mused the *Times*, "that if you had it you'd lock up the desk and take a trip around the world."[8] Rube pitched his team to a 5–4 victory in "the hardest battle of his life ... a bitter uphill 11-inning contest ... that will go down in history as one of the classic pitching duels of the national game."[9]

The Pirates got on the board first, Honus Wagner driving in Bobby Byrne with a single. But O'Toole walked the bases full in the bottom of the inning and gave up a sacrifice fly; a double play ended the threat, and the score was tied at one. In the fifth the Pirates scored two more, helped by O'Toole's double and a critical throwing error by Doyle. The Giants answered with one run in their half, and the score stood at 3–2 Pirates after five full innings.

Now, "when the fray was hottest and the excitement was on a high wave,"[10] the skies darkened and rain came down in torrents. Umpire Rigler suspended play and announced that if play had not resumed after 20 minutes the game would be called and Pittsburgh declared the winner, ending Rube's streak at 13. But the storm passed, and the game continued, "not one of the fans having left the yard to return home and face the wrath of their wives."[11] Back-to-back doubles by Devore and Murray in the eighth tied the score at three, and the game went into extra frames. In the 11th, Wagner, "the hammering Teuton," stroked a triple to the center-field wall and Dots Miller walked. John Wilson drove Wagner in with a fly ball, and the Pirates led by one. Miller worked his way around to third and, with two out, tried to steal home. The move took Rube by surprise, who threw hurriedly to the plate. Meyers scooped the ball out of the dirt and tagged Miller out on a close play; Miller argued so strenuously that his teammates had to pull him away from Rigler.

In the bottom of the inning, Snodgrass popped out to Wagner at short, and Giant hopes were fading. But as Rube watched nervously from the bench, Red Murray lined a single and Beals Becker smashed a triple to right-center. Moments later Herzog brought Becker home with the winning run, and for his efforts was mobbed at first base by his teammates and hundreds of fans. "The mighty O'Toole had cracked," said the *Times*, "but the mighty Marquard proved himself to be a foeman worthy of his steel, for not once during the torrid strife did he waver for a moment. Boys who saw the game will tell their children about it some day, and then again their children will also tell how their granddaddies were present."[12]

Despite the extended outing, only two days later in Boston Rube threw again, this time in relief of Ames. He entered the game with two outs in the eighth and the score tied at five. He pitched scoreless ball and gained the victory, his 15th straight, when the Giants scored a run in the bottom of the 10th inning.

Rube took his regular turn as a starter on June 21, still in Boston, but perhaps the extra work had fatigued him. The Braves touched him for six hits and two runs in the first three innings, and McGraw was sufficiently concerned to send Tesreau to the bullpen to warm up. But Rube settled down, allowing only four more hits the rest of the way, and the Giants won 5–2. By winning his 16th consecutive game, noted the *Times*, Rube had "clinched his hold on the ladder of fame."[13]

Philadelphia invaded New York on June 25. Once again Alexander pitched for the Phillies, and once again Rube defeated him, this time by a score of 2–1. A steady rain kept the normal crowd away from the park, but both teams played well despite the wet weather. In the bottom of the third inning, Rube singled up the middle and took third on Snodgrass' double. Doyle drove him home with a long fly ball, and Meyers singled in Snodgrass. Rube was perfect on the mound for five innings, but in the sixth Bill Killifer homered to left for the only Phillies run of the day. In gaining his 17th consecutive victory, Rube was never better. He gave up only five hits and walked one and "exerted such hypnotic influence over the horsehide bulb that he had the Phils wiggledy-eyed trying to follow its zigzag actions as it dipped, snapped, twisted, and spun over the platter. Sometimes the ball floated up majestically and then fell limpid and dead into Meyers' big mitt; other times it shot from Rube's fork hand with the speed of a rifle ball in a hurry, and zipped playfully over and under the Quaker bats."[14]

On June 29 the Giants staked Rube to a six-run lead against Boston, and he barely held on for an 8–6 victory over the last-place Braves, who hit safely in every inning but the second. On July 3 he beat Nap Rucker and Brooklyn 2–1 in the first game of a doubleheader at the Polo Grounds. Between games Rube took a seat of honor in the box of Giant treasurer John Whalen. He lit a cigar and welcomed dozens of fans, young and old alike, who pressed him for autographs and handshakes. The next day he treated himself to an exquisite stickpin with opal clusters and proudly displayed it to his teammates. Since the season began, Rube had won 19 straight ballgames. And the Giants had now won 16 in a row, leaving them with an amazing record of 54 wins and only 11 losses, fully 15 games ahead of Chicago and Pittsburgh. As they prepared to embark on their second western swing of the year, they considered themselves invincible.

Rube on his way to a record 19 straight victories, 1912. Photo courtesy National Baseball Library.

Giants supporters were not limited to New York. As Rube's winning streak mounted, his friends and family back in Ohio followed the team's progress closely because several Cleveland newspapers contained daily coverage of Giant games. When Rube's streak reached 19 games, the Cleveland *News* ran a lengthy story on the Marquard family, featuring photographs of Rube's father, stepmother, and grandmother, still alive at the age of 78. "Everybody is happy in the Marquard household on West 48th street," wrote Ed Bang. "This is especially true about every fourth day when Rube goes to the firing line and adds another victory to his already large string." Mrs. Marquard was quoted as saying, "He's a great pitcher and a good boy. We all love Rube and are immensely pleased with his success."[15] Any trace of bitterness between father and son about baseball as a career had long since faded. "His father is probably prouder of Rube's wonderful work than the boy is himself."[16]

Perhaps the *New York Times* knew something in its headline of July 8, "Marquard Seeks Record in the West; Chicago May Break the Rube's Winning Streak in Battle Today."[17] For the Cubs did just that, sending Rube to the showers after six innings and leading the Giants 6–2. They scored two runs in the second, fourth, and sixth innings, collecting eight hits and three bases on balls and taking advantage of three New York errors. When Josh Devore pinch-hit for Rube in the top of the seventh, the crowd "yelled in glee at the announcement, for it meant that the Cubs had driven the southpaw from the slab."[18] Not all of the crowd participation came from inside the stadium. Perched on a tree outside the park was a "female lunatic" named Mary Porter. Her derogatory and profane screams, aimed at Rube, could be heard throughout the game until finally the fire department arrived and forcibly removed her, transporting her to the detention hospital for the insane. "That poor woman certainly proved to be a jinx," said Rube after the game. "Her shrill shrieks affected me more than the cries of all the fans inside the park."[19] Chicago rookie right-hander Jimmy Lavender entered the game on an impressive streak of his own, having thrown three consecutive shutouts. He was in control all day, allowing only five hits and striking out seven, and was on his way to 23 wins in 1912. Rube's record for the season now stood at 19–1.

Rube seemed relieved that the streak was at last over. "Of course I am sorry I did not win my twentieth game," he said. "I would be a fool to deny it.... I am not worrying over my first defeat a little bit. In fact, I feel easier in my mind now that the strain is off. I did worry nights before every game and now that I have done it in 19 straight wins I am perfectly satisfied. I can go into every game I pitch hereafter and not be bothered with any old records or new ones."[20] (At least one member of the Pittsburgh team thought Rube was downplaying his symptoms. "He was almost a physical wreck when we met him in the east before the present trip. Had he won a few more games Marquard would have been a fit candidate for the bug house," one unidentified Pirate told *Sporting Life*.[21]) That night, acting on the advice of his teammates, he took his new opal stickpin, which had obviously brought him bad luck, and ceremoniously tossed it into the Chicago River.

The winning streak was celebrated in feature articles in the *Sporting News*, *Sporting Life*, *Baseball* magazine and even the *Literary Digest*, as well as in newspapers across the country. Rube had defeated each team in the league at least twice, downing Brooklyn three times and Boston and Philadelphia four times each. Opposing pitchers Nap Rucker, Grover Alexander, and Marty O'Toole were bested twice apiece. In 19 games Rube surrendered 142 hits and 49 runs (at least eight of which were unearned), and 16 times he pitched complete games. At the time of his 19th victory in the first week of July, only two other pitchers, Benton of Cincinnati and Larry Cheney of Chicago, had as many as 10 wins.

Coincidentally, on the day that Rube's streak ended, Boston's Joe Wood of the American League began a streak of consecutive victories that would reach 16 games. Only a week earlier, the Senators' Walter Johnson began his streak, which also totaled 16 games.

In midsummer the Giants cooled from their .750 winning percentage pace but still remained comfortably in first place. On July 21, Rube beat Cincinnati 11–1, allowing only four hits, but struck out only one batter, a sign that fatigue and hotter weather were beginning to affect his performance. But if McGraw noticed, he was not overly concerned. On July 23 he scheduled an exhibition game in Toronto against the Leafs and had Rube throw three innings to the satisfaction of a crowd of 12,500. Only two days later Rube started against Chicago at the Polo Grounds. An enormous crowd of over 38,000 people turned out on the Saturday afternoon, not just to see the second-place Cubs — they were still a full 10 games behind the Giants — but because the game promised a rematch of the Marquard–Jimmy Lavender game that had ended Rube's streak a few weeks earlier. When Rube took the mound, the crowd roared in such fashion that it made "the whole upper end of Manhattan Island shake when it burst forth in unrestrained acclaim."[22] But Rube was battered for seven runs in seven innings, and when he left, the Giants trailed 7–2, on their way to a 7–6 loss. It was the first time Rube had been defeated all year in New York.

Rube proceeded to lose seven of his next nine decisions. He was hit particularly hard by Pittsburgh's Honus Wagner, who launched a tremendous home run on August 5, then hit for the cycle two weeks later. Wagner was slowing down — at age 38 he was now the oldest player in the league — and his skills were not what they once were, but he never had trouble against Rube. Of the 10 homers he hit in 1912, three were at Rube's expense. The strains of the winning streak had caught up with Rube, opined the *Times*. Rube had "cracked ... his greatness dissolved into oblivion."[23] But just as he had slumped following his midseason sale to the Giants back in 1908, the better explanation was that Rube was tired, both physically and mentally. He did not pitch badly in August and early September, usually going the distance and only twice giving up more than five runs in an outing. But his fastball clearly had lost some of its zip, and perhaps the lack of a tight pennant race caused him to relax more than he might have. He was not overly concerned with his record as the summer wound down because he knew McGraw had no intention of pulling him from the rotation, and he remained confident that he would establish himself again in the World Series. He experimented with a spitball and gave it a unique name which reflected his newly acquired musical tastes: the ragtime drop.

Neither did the fans turn against Rube, as they had in the "lemon" years. In fact he remained as popular as ever. On one occasion in August he appeared, for a fee, at a semipro game in the Bronx. Even though he was dressed in street clothes, he was persuaded to pitch a few innings and was fined $25 by the National Commission for the unsanctioned appearance. His likeness appeared on folding fans which women used to cool themselves on hot summer days at the ballyard. Rube endorsed products like Coca-Cola and men's clothing. He was, for a time, a light smoker, and in July the Miners Extra and Honest Long Cut Tobacco companies issued their T-227 baseball card set. The set featured only four of the country's most popular stars: Ty Cobb, Home Run Baker, Chief Bender, and Rube. But perhaps the best example of Rube's enormous appeal was that he became, that wonderful summer of 1912, a movie star.

The Kalem Moving Picture Company produced *Rube Marquard Wins*, starring "National Hero" Rube and actress Alice Joyce. The silent film was shot in just a few days on location in New York City and at the Polo Grounds and was released on August 24. The storyline centered around Rube's success on the diamond, of course, and just as predictably involved a lovely and innocent heroine and some sinister villains.

Alice attends a ballgame and by chance meets "the Champ," Rube. Days later she takes in a practice session, and Rube provides a pitching demonstration for her. As Rube leaves the park, some gamblers approach him and try to convince him to sell out the next game, but Rube is aghast at the idea and knocks one of the crooks to the ground.

The villains do not go away. The next day they miraculously induce Rube to meet them at their office at the Metropolitan Tower, where they lock him into a room high above the city streets. Rube opens a window and frantically waves his handkerchief in a signal of distress, and by some miracle he is spotted by Alice from her hotel room. "Now, what can Marquard be doing in the Tower at that time of day?" she wonders. She checks the paper and discovers he should be at the Polo Grounds, preparing to pitch. Determined to investigate she rushes across the street to the Metropolitan and informs the attendant of her suspicions. They free Rube, and Alice accompanies him to the park, where he arrives in time to win the game for the Giants. That night Alice is presented with flowers of thanks from Rube and some of his teammates, and all ends well.

It is not known how the film fared at the box office, but *Moving Picture World* magazine gave it a favorable review, predicting a hit sure to appeal to the "male end of the patronage." Rube was complimented as well. "Marquard takes to the camera as he does to baseball — just naturally. Perhaps his vaudeville experience stood him in good stead or maybe it was his known modesty.... There is, of course, a plot, but it is an excuse only; the interest will center in the baseball pictures, taken at the Polo Grounds. They are excellent."[24]

At last the regular season came to a close. Rube's final numbers for the year were 26 wins (which tied for the league lead with Chicago's Cheney) and 11 losses, a winning percentage of .703. He struck out 175 men, down a bit from 1911 but still the third most in the league, and his 295 innings pitched would be the highest total of his career. National League sportswriters recognized his dominance; Rube finished in eighth place and first among pitchers in the voting for the Chalmers Award, the precursor to the Most Valuable Player award. The Chalmers Award was given to "the one player who should prove himself as the most important and useful player to his club and to the league at large in point of department and services rendered."

There was a somber episode on September 9 when it was discovered that Bugs Raymond had been killed in Chicago. Bugs had technically been reinstated by the National Commission back in May and ordered to report to the Giants, but McGraw had tersely told the press, "I have no use for him."[25] He had steadily gone downhill all summer, attempting to care for his wife and children but mainly frequenting saloons and cadging drinks. He was found dead in a shabby room at the Hotel Valey, and originally it was suspected that the cause of death was heart failure, aggravated by the extreme heat. But a coroner's inquest revealed a fractured skull, and soon a 23-year-old transient named Fred Cigranz was arrested when he admitted he had beaten Bugs to death in an argument over alcohol. In the thick of the pennant race, *Sporting Life* found space for a brief eulogy of the former pitcher: "[Bugs was] one of the saddest figures in base ball, a man who, had he been able to curb his appetite for strong drink, would have undoubtedly been known as one of the really great pitchers in the game. Perhaps the most fitting sentiment of the career of Arthur L., better known as 'Bugs' Raymond may be best expressed in the epitaph: 'What he might have been!'"[26]

The Giants clinched the pennant on September 26 with a doubleheader sweep over Boston. Mathewson won the opener 8–3 for his 23d victory of the year. In the second game, rookie Al Demaree, signed after recording 25 wins for Mobile of the Southern League, threw a seven-hitter in his major league debut, shutting out the Braves 4–0. The Thursday afternoon crowd of 10,000 stormed the Polo Grounds in celebration of a second straight National League championship. This time the opponent in the World Series would be the Red Sox of Boston.

Once again Rube contracted with the Associated Press to cover the Series in a syndicated column. This year the *Plain Dealer* back in Cleveland was picking up his articles, a fact that pleased him and hometown friends and family, as well. Daily coverage by ballplayers had become a very popular idea; a variety of publications also printed game-by-game reports of the 1912 Series by Chief Meyers, Jeff Tesreau, Josh Devore, Boston shortstop Heinie Wagner, Ty Cobb, Walter Johnson, and the managers of both clubs, among many others.

Despite New York's tremendous year, Boston was favored to win the World Series. Managed by Jake Stahl, the Red Sox had won a record 105 games, clinching the pennant on September 16. The heart of the team was its outfielders Duffy Lewis, Tris Speaker, and Harry Hooper (all future Hall of Famers, and even today considered one of the finest, if not the finest, outfield group the game has known). Speaker had particularly excelled during the regular season; he was among the league leaders in 11 offensive categories.

Player-manager Jake Stahl manned first base, while Steve Yerkes, Larry Gardner, and Heinie Wagner rounded out the infield. The pitching staff was led by babyfaced Joe Wood, called Smoky Joe, who was enjoying one of the finest seasons any pitcher ever had. A Kansas native and, like Rube, a product of the American Association (he pitched in 1907 and 1908 for Kansas City), he won 34 games in 1912 and lost only 5. He struck out 258 hitters (second only to Walter Johnson) and tossed 10 shutouts. His ERA was 1.91; he was, for the year, nearly unhittable. Joining him on the staff were steady veteran Ray Collins, rookie Hugh Bedient, and second-year man Buck O'Brien, both 20-game winners.

Boston had last won the American League pennant in 1904 and should have played the Giants in the second World Series. But McGraw was of the opinion that the new league played an inferior brand of baseball and refused to allow his club to participate. The snub was not quickly forgotten, even eight years later, and may have given Boston an extra incentive. Although McGraw respected the Red Sox, he knew little about them and just assumed his club was superior in most respects. He was not a great believer in scouting the opposition in advance, relying instead on reputation and any other scattered information gleaned from friends and coaches who might know something. In late September both teams were in Philadelphia for series against the Phillies and the A's. McGraw could not be bothered to watch the Sox play himself but was content to send Rube and Mathewson to attend and file a report.

While New York fans had the well-deserved reputation of being enthusiastic and knowledgeable, the Red Sox boasted a special group of "bugs" who had gained a national reputation for their devotion to the team. The "Royal Rooters" was led by tavern owner Mike "Nuf Sed" McGreevey, and his group of 300 was in attendance at the Polo Grounds for game one of the Series. Wearing bright red sweaters with matching hatbands and sashes and carrying pennants which read "Red Sox, World's Champions," the Rooters marched confidently across the playing field led by a 30-piece brass band and took their seats in a special section near the right-field foul pole. Boston mayor John J. Fitzgerald was an honorary member of the Royal Rooters, and he left his box seat alongside New York mayor Gaynor and ran to the Rooters' section. "Honey Fitz" grabbed a megaphone and led the group in a boisterous version of their theme song, "Tessie":

> *Carrigan, Carrigan*
> *Speaker, Lewis, Wood and Stahl.*
> *Bradley, Engle, Pape and Hall.*
> *Wagner, Gardner, Hooper, too.*
> *Hit them! Hit them! Do boys, do.*[27]

The balance of the crowd of 35,730, however, soon muffled any more singing with its own cheers for the Giants.

McGraw surprised everyone and named Tesreau as his starting pitcher, to face Wood. Despite his fabulous year, Wood was so nervous before the game that he could not speak, and he quickly fell behind. The Giants scored two runs in the third inning when Murray singled in Devore and Doyle. But Wood composed himself and seemed to get faster as the game progressed; his fastball had tremendous movement and his control was nearly perfect. Tesreau was not overpowering but was effective, mixing a spitball in with his fastball and changeup; he pitched shutout ball until the top of the sixth. Then Speaker lifted a high fly ball to left field. It was Devore's play, but Snodgrass raced over from center and called him off. The ball glanced off Snow's glove and rolled all the way to the fence, Speaker pulling into third. The official scorer gave him a triple, but everyone in the park knew Snodgrass had bungled the play. Lewis grounded to Doyle and Speaker scored; the Giants' lead had been cut to 2–1.

In the top of the seventh, Boston strung together four base hits, including Hooper's double and Steve Yerkes' two-run single, and the Red Sox took a 4–2 lead. Wood continued to mow down New York hitters, and as the Royal Rooters screamed, Boston took the lead into the bottom of the ninth.

With one out, Merkle singled past a diving Heinie Wagner at short. After Herzog's pop fly fell safely in short right field, Chief Meyers singled down the first base line, scoring Merkle and sending Herzog to third: He took second on Hooper's strong throw to the plate. (This throw, which was so remarkable that sportswriter Hugh Fullerton later called it the most important of the Series, was an excellent illustration of Hooper's sparkling play in the clutch.) Now the Giants trailed 4–3 and had runners on second and third, and the stadium was shaking with noise. But Wood was ready for the task, striking out Fletcher and then Crandall to end the game. It was the first time Crandall had ever struck out at the Polo Grounds, Wood fanning him on a full count fastball over the outside corner which he called "one of the fastest balls I ever threw in my life."[28] The victory was Wood's most thrilling moment in his career. Boston had won the first game of the Series in dramatic fashion, but much more excitement was yet to come.

Game two was played in Boston the very next day, October 9. Mathewson opposed Ray Collins in an 11-inning contest that was tied at six runs apiece when it was called because of darkness. Ty Cobb, covering the Series with a syndicated column, called it "the greatest game of baseball ever played,"[29] but McGraw disagreed, as he watched Matty get pounded for 10 hits and the Giants make five errors behind him. None was more costly than the last. With New York ahead 6–5 in the bottom of the 10th, Speaker hammered a long drive to the center-field wall. He reached third easily and then headed for home when Shafer bobbled Becker's relay. The throw to the plate was in plenty of time, but Wilson dropped the ball. Speaker slid wide and had to scramble back to touch home an instant before the lunging catcher. The score was still tied an inning later when the game was called.

Rube awoke the next morning to this headline in the Boston *Post*: "With Matty Out of the Way, the Sox Fear No Giant Twirler."[30] But Rube proved the paper wrong that afternoon, for he was brilliant in leading the Giants to a 2–1 victory at Fenway Park. He struck out six, walked only one, and pitched scoreless ball until the ninth inning. With one out, Lewis chopped a bouncer to Merkle at first, but Rube was late in covering the bag and Lewis was aboard. Gardner doubled off the right-field wall, and the Sox were within one. Stahl drove a line drive straight up the box; Rube somehow knocked it down and threw to third to catch Gardner. Wagner bounced to Fletcher at short, but Merkle dropped his throw, and Henrickson, running for Stahl, advanced to third. Wagner then surprised everyone by stealing second, and now with two out the tying and winning runs were in scoring position.

Forrest Cady stepped in at the plate, and with the game on the line smashed a tremendous drive toward right-center. Josh Devore "ran faster than he had ever run in his life.... No one dreamed he could ever reach that ball.... The Boston crowd was already celebrating a second victory and counting the series won. The bands were blaring, the bass drums rumbling, and the cymbals were crashing. The grandstands and the bleachers were afire with waving red flags."[31] Devore lunged at the last instant and managed to hold onto the ball, securing the Giant victory and Rube's first World Series win.

Rube had "redeemed himself," according to the *Times*. "In midseason, after being hailed as the game's greatest hero in 20 years, with his record of nineteen straight victories, the slim southpaw found that much of his strength had been spent and his cunning had gone in the building up of his remarkable pitching feat.... But today he was himself again."[32]

McGraw was generous in his praise. "That last wonderful catch and Marquard's pitching were easily the main features of the game. I had known for some time that the Rube was there and in shape to pitch a gilt-edged battle.... He twirled a grand, steady game."[33] In his column Rube accepted a mere "one-ninth of the credit" for the victory. He felt strong before the game, he wrote, and the encouragement he received from McGraw inspired him:

> I thought of the days when I was called the $11,000 lemon and names by the fans; thought how McGraw's best friends pleaded with him to tie the can to me; thought of the many blunders I had made in the past that cost the Giants victories, and now I had the opportunity to prove to the whole world that McGraw was right when he retained me.... I wanted to win for myself; I wanted to win for the Giants, but more than all I wanted to win for McGraw's sake, the best friend I ever had. And I made good for him. This pleases me more than anything else.[34]

The Giants and Jeff Tesreau were again overmatched by Smoky Joe Wood in game four at the Polo Grounds. Over 36,000 fans watched in awe as Wood struck out eight and gained a 3–1 victory, his second of the Series. The next day Giant bats were just as quiet, this time against Hugh Bedient, and the Sox beat Mathewson 2–1. They now led the Series three games to one, and McGraw called on Rube to stave off a Boston championship.

Once again Rube awoke to a disturbing headline, although this one was far more serious than a ballgame prediction. In Milwaukee former president Theodore Roosevelt was shot in the chest as he prepared to give a speech; undaunted, Teddy gave the speech anyway and suffered no serious complications. And once again Rube came up with an outstanding performance at the ballpark, this time winning 5–2. The Giants stroked Buck O'Brien for six hits and all their runs in the first inning, and Rube was in control the rest of the way.

His fastball rode in on Red Sox hitters, and as they swung away at pitches at the letters, they popped up or flew out all day long: Of the 27 outs in the game, fully 18 were on fly balls. Rube joined Wood in pitching his second complete-game victory of the Series; now in 18 innings he had allowed 14 hits and one earned run. Against Rube, said McGraw, the Red Sox "never had a chance."[35]

With the Sox now ahead in the Series three games to two, the clubs returned to Boston on October 15 for game seven, and with Smoky Joe Wood pitching they were decided favorites. For once the controversy took place off the playing field. Boston management inexplicably sold the block of seats normally reserved for the Royal Rooters to other fans. The Rooters tried to storm the field and actually succeeded in knocking down parts of the outfield wall; they were finally subdued by mounted police. The disturbance caused a delay in the start of the game of some 30 minutes and threw the pitchers' warm-up schedule off kilter. Although he refused to use it as an excuse, Joe Wood was clearly affected by the irregularity, for he was hit harder than in any other start all season. He lasted only one inning, giving up 7 hits and 6 runs on only 13 balls thrown, and the Giants went on to win 11–4. "The idol of Boston fandom is no longer the hero he was," gloated the *Times*. "To-night, instead of singing paeans of joy over him, the Boston fans are mentioning his name only in whispers, and deepest gloom prevails wherever baseball is discussed."[36]

The toss of a coin determined that the eighth and deciding game would be played in Boston, on October 16. In protest of the treatment the Royal Rooters had received and under the boycott directive of McGreevey (and with the editorial support of the *Boston Globe*), only 17,000 fans, half of Fenway's capacity, turned out. Those who stayed home missed one of the most exciting and infamous World Series games ever played.

The Giants touched Bedient for the game's first run in the third inning. Devore walked and was sacrificed to second, and Murray lined a sinking drive to center field. Speaker dove for the ball, but it skipped under his glove, rolling nearly to the wall. Merkle grounded out to end the inning, but the Giants had the lead. They threatened again in the fifth, but Hooper made a tremendous catch — some fans swore with his bare hand — while diving into the temporary bleachers in right field. Joe Wood later described the catch as "impossible to believe even when you saw it."[37]

For six innings it looked as though one run was all Mathewson would need. He skillfully changed speeds and kept the Sox hitters off balance, but then he ran into trouble in the bottom of the seventh. Stahl popped a Texas leaguer into short center field. Shafer and Snodgrass each called for it but, neither took it, and the hustling Stahl slid safely into second base. With two outs, Olaf Henriksen hit for Bedient. In his only plate appearance of the Series, Henriksen took two called strikes and then drilled a double down the third base line. Stahl scored easily, and the score was tied at one.

Smoky Joe Wood came on to pitch for Boston, providing at last, if only for a few innings, the anticipated Wood-Mathewson matchup. The game moved into extra innings. In the top of the 10th, New York took the lead again when Murray doubled and Merkle, seeking to exorcise the ghosts of his 1908 baserunning blunder, lined a single to center; Murray scored when Speaker bobbled the ball. The next hitter, Chief Meyers, drilled a shot straight back at Wood, who knocked it down with his throwing hand and threw Meyers out, ending the inning. Now the Giants were only three outs from their first World Championship in seven years, and Matty walked confidently out to the mound.

McGraw had little doubt but that Matty would finish off the Red Sox, but as an extra precaution he sent Rube out to the bullpen in deep center field in case he needed to get loose quickly. It gave Rube a bird's-eye view of perhaps the most famous error in baseball history. Pinch hitter Clyde Engle stepped in for Wood. Smoky Joe was a good hitter (several years later, when his arm went bad, he made it to the major leagues as an outfielder), but the drive off Meyers' bat had swelled his hand, making it impossible for him to swing the bat. Engle lofted a lazy fly ball to left-center field, and the crowd groaned as Snodgrass called off Murray and settled under it. Rube recalled later that as the ball came down only a few feet from him, he called out, "Fred, squeeze that son of a so-and-so!"[38] But to the shock of players and fans alike, Snow dropped it onto the outfield grass, and as the fans roared, Engle, representing the tying run, stood safely on second base.

Harry Hooper came up next and tried to bunt Engle over to third, but he fouled the first pitch off. The Giants still expected the sacrifice, and Mathewson held Engle close at second, Snodgrass playing shallow in center in case a pickoff throw got away. But Hooper crossed them up and swung away and cracked a long drive to deep left-center field. "Ninety-nine times out of a hundred no outfielder could possibly have come close to that ball," Hooper said. "But in some way, I don't know how, Snodgrass ran like the wind, and dang if he didn't catch it. I think he *outran* the ball. Robbed me of a sure triple."[39] Snodgrass crashed against the wall, wheeled, and threw back to second base and nearly doubled off a sliding Engle, who had already rounded third base on the drive.

Now Mathewson's usually impeccable control failed him as he walked Yerkes. With one out, Speaker stepped in and lifted a high pop fly into foul territory near the first base coach's box. It was Merkle's ball, but he froze, called off by shouts from the Boston bench or perhaps from Mathewson himself. The pitcher inexplicably called for Meyers to take it, but the lumbering Chief couldn't quite catch up to it and the ball fell untouched. Reprieved, Speaker called out to Matty that the misplay "would cost him the ballgame."[40] On the next pitch, he knocked a single to right, scoring Engle and sending Yerkes to third. Lewis was walked intentionally to load the bases and set up the force at any bag, but Gardner drove a deep fly ball to Devore, scoring the tagging Yerkes with the winning run. Hundreds of jubilant Boston fans stormed the field, mobbing their heroes in celebration. The stunned Giants watched the scene in disbelief, losers of the World Series for the second year in a row.

The newspapers were merciless in their criticism of Snodgrass. "Sox Champions on Muffed Fly" and "Game Kicked Away on Snodgrass Error" were typical headlines. The *Times*, noting that the misplay cost the Giants nearly $30,000, began its story this way: "Write in the pages of world's series baseball history the name of Snodgrass. Write it in large and black. Not as a hero; truly not. Put him rather with Merkle, who was in such a hurry that he gave away a National League championship. Snodgrass was in such a hurry that he gave away a world championship."[41]

None of the Giants, including McGraw, ever publicly criticized Snodgrass for the error (or errors, for that matter; his failure to grab Stahl's pop fly in the seventh led to the Sox's first run). To a man they agreed that mistakes were part of the game, and no player was immune from them. It was the misplay of Speaker's pop foul, after all, that had truly cost them the game. They did have to console Snodgrass, of course. After the game he packed his gear and rode in silence to the hotel. Finally after two hours, he was able to mutter his first words since the muff: "Boys, I lost the championship for you."[42]

The defeated club arrived back in New York that night just before midnight. A parade and special music had been planned in anticipation of a Series victory; now only a small crowd of fans greeted them at the West 125th Street station. Snodgrass was the first Giant off the train (Mathewson rode on alone to Grand Central; even in defeat special rules applied for him), and Snow looked "a little sheepish as his friends crowded around him and told him not to fret."[43] In his column the next day, Rube wrote what every member of the Giants was thinking: "I don't like to take glory away from a winner, but the Red Sox are the luckiest world's champions that ever lived."[44]

CHAPTER 10

Scandal

In the summer and fall in New York, it was rumored that the city's most eligible bachelor, Rube Marquard, was engaged to be married to a showgirl named Shirley Kellogg, who had appeared, among other productions, in *The Follies of 1910*. To be sure, Rube and Shirley enjoyed each other's company and had been seen together on several occasions dining at finer restaurants and stepping out along the Great White Way. What Miss Kellogg assumed of the relationship and what she may have told her family and friends can only be guessed, but Rube had no intentions of marrying her. He was infatuated with Blossom Seeley.

Blossom Katherine Seeley was born on July 16, 1891, in San Francisco, and show business was the only life she ever knew. Her father had lost his legs in a construction accident, and it was probably her mother, Bertha, who first recognized her talent and guided her toward the stage. By the age of 10, "The Little Blossom," as she was billed, was already a veteran of San Francisco and Los Angeles musical revues and theater productions, including shows at the famed Grauman's Theater. Her start in show business at such an early age allowed her to develop a toughness and savvy that would steady her through the ups and downs that any entertainer's career would hold. In 1906 she gave new meaning to the adage "the show must go on": she was onstage performing when San Francisco was shaken with its monstrous earthquake. As she grew older, she developed a brassy, sexy singing style that later would be emulated by Sophie Tucker and Mae West. She traveled the burlesque and vaudeville circuits of the country and first appeared in New York in 1910 at the Washburton Theater. Her act included such numbers as "Put Your Arms Around Me, Honey" and the popular "Toddlin' the Todalo." The latter earned her the nickname "The Queen of Syncopation," and show business insiders predicted stardom. "When Blossom starts those hands agoing, and begins to toddle," said *Variety* magazine, "you just have to hold tight for fear of getting up and toddling right along with her."[1]

Blossom's big break came in 1911, when producer (and comedian) Lew Fields spotted her and cast her in *The Henpecks*. Her rendition of "Frisco Toddler," a song written especially for her, was a showstopper and earned her great acclaim. The next year she costarred with Al Jolson in *Whirl of Society*, the first of many appearances the two would make together, and between Broadway productions she continued to perform in vaudeville, always as a headliner. During July and August of 1912, she appeared at Hammerstein's Victoria Theater before sellout crowds that greatly enjoyed her saucy mix of song, dance, and comedy. Her husband of one year, Joe Kane, had abandoned his own singing career for hers, and under his direction her career continued to escalate. She was considered, along with her good friend Fannie Brice, the brightest young star of the stage, and at 21 years of age she was having the time of her life.

In September, Blossom was in Chicago, appearing in a three-act musical comedy called *The Charity Girl*. Producers George Lederer, Charles Dillingham, and William Connor had revised the show after a successful run in London, adding ornate backgrounds, extravagant costumes, and an all-American cast. On October 2 the show moved to New York, where it was booked at the Globe Theater on Broadway. Blossom and costars Ralph Herz and Marie Flynn performed an eclectic combination of ragtime, comedic and light operatic numbers. (Blossom's one bawdy solo was "universally condemned for its vulgarity" and dropped after one performance.[2]) *The Charity Girl* opened to mixed reviews in Manhattan, critics wondering whether metropolitan audiences could appreciate the show's European flavor. Modifications were scheduled to begin, but when Lederer's wife was thrown from her horse in Central Park he opted to close the production down instead. It was to reopen in Boston at the end of the month, but Blossom chose not to go. Her husband had booked her to appear in a brand new vaudeville act costarring baseball star Rube Marquard.

Kane and Blossom met with Rube at the Endicott Hotel, where Rube now lived, and made plans for the show. The act would be called "Breaking the Record, or The 19th Straight," and would be written in large part by Thomas J. Gray, a respected veteran composer and lyricist. Kane could assure that each star would receive $1,500 per week, and they were scheduled to be the headline act at Hammerstein's Victoria beginning October 28. Within a few days of the conclusion of the World Series, Kane arranged for rehearsals to begin. The electricity between Rube and Blossom was apparent to everyone, and they made no secret of the affection they felt for each other. Almost immediately they began a love affair.

Rube and Blossom were excited to be together and looked forward to their show's opening, but their enthusiasm was tempered when Mabel Hite died of cancer on October 22. Mabel had been ill most of the summer, but the news still came as a great shock to the vaudeville community. She passed away suddenly at her home on West 111th Street, alone save for the company of her attending Christian Science nurse. Mike Donlin was touring with his act in Youngstown, Ohio, and returned to New York immediately. Despite the circumstances, Rube

Sheet music from 1912, when Marquard and Seeley toured the vaudeville stages of America. Courtesy National Baseball Library.

and Blossom were glad to see Mike again and reminisce about Mabel because both believed that she was the one who had brought them together.

"Breaking the Record" was a smash. The 24-minute act was a combination of music, comedy, and simple dance and filled the Victoria for a solid week. The curtain went up to reveal a backdrop depicting the entrance to the clubhouse of the Polo Grounds. Blossom, as the pert and innocent baseball fan dressed in a white spring dress, happens to meet the uniformed Rube as he arrives at the park. They flirt, and Rube promises to do his best for her in the ballgame. He enters the clubhouse and can next be seen through a transparent screen throwing baseballs to an offstage catcher, while Blossom sings "The Marquard Glide," a rollicking ragtime number they had helped write:

> *All you fans, all you fans*
> *Clap your hands, clap your hands*
> *When you hear, when you hear*
> *The tune that I'm goin' to croon*
> *For it's there, it's a bear*
> *Right from the home plate, Gee! boys but it's great!*
> *Here she goes, on your toes.*
> *Take your place, take your place*
> *On your base, on your base*
> *Just you hear that band*
> *Don't it sound just grand!*
> *Hear them shout, hit it out*
> *It makes a big score, it makes you want more*
> *Feel the sway, come this way.*
> *We'll do that Marquard glide, yes, that Marquard glide*
> *Matty, Meyers and McGraw*
> *Murray, Snodgrass and Devore*
> *Herzog, too! Fletch and Doyle*
> *Make that band of music toil*
> *Oh, that Marquard glide!*
> *Oh, that Marquard glide!*
> *He's going down to second, watch him slide!*
> *He's king in the pitchers box!*
> *Stood up through all the knocks*
> *Had it on those Red Sox*
> *You can bet all your rocks on Reuben! Reuben!*
> *He's some pitcher, so we'll all do that Marquard*
> *All do that Marquard, all do that Marquard glide.*[3]

To great applause, the "game" over, the stars sing a duet called "Baseball," and when Blossom exits, Rube has the stage alone. He sings a verse all by himself; the audience loves it, and so he sings it again. Now Blossom reappears, this time in a beautiful blue and pink gown. She sings as Rube quickly moves offstage and changes into a tuxedo. When he returns, the pair perform an up-tempo dance number. The ovation from the audience is deafening, and there are a number of curtain calls.

The act, and particularly Rube's performance, was favorably reviewed in

Variety: "Interest in the Giants' southpaw was palpitating and intense.... The mere presence of the big twirler was what made the act. The vehicle will carry the pair nicely.... Rube is making money for the Victoria.... The combination [of Rube and Blossom] is invincible. Certainly it resulted in the best business the 42nd street house has seen this long time."[4]

Sometime during the first week's engagement Blossom told her husband about her romance with Rube. An argument ensued, and Blossom later claimed that Kane threatened her with a gun. She left him alone at his Seventh Avenue hotel and moved in with Rube. Blossom found a city magistrate willing to issue a temporary restraining order against Kane; though he was still her manager and entitled to a $100 weekly fee, he was now barred from the premises of the Victoria. When Rube and Blossom decided to vacation for two days in Atlantic City, Kane filed a criminal complaint against Rube alleging adultery, for which conviction could mean imprisonment of up to one year. A warrant for Rube's arrest was issued.

The situation got uglier. The love-struck couple registered at Atlantic City's Hotel Dunlop under the names "Rube Marquard and wife." Joe Kane maintained later that he and two private detectives followed the lovers to the hotel, bribed a bellboy into identifying their room, and broke down the door at three in the morning. When they informed Rube that a constable was waiting downstairs in the lobby with an arrest warrant, Rube asked for a few moments to dress and promised to come down shortly. Rube's version of events was much different: he claimed that when the intruders broke into the room he chased them down the hall with tails between their legs. Wherever the truth lay, subsequent newspaper accounts agree that Rube and Blossom left the building via the fire escape and caught a train to Philadelphia. As John McGraw, appearing at the Colonial Theater with his "Inside Baseball" routine, watched disgustedly, the newspaper headlines chronicled every detail of the entire scandalous story.

Both sides cooled down considerably in the following weeks. Rube hired an attorney who convinced the court that his client would appear in court voluntarily on a summons and had the warrant quashed. Kane realized that he had no hope of winning Blossom back but was so humiliated by the affair that he filed suit against Rube for $25,000, alleging alienation of affections, serving the papers himself as Rube and Blossom dined at the Folies-Bergère. His complaint maintained that Rube had "persuaded Blossom that her husband was not the right person for her to cherish" and that he had robbed Kane of his wife's affections by "attentions, numerous gifts, and by abusing, slandering and belittling him." Rube had, in addition to the Atlantic City escapade, gone so far as to kiss Blossom "in the presence of several people at a tavern in Central Park."[5]

Rube and Blossom hired new management and got back to the safety of the stage, appearing for a week at the Union Square Theater. Their act remained essentially the same, although Blossom added a fiery medley called "Those

Ragtime Melodies." They next appeared at the Fifth Avenue Theater for the week preceding Thanksgiving, and then they hit the road.

"Marquard & Seeley," as they were now billed, began a nationwide tour, headlining at vaudeville theaters in larger cities across the country. While not always meeting critical success, they routinely played to packed houses of adoring crowds. Aggressive press agents described Rube as the all–American success story who had transformed himself from lemon to peach, the pitcher who had won an unprecedented 19 straight games, the World Series hero. His partner was the electrifying "hottest girl in town," who sizzled on stage like no other, and together they had conquered New York and met similar success on the national scene. They were greeted at train stations by photographers and journalists; they stayed at luxurious hotels in Chicago, Kansas City, St. Louis, and every city they played, and they dined in the most elegant restaurants. They thought that the dizzying months they spent on tour together were the most exciting they had known. They were in love with each other, and in love with the lives they led.

Rube now believed that he was in a good position to parlay his show business popularity into a raise in salary from the Giants. In St. Louis over Christmas, he took his case to the press, advising McGraw through the newspapers that his current contract, still with two years left to run, should give way to a new three-year deal at $10,000 per year. He reminded readers that he had won as many games as Mathewson for two years in a row and was a two-game winner in the recent World Series. If his demands weren't met, he promised, "I'll remain in vaudeville. That's no dream, either. Miss Seeley and myself are booked for the next 22 weeks. That will keep us busy until June 1st."[6]

John McGraw was in Pittsburgh when the story broke, and having gone through the same routine with Mike Donlin a few years before, he was neither surprised or impressed. "That kind of talk makes me tired," he said. "His declaration that he won't sign unless he gets $10,000 a year is foolishness. He is signed for three years now and he'll report on time just like all the other players next spring." McGraw could not resist taking a personal shot, as well. "Marquard hasn't done himself or the New York club any good by his actions this winter.... Regarding all his troubles, I don't care to say anymore except that it is unfortunate that his conduct has made it unpleasant for all the rest of us on the team. Let him get all the free advertising he can, but let him use some sense in choosing his methods."[7]

While Rube's declarations no doubt caused some Giants fans to worry, the sportswriters of at least one national publication were not sympathetic. "The Rube is scarcely serious in his demand for $10,000 a year," wrote William McBeth of the *Sporting News*. "Such assertions have been made, it is believed, for the object of publicity, but the fact that Marquard went all to pieces last year after winning 19 straight games and that he has been hitting the high places all winter is another matter. McGraw will count nothing on this fellow till he proves he is still the great tosser which, for his innate foolishness, he should be."[8]

Rube and his new bride Blossom Seeley. This photograph was taken by Christy Mathewson. Photo courtesy National Baseball Library.

The *Sporting News* was not content merely to criticize Rube's baseball dealings but took the opportunity to comment upon his personal life and the appropriateness of the stage act, as well. For moral reasons alone, it stated in its February 13, 1913, edition, Rube deserved to be "pulled into oblivion. Perhaps it would be fitting to say that not the Rube, but the scandal that hovered about himself and his 'partner' in this act was the drawing card, for it was ever thus. All an 'actress' has to do to insure S.R.O. business is to get chased out of a hotel with another man, her husband and a policeman being the chasers. There are always enough people who delight in this sort of scandal to fill a theater when the principals in the case appear, even in Denver, which is a fairly respectable city."[9]

While Rube haggled with McGraw over his contract, Blossom successfully negotiated an end to her marriage. She granted Kane an uncontested divorce on January 15, 1913, and declined to press charges against him for the alleged assault with a weapon. The parties continued to dicker over the alienation of affections lawsuit Kane had filed against Rube, but within a few months Kane accepted a settlement of $4,000 and that case, too, was resolved.

But as spring training began in early March, Rube still insisted that he would not honor his contract, and he did not report to Marlin Springs with his teammates. While the *Sporting News* wondered whether the Giants, without Rube, could stave off Pittsburgh and gain a third successive National League pennant, John McGraw was not eager to find out. He dispatched scout Dick Kinsella to the West Coast to try and talk some sense into his star left-hander.

Kinsella caught up with Rube in Los Angeles, and while he had no immediate success in persuading Rube to end his holdout and depart for Texas, he did arrange for him to work out informally for a few days with the Chicago White Sox, who trained nearby. The show moved to San Francisco and played for a week at the Orpheum Theater. There Rube and Blossom were the headliners on a bill which included the usual assorted collection of vaudeville entertainers: Apdale's Zoological Circus, comedians Diamond and Brennan, singer Eddy Howard, and Rosner's Augmented Hungarian Orchestra, among others. Finally when McGraw sent a wire authorizing Kinsella to offer Rube a raise of $2,500, it appeared a deal was imminent. But before it could be finalized, there was another matter for Rube to attend to — his marriage.

On Wednesday, March 12, Rube and Blossom finished their 2:15 matinee performance and walked two blocks down O'Farrell Street to St. Mark's Lutheran Church, where at four o'clock in the afternoon they were married, the ceremony being conducted by the Reverend Henry S. Feix. The only witnesses to the wedding were James Cullen, who managed the Orpheum, and his wife. A number of journalists and photographers, however, had been alerted and waited outside the church. The happy couple hustled back to the theater for the evening performance, and later that night Rube signed his new contract with the Giants. "McGraw commissioned me to corral Rube," said Kinsella. "I used my own judgment in drawing up the contract, but it will stand. Rube held out at first, because he wasn't sure what his bride thought about it, but when she agreed he did not hesitate."[10] There was no time for a honeymoon, although Rube and Blossom hoped to travel to Europe after the 1913 season. They canceled the remainder of their theatrical engagements and in a few days caught the train for Texas, where they met the team in Galveston.

"The two best things in the world have happened to me," Rube told a reporter in an article picked up by the Cleveland *Press*. "Marriage and baseball. We're a great battery, this little girl and I, and with her rooting for me in the grandstand this season I expect to break all previous records, including the one of 19 straight games. We are through with show business for the time being. I do not feel that I have lost much by missing the front end of the training season, because, you see, I have kept myself in pretty good form while on the road." And what did Blossom think of her new spouse's return to baseball? "Well, you know I am the most enthusiastic little girl in the country," she said, "and anyway, anything that suits Rube suits me."[11]

W. A. Phalon of the *Sporting News* had a slightly more caustic reaction:

Glad news from afar. Rube Marquard has announced that out of the greatness of his heart he will condescend to play ball and will rejoin the Giants, thus saving the Polo Grounds, the National League Circuit, and the whole foundation of base ball, from utter ruin. What on earth could the game have done without Mr. R. Marquard? Can you imagine base ball groping, stumbling, staggering along from April to October without Mr. Marquard? There would have been nothing but empty stands and grass-grown bleachers — but Mr. Marquard, most generous of heroes, has consented to play ball, and the universe is saved![12]

CHAPTER 11

The Best Left-Handed Pitcher in Baseball

Despite the cold April weather, nearly 22,000 baseball fans turned out at the Polo Grounds on April 10 to see the first game of the 1913 season. As a 12-piece band played, McGraw was presented with two large floral horseshoes made of Killarney roses, one from the Friars Club and one from the Lambs Club. Before Mayor Gaynor threw out the first ball, each of the Giants was introduced. Christy Mathewson, now beginning his 13th year, was loudly cheered, of course, as were Doyle, Herzog, and the others. Even Snodgrass ignored the numerous catcalls and doffed his cap. Many fans were eager to get a glimpse of the newest Giant: Olympic champion Jim Thorpe had won gold medals in both the decathlon and the pentathlon in the 1912 Games in Stockholm, and his unparalleled athletic abilities had so intrigued McGraw that he won a spot on the roster, as well, despite very brief minor league baseball experience. Initial speculation was that Thorpe could play all infield and outfield positions and could even pitch if needed. But he was to see only occasional duty in his first year, mainly as a pinch runner. Still, his gate attraction was easily enough to justify the $5,000 contract McGraw had tendered.

The biggest cheer from the crowd, however, came for Rube. He was a little apprehensive before he took the field, worrying that perhaps his off-season travails and spring training holdout would cost him some fan support, but now, like the entertainer he had become, he made the most of the opportunity. He grinned broadly and ran over to Blossom, seated in the box seats near the Giants' bench, and together they waved and posed for the photographers. Now four months pregnant, she gazed at him adoringly, wrapped tightly in the fur coat he had bought her. He blew her a kiss, retired to the dugout, and watched Jeff Tesreau get blasted 8–0 by the Boston Braves.

The only change to New York's starting lineup found George Burns in left field for Devore. Nicknamed for his hometown, "Utica George" had played sparingly in 1912 but had a terrific training camp in Marlin Springs. Very fast on the basepaths and always hustling in the field, he quickly became a favorite of the fans and of McGraw, as well. He would become a fixture in the Giant outfield for the next nine years, consistently hitting .300 and five times leading the league in runs scored. By the end of the first month of the season, McGraw had become so impressed with Burns that he traded Devore away, along with Leon Ames and utility player Heinie Groh, to Cincinnati for pitcher Art Fromme.

Since Rube had missed most of camp, he worked his arm into shape slowly, throwing in the bullpen before games under Wilbert Robinson's watchful eye. A mild case of tonsillitis delayed his first appearance on the mound until April 21, in Boston. He gave up nine hits but beat the Braves 4–3, the Giants profiting by several Boston errors and scoring three unearned runs. Against Philadelphia on May 5, he was blasted by three home runs, two by Sherwood McGee and one by Gavvy Cravath, and took a 6–3 loss. Four days later the Reds, now managed by Joe Tinker, beat him 3–1, all the Cincinnati runs coming in the sixth inning when John Bates doubled with the bases loaded. Rube's inconsistent start and his show business experiences provided easy fodder for the newspaper columnists' observations. "During seven of the eight innings that he occupied the mound, Marquard acted like a pitcher," noted Aulick of the *Times*. "In the other inning he pitched like an actor.... The harsh treatment to which the southpaw was subjected in this session made him long for those happy winter days out in Kokomo when the matinee crowds showed how much an actor is appreciated."[1]

Giant hitters struggled in the early part of the season, and the club limped along at a .500 pace. Mathewson won 12 of his first 16 starts, however, almost single-handedly keeping the club within striking distance of Philadelphia. Rube gradually got into pitching shape, and while his record was only 5–7 at the end of June he showed signs of returning to top form. On May 19, he threw eleven strong innings against Pittsburgh and their fine right-hander Howie Camnitz, coming out of the game with the score tied at one. A week later he beat Boston 7–2 for his first complete game victory of the year. With the warmer weather the New York bats began to heat up as well. They won series against Brooklyn, Boston, and Chicago and gradually made up ground against the Phillies, and when they traveled to Philadelphia for a four-game set beginning June 30 they were only a half-game back.

Fifteen thousand raucous fans attended what was supposed to be a pitcher's duel between Tesreau and Grover Alexander, but both hurlers were shelled early and gave way to relievers. McGraw stationed himself in the third base coach's box, directly in front of the Phillies bench, and was in a particularly combative mood. He continually chided and challenged Philadelphia players on the bench and those fans within earshot. At one point umpire Klem warned McGraw to keep quiet, but it did little good. The offensive show continued into extra innings, and finally in the 10th inning Snodgrass, who had four hits on the day, scored the winning run on Herzog's single, the Giants holding on for an 11–10 victory. For the first time this season, they were in first place, now a half-game ahead of the Phillies.

Directly after the game, McGraw met up with Phillies manager Red Dooin and, along with several players from both teams, began to walk across the outfield grass toward the clubhouses. A large group of Philadelphia fans, angry at the game's outcome and their club's loss of first place, left their seats and encircled McGraw and the others. Suddenly McGraw was pushed down from behind by either a Philadelphia fan or, as some of the Giants later claimed, Phillies pitcher Addison "Eddie" Brennan. The crowd surged around McGraw and kicked him repeatedly, opening up a large gash on his chin and another on his cheek. McGraw struggled furiously and attempted to get off the ground and fight back but was held down until Dooin and Giant players Art Wilson and Grover Hartley came to his rescue. Finally some policemen were able to push through the mob, which now numbered perhaps 2,000 people, and they broke up the melee. McGraw was treated for cuts and abrasions and hurriedly filed his report of the incident to the National League. This time, he believed, he was not the antagonist but an innocent victim and would not be punished for his role in the fracas. Later in the week league president John Heydler personally traveled to Philadelphia and interviewed witnesses and combatants. After reviewing all the evidence, he suspended both McGraw and Brennan for five games, finding that they had "engaged in personalities during the game which were the direct causation of the incident."[2] Brennan was also fined $100.

If the Philadelphia ballclub, or their fans for that matter, thought that the fracas would intimidate the Giants, they were very much mistaken. The next day, July 1, with McGraw safely on the bench, New York clubbed four Phillies pitchers, including Alexander again, for 17 hits and 10 runs, and Rube tossed a 4-hit shutout. Just over 10,000 "baseball rooters and fight fans"[3] witnessed the slaughter. In the "torrid white heat Rube made his graceful shoots cut mysterious capers around the plate"[4] and joined in the fun by banging out two hits and stealing a base. The following day the Giants again hit safely 17 times, this time winning 8–4 behind Mathewson. They then won the finale 4–2, with Demaree on the mound, again beating Alexander. With the series sweep, they were suddenly 20 games above .500, and their prospects looked bright.

Their hot hitting continued into the summer. On the Fourth of July they took a doubleheader from the Dodgers at brand new Ebbets Field. (The park was so new, in fact, that it would not be formally dedicated for another two weeks.) A huge crowd of 43,000—"there hasn't been so many folks at one place on one day in Flatbush since George Washington paraded around the Revolutionary League"[5]—withstood the 100-degree temperature and saw Tesreau and Rube notch the wins for the Giants. On July 8, Rube relieved Tesreau and saved a 6–5 win over the Cubs, then threw a five-hit shutout against them the very next day. It was the Giants' 14th straight victory and their 33d victory of 40 games, and they were once again threatening to run away with the pennant.

According to the *Times*, Rube had now "fully recovered from the temperamental effects of the vaudeville season"⁶ and was back in fine form. On July 19 he pitched near-perfect ball for five innings against the Cardinals. The only runner to get on base was Possom Whitted, who walked, stole second, and was promptly picked off base. Rube finished with a 6–3 win and followed that performance by shutting out Pittsburgh on two hits and then downing the Cardinals again 2–1. Suddenly he had won nine games in a row, and baseball fans and the press began to wonder whether he might match his streak of 1912. Whether he could or not, there was no longer any question but that Rube was the best left-handed pitcher in either league. On July 27, President Hempstead extended Rube's contract through 1916, with an option for a year after that.

With Devore now gone from the club, Rube was assigned to room with Al Demaree, McGraw hoping that the young pitcher could benefit from a mentor, as Rube had learned from Mathewson. Rube enjoyed the responsibility and found Demaree to be a willing pupil. The most important thing, he preached, was to get ahead of the hitters and allow the defense behind you to do their jobs. It was not necessary to try and strike out every hitter, and a seasoned pitcher could, if he was smart about it, "coast" through certain parts of the ballgame and save his best stuff for critical moments: "pitching in the pinch" Mathewson called it. Demaree never achieved the spectacular success of Rube or Matty, but he did last eight years in the big leagues and managed to win 80 games.

Back in New York, Rube and Blossom purchased an upscale apartment on West 99th Street that would be their home for the next three years. For a while at least, in the summer of 1913, Blossom was satisfied to stay home and prepare for the new baby's arrival, and Rube settled into a comfortable routine. He arose at 8:30 every morning and took a 15- or 20-minute walk with his wife. He enjoyed a generous breakfast of fruit, eggs, and toast, always washed down with iced tea. All the Giants had to be at the Polo Grounds by 10 A.M. for scouting reports, team meetings, or rubdowns in the spartan training room. Mornings at the park were also reserved for extra batting practice or informal defensive drills, although Giant pitchers were allowed, and expected, to follow their own running and throwing regimens.

At noon the players were free to leave for lunch, take a quick nap, or simply loaf around the clubhouse. (Surprisingly, McGraw did not allow cardplaying in the clubhouse, although checkers or chess was permitted.) Rube almost always went home to rest and visit with Blossom; he never ate lunch on game days. All the Giants were due back at the park by 2 P.M. and had to be dressed and on the field by 2:30 P.M. McGraw usually went over the opposing lineup with the pitchers, discussing their various weaknesses or tendencies. If Rube was throwing that day, he would warm up about 20 minutes before game time, always in deep right-center field and only with Meyers, whether the Chief was scheduled to work behind the plate or not. If it was not his turn to pitch, Rube tossed lightly with one of the other pitchers and then hit fungoes to the outfielders.

Ballgames in those days seldom went over two hours in length and often were over in an hour and a half. After the game Rube showered or "took a plunge" in what passed for the team whirlpool, then returned home to Blossom. If there was another Marquard victory to celebrate, they might have dinner downtown at one of the popular restaurants along the Broadway theater district, like Rector's, Louis Martin's, or Delmonico's. At any of these finer establishments, they could dine in style and enjoy the company of the "fast crowd"—actors, actresses, chorus girls, theater patrons, wealthy stockbrokers, and sporting enthusiasts. Many of these restaurants were famous not only for the fancy food they served and the ornate decor they provided, but because they placed their guests on display, and Rube and Blossom welcomed the attention. Their unique combination of baseball and show business stardom, their good looks and personal charm, and their willingness to spend their money qualified them as one of the most glamorous and well-known couples in New York. Many personalities could claim to be the "toast of Broadway," but Rube and Blossom came as close to deserving that moniker as anyone.

They did not always need the dazzle of the Great White Way, however. On many nights they were content to stay home for supper, read the papers, talk about the day's game or make show business plans for the fall. They adored each other and never tired of each other's company. Blossom had no cooking skills to speak of, and they often had food delivered to their apartment. Rube had a firm rule that could not be broken: During the season he never ate meat of any kind. Blossom's mother arrived from California in midsummer as the baby's due date approached, and she stayed in the spare bedroom that would become the nursery. Whether Rube and Blossom stayed in or went out for the evening, at the Marquard household it was lights out by 10:30 every night.

Rube's winning streak was in jeopardy on July 31 in Chicago. He left the game with the score tied at four, two Cubs on base and one out in the eighth. Art Fromme came on and put out the fire, only to lose the game in the ninth. Four days later in Pittsburgh it was Rube who came on in relief, again in the eighth, and struck out Claude Hendrix on three pitches to end a Pirate threat. The Giants scored the winning run in the ninth on a successful double steal by Murray and Snodgrass, and Rube had his 10th straight victory. It was his 15th win of the season against only seven losses.

But Rube's streak ended the very next night against the Pirates. He gave up five hits and five runs and contributed heavily to his defeat by throwing a wild pitch and allowing a groundball to roll through his legs. He was driven from the box in the third inning, and to the crowd of about 10,000 "it seemed as good for them as the winning of the pennant, for a victory at the expense of the portsider is a very rare thing."[7]

By the middle of August, the Giants had stretched their lead in the National

League to 12 games, and even some mild dissension in the ranks seemed unlikely to derail another pennant. McGraw confronted five of his players at the hotel in Cincinnati as they returned past curfew and well under the influence of alcohol. Angry words were exchanged, and some of the players (none of whom were regulars) questioned the wisdom of McGraw's recent trade of veteran Doc Crandall to St. Louis for Larry McLean, a backup catcher and, coincidentally, a notorious drinker himself. Blows were exchanged, McGraw getting the worst of it and ending up with a bloody nose, but the incident was quickly forgotten. The next day McLean got two hits in his Giant debut (Chief Meyers had broken his thumb), and Mathewson coasted to an 11–2 victory. McGraw would tolerate McLean's carousing as long as he produced and for the rest of the season he did. He hit .320 in 30 games and handled himself well behind the plate.

On August 20, Rube was beaten by his old nemesis, Pittsburgh, Hans Wagner once again leading the way with three hits, three RBI, and a stolen base in the 4–1 game. The loss was the rubber game of a five-game set with the Pirates, and it marked the first time since May of 1912 that the Giants had lost a series at the Polo Grounds. Blossom was one of 8,000 fans who attended the contest, and while she could not have been pleased with the result, she surely appreciated her mention in the following day's *New York Times* column, which referred to her as "one unusually pretty girl."[8] Even in defeat Rube and Blossom seemed to come out ahead.

If there were any questions, as in previous years, about Rube's stamina in the latter part of the season, he answered them on Labor Day. He threw all 14 innings against Boston, striking out nine and finally winning 3–2 when Murray drove in Merkle in the bottom of the 14th. (The first game of the holiday doubleheader had gone 10 innings, the Giants winning by the same 3–2 score. Crandall, having already been released by the Cardinals, got the win in relief of Tesreau.) While Rube's performance was nice, and the Giants' position on top of the standings seemed secure heading into the stretch, there was another reason to celebrate: earlier in the day Blossom had given birth to a healthy baby boy named Richard William Marquard, Jr.

The Giants were not seriously challenged in September, and McGraw told the newspapers that overconfidence was the only thing he feared could rob the club of another flag. In the American League, Connie Mack's Athletics were in first place ahead of the surprising Washington Senators and the Cleveland Naps, led by slugging sensation Joe Jackson, and it was expected that a rematch of the 1911 World Series was in store. A prelude of sorts occurred on September 7 when the Giants and A's played a charity exhibition game in Newark for the benefit of St. Joseph's Parish Grade School. Although no regular players were used, over 7,000 fans turned out for the good cause and were treated to an 11-inning, 1–1 tie. Most of them came mainly to see Jim Thorpe perform; although the Olympic hero went hitless in four at-bats he did display his blazing speed in the outfield, sprinting to the left field foul pole and making a fine catch of Harry Davis' drive.

Rube (left) and his friend Chief Meyers, both now with the Brooklyn Robins. Photo courtesy Charles Guggenheimer collection.

The A's clinched the pennant, their fifth in the 13-year history of the American League, on September 22 with a doubleheader sweep of the Tigers. Two days later the Giants were shut out 4–0 by Nap Rucker and the Dodgers but claimed the pennant anyway when Boston beat the Phillies, eliminating them from the race. As was his custom, Mack rested his players as much as possible for the last two weeks of the regular season and sent his scouts to watch the Giants finish out their schedule. On September 26 those scouts, along with A's players Eddie Collins, Eddie Plank, and Danny Murphy, watched Rube throw against Brooklyn. Rube hit the first two Dodgers, Herbie Moran and George Cutshaw, in the ribs — perhaps to send a message to Frank Baker? — but then settled down as the Giants banged out 16 hits in their 8–2 victory. It was Rube's 23d win of the season against only 10 losses. While not quite the power pitcher he once was — his season's strikeouts totaled 151, compared to 237 in 1911 and 175 in 1912 — he had virtually overcome the control problems that plagued his early years. He walked only 47 men in 288 innings, and his ERA was a fine 2.50. For the three pennant-winning years of 1911, 1912 and 1913, Rube's record was 73 and 28, numbers which mirrored Mathewson's 74 and 36.

The Series was scheduled to begin on October 7 at the Polo Grounds. Two days prior, on Sunday, Rube and several of his teammates, including Mathewson, Snodgrass, Fletcher, Meyers, and Thorpe, gathered at the Grace Methodist Episcopal Church on 10th Street in Manhattan. The Reverend Doctor James Reisner held a special "baseball service," honoring the champions and praising them as "high types of manhood to be held up as examples for the general run of folks to emulate."[9] John McGraw did not attend, but his letter to the congregation was read: "Naturally I think baseball the most admirable pastime in the world.... I know of nothing to which I would quicker recommend young men than baseball in its amateur and professional capacity. For almost all of my life I have been a participant and a student of the American national sport, and I know that everything in connection with it is for the betterment of those who participate in it."[10] Telegrams from Connie Mack and ballplayer-turned-evangelist Billy Sunday were also read. (Sunday toned his message down considerably; "This rum-sodden world is breaking the speed limit on its way to Hell" was his usual theme.) It was questionable, however, how many in the congregation were paying attention; most seemed to be eyeing the ballplayers in the front pews. When the service was over, the Giants passed out team photographs, and Al Demaree, who was a talented cartoonist as well as a fine pitcher, gave away some of his drawings.

Whether Divine Providence was on his side or not, McGraw was confident going into the Series and boldly predicted victory. Ignoring the National Commission's order that no players or manager cover any World Series games themselves or through ghost-writers (the ban was never enforced), McGraw authored a series of columns for the *Times*, comparing his club to the A's and explaining why this year would bring about a different result than the past two. While no player stood out offensively, noted McGraw, as a team the Giants were steady and efficiently productive. They had led the league with a batting average of .273 (oddly, Meyers at .312 in 378 at-bats was the only regular to hit .300). The pitching staff was perhaps the strongest of McGraw's long tenure as manager. It boasted three 20-game winners in Mathewson (25), Marquard (23), and Tesreau (22), and Demaree, in his first year as a starter, had contributed 13 more. The first three pitchers were among the league leaders in nearly every pitching category, and as the Series was set to begin each starter was healthy, rested, and confident.

Rube in particular felt certain that he and the team would have a good Series. In an interview granted to the Cleveland *Leader*, he claimed to have his Series money already spent. "Sure as you're born we'll win the world's championship this time. Luck cannot break against us always. We should have won our last two starts. Two home runs by Frank Baker stopped us in 1911. We simply threw away the series with the Red Sox last fall. I'd like nothing better than to whip them single-handedly. When I say that I can beat the Athletics I mean it. It is no braggadocio, either. I gave them the battle of their lives in 1911, when I was blind with nervousness.... Certainly I shall face Mack's team with all the confidence in the world."[11]

The A's were essentially the same team they were in 1911. Collins, Baker, Murphy, and McInnis had enjoyed typically productive years at the plate. It was thought, however, that their one weakness was on the mound. Chief Bender was the only starter to win 20 games, although Eddie Plank threw a lead-leading 7 shutouts among his 15 victories. But Jack Coombs, who had won 80 games the previous three years, suffered from severe back troubles and started only two games all year. He spent the Series in Philadelphia's University Hospital in traction and was kept abreast of each game by his wife, who provided play-by-play over the telephone.

Fifteen minutes before the start of the first game McGraw still had not decided on his pitcher. He watched both Rube and Mathewson warm up, and both seemed sharp. Finally, taking note of the overcast day and warm weather, he settled on Rube, figuring that the conditions would make his fastball tougher to hit. While McGraw watched his pitchers, the stands filled to capacity, more than 36,000 strong. In addition to the usual Giant fans, representatives of major league baseball and the political and show business worlds were in attendance. Old-time magnate Albert Spalding, nearing the end of his life, shared a box with the Chicago White Sox president Charles Comiskey, Ban Johnson, and Thomas Lynch. Nearby sat the governors of New York and Pennsylvania. Entertainers George M. Cohan and Al Jolson, among many others, joined Blossom and Thomas Gray in a section of seats along the first base line and smiled for an endless stream of photographers.

When the pregame festivities concluded, Rube took the hill. A's leadoff hitter Eddie Murphy swung at the first pitch, a fastball, and flied to Murray in right. Oldring knocked a single but was immediately picked off first base; his protestation to umpire Klem that Rube had balked gained him little sympathy. Collins then drilled another clean base hit, however, and the crowd leaned forward nervously as Baker settled in at the plate. He took a vicious cut but was late and skied a fly ball to Burns in left-center for the third out. In the first inning, Rube had thrown six pitches: all fastballs and all strikes.

His opponent, Chief Bender, relied this day almost exclusively on his breaking ball. He frequently fell behind in the count but threw strikes when he needed to, not walking a batter all day despite throwing 113 pitches. The Giants scored the first run of the game in the third. Merkle beat out a high hopper to Barry at short, and Rube laid down a perfect bunt, moving the runner to second. Tilly Shafer, playing because Snodgrass had suffered a charley horse during pregame warmups, lined out to Amos Strunk in center, but Doyle singled to right, plating Merkle and giving the Giants the early lead.

It did not last for long. In the top of the fourth, Collins slammed a triple to the gap in right-center field. Baker fouled off the first pitch, and then Rube aimed a fastball to the outside corner. It sailed inside instead, and Baker grounded a single off the glove of a diving Doyle at second. "It was a hard ball to handle," Rube later wrote (like McGraw he ignored the ban against newspaper columns), "but ordinarily I think Larry would have taken care of it."[12] The score was now tied, and McGraw immediately sent Mathewson to the pen to warm up. Stuffy McInnis sacrificed Baker to second, and Strunk lined straight back towards the box. Rube knocked it down and fired to third to catch the gambling Baker, and now with two out it looked as if the Giants would get out of the inning. But Barry smashed a liner directly over the third base bag for a double, sending Strunk to third. Then Schang lofted a drive into right center. "Almost any player would have taken a nap and then caught it," moaned the *Times* the next day, "but unfortunately Shafer was out there because his chum, Snodgrass, who made an equally historic muff, was damaged goods and couldn't play. Shafer ran at the ball, backed around it, jumped, hit it with his hands, and let it go on to the fence for three bases.... The official scorers, a trifle worse on form than usual, scored it a three-base hit."[13]

Later Rube second-guessed his decision to pitch to Schang, calling it a "prime mistake. Schang was a new man to [Meyers and myself], and all we knew was that he liked a fastball. My notion was to walk him and take a chance on Bender with the bases choked. Meyers thought we could fool him and ordered a slow ball. I failed to deliver. And there you are for another of my blunders."[14]

While the Giants now trailed 3–1, the final blow was struck in the fifth inning, and once again Baker was the culprit. Rube easily retired Murphy and Oldring but walked Collins on five pitches. As Rube concentrated on Baker, Collins stole second standing up. Again Meyers signaled for an outside pitch, but Rube's curveball hardly broke and came spinning across the inside corner of the plate, only inches above the knee. "As soon as it was free I looked for Baker to give it a ride," wrote Rube. And that he did, sending a shot far into the air in right, and "somebody in the rightfield stand, down near the bleacher barrier, got a choice souvenir."[15] The A's lead was now 5–1.

Cy McCormick batted for Rube in the bottom of the inning and ignited a three-run rally with a single, but it was all the Giants could manage. Tesreau finished up and surrendered a meaningless run in the eighth, and Bender, backed by superb infield play, held on for the 6–4 Athletic victory. "The contest was full of opportunities for my club to win," wrote McGraw, "and it lost. I can take that contest apart and show any number of places where we should have grabbed it, but this is not an article of regret."[16] Rube attributed the loss to overconfidence and a lack of control. "I had more stuff than Bender," he wrote. "I'll admit that I was nervous. The trouble with me was, I could not get the ball over exactly where I wanted to put it. If I had the control to pitch to Baker as Meyers ordered, we would have won this game."[17] The headline in the Cleveland *Plain Dealer* put it more simply: "Baker Just as Safe as a Train Wreck."[18]

With Mathewson prepared to take on 39-year-old Eddie Plank in game two in Philadelphia, the Giants suddenly found themselves ailing. Chief Meyers, while warming up Matty, split a finger so badly that he was lost for the rest of the Series. Merkle had twisted an ankle so severely in the first game that he would miss two games. Snodgrass, still limping badly, started the game at first base but aggravated his injury while running the bases in the second inning. McGraw called on Hooks Wiltse to play first, and he handled himself well even though he refused to wear a first baseman's mitt, preferring to use his regular glove.

For nine innings the clubs battled to a scoreless tie before a full house of some 20,000. (The crowd was smaller than might be expected because no fans were allowed to stand in the outfield behind a temporary wall, pursuant to National Commission orders. Large numbers, however, viewed the action from the rooftops beyond the right-field wall, across 20th Street.) In the top of the 10th inning, Larry McLean singled and Eddie Grant ran for the slow-footed catcher. Wiltse rolled out to first, and Grant took second. Now Matty, with one hit to his credit already on the day, stroked another to center field, scoring Grant with the first run of the game, and the A's fell apart. Herzog drilled a groundball to Collins at third, a sure doubleplay ball, but Collins's throw to second hit Mathewson in the shoulder. Plank's next pitch hit Doyle in the back, and the bases were loaded. Art Fletcher hit a routine grounder towards Baker at third, another potential doubleplay ball. But the ball took a wild bounce over Baker's head into left field, and two runners scored. Burns and Shafer were retired, but the Giants led 3–0.

The A's did not go quietly in the last half of the ninth inning, loading the bases with only one out and Collins coming up. With a full count, the A's captain watched a curveball float by for a called strike three; the usually even-tempered Collins argued the call strenuously with umpire Tom Connolly to no avail. Now came Baker to the plate, and another home run, of course, would give the A's the lead. This time, though, he didn't quite come through. He smashed a wicked grounder to Wiltse at first; the ball hit so hard that Hooks could only manage to get a glove on it — perhaps in self-defense — and deflect it into short right field. But the hustling Doyle sprinted over to back up the play, gathered in the ball, and fired it back to Wiltse to nip Baker for the final out. Mathewson, with a brilliant performance at bat and on the mound, had evened the Series at one game apiece.

In game three in New York, the A's jumped to a five-run lead after two innings and coasted to an 8–2 triumph. They battered Jeff Tesreau and Doc Crandall for 11 hits, led by 3 singles and 3 RBI from Collins. Twenty-year-old rookie "Bullet Joe" Bush shut down the Giants on five hits, and the visiting team had now won each of the first three games of the Series. But this trend did not continue in Philadelphia in game four. Again the A's got off to an early lead, this time 6–0, and they held on for a 6–5 win behind Bender. Al Demaree started for the Giants and lasted four innings, Rube relieving and finishing up. Collins and Baker were held hitless this time, but Wally Schang touched both pitchers for singles in clutch situations, driving in three of the A's runs.

In his column Rube declared that he would have won the game had he been the starter. He now knew the Athletic hitters, he wrote, and had practically begged McGraw to start him, but by the time he entered the game it was too late. Rube also criticized Demaree, writing that his pitch selection was poor and that a defect in his delivery had allowed Collins to steal a base in the first inning, although it did not lead to a run. Some of Rube's comments were not appreciated by his teammates, and in the weeks ahead he would learn of their displeasure.

With the Giants now down three games to one, the teams returned to New York for the fifth game, and again Mathewson was matched against Plank. The A's struck first as Baker drove home Oldring with a sacrifice fly in the top of the first. The turning point of the game, however, came two innings later. Eddie Murphy led off with a single, and when Doyle booted Oldring's groundball, the A's had runners on first and second. Collins bunted the runners over, and again Baker stepped in. Mathewson offered him nothing inside, but Baker surprised the Giants by dropping a bunt down the first base line. Merkle fielded it and waited to tag out Baker, but he stopped short, and then backed up to avoid the tag. As Murphy rushed toward home, the confused Merkle couldn't decide what to do. Finally he threw home but too late to get Murphy, and Baker sprinted safely to first. "There never was a ballplayer who is so closely pursued by ill luck as Merkle," said the *Times*. "His baseball mistakes have always come at critical times. He falls down when the cost is greatest."[19] McInnis drove in Oldring with a sacrifice fly to left, and the A's led 3–0.

Plank mystified New York hitters all day, allowing only two hits and one run. His sharp-breaking curveball had the Giants driving the ball into the dirt; 14 outs came on grounders to the infield. Mclean drove in Shafer for the only Giant run of the day in the fifth inning, and the A's won 3–1. In two games Plank had allowed only nine hits and two earned runs in 19 innings, and once again Connie Mack's team took home the championship. McGraw's Giants had now matched the Detroit Tigers' record for futility by losing three straight World Series.

But once again Rube had little time to mourn the World Series loss. As much as he and Blossom were enjoying their new baby, the vaudeville stage was beckoning, and to the tune of $1,000 per week. Under the direction of Thomas Gray, a brand new act was put together, and Marquard & Seeley was booked to appear at the incredible Palace Theater.

The Palace was in its first year of operation. Built by Martin Beck, an unsuccessful actor who had become a theater manager, the Palace, at the corner of 47th and Broadway, had leapt into prominence when first Ethel Barrymore and then Sarah Bernhardt appeared there. It quickly gained a reputation as the mecca of all vaudeville venues. Performers agreed: if you played the Palace, you had achieved the ultimate in the show business world.

Rube and Blossom's act, entitled "The Suffragette Pitcher," was a lively paced mixture of comedy and song centered around Blossom's considerable talents and Rube's newly discovered ability to poke fun at himself. They commanded star billing, appearing seventh out of eight acts, following the likes of comedian Joseph Jefferson and singer Gertrude Barnes, whose hit song was called "I'm Going Back to Hackensack." The 19-minute sketch opened in the newlyweds' apartment with a clever role switch: Rube played the homemaker and Blossom the owner and star player of a womens' pro baseball team. On the eve of the big game, went the plot, Blossom convinces her husband to help them out on the field and he does, dressed in female clothing. Audiences were amused to learn that Rube was to play one of the infield positions. "I'd put you in to pitch, Rube, if you had another good game left in you," Blossom teases. As Rube pantomimes some baseball maneuvers, swinging a bat and fielding imaginary grounders, Blossom sings her solo, called "My Base Ball Man." After Rube is discovered by the umpire and put out of the game, he joins Blossom for a song and dance at the front of the stage. Their act always received great applause, and they usually received several curtain calls. (While the act was the high point of the evening, there was one more act on the bill for those patrons who wished to remain: "Volant and the Flying Piano.")

Audiences and critics loved "The Suffragette Pitcher." "Tommy Gray has given the pair the best act they have had yet," raved *Variety*. "It should pass on the road as well as in the New York houses. Rube's still a curiosity by reason of his Giants' connection, while Blossom has ability to entertain without any call on the Marquard diamond prestige."[20] Wrote another reviewer, "Mr. Marquard seems to get as much fun out of his singing and dancing as does the audience. Rube is some dancer.... Miss Seeley appeared very pretty in a soft pink charmeuse gown. A little cap of lace and rhinestones is worn with it."[21] The management at the Palace knew it had a huge hit on its hands. It delighted in placing the "Sold

Out!" sign on the sidewalk out front, and inside the lobby there hung an oversize poster of Rube throwing a baseball. Rube didn't even mind that the artist portrayed him throwing with his right hand.

After two weeks at the Palace, Rube and Blossom again hit the road. With a new baby and the family in sound shape financially, Rube was not particularly thrilled with the idea of an extended tour, but Blossom, after a summers' inactivity, convinced him that they must take advantage of their enormous popularity. Her mother agreed to stay and care for Richard, Jr., while his parents were away, and after an enjoyable Thanksgiving in New York, Rube and Blossom packed their trunks and were gone.

Again Marquard & Seeley headlined at major theaters in the northeast. They appeared in Boston and Hartford and at the Allegheny Theater in Philadelphia, where they competed against A's stars Bullet Joe Bush, Home Run Baker, and Wally Schang, whose act played directly across the street. From Pennsylvania the pair rolled through the Midwest, entertaining sold-out crowds in Cincinnati, Akron, and Cleveland. (There is no record of whether Rube's family came out to see Rube and his partner, though it seems certain that they did.) Then they traveled through Indiana, Illinois, and Iowa. They returned to New York for the Christmas holidays but hurried back out on the road again a week later. They played familiar theaters in familiar cities like Omaha, St. Louis, and Denver, for the most part delighting audiences and receiving good reviews. Finally, some $10,000 richer, they made their way home and enjoyed another successful week's run at the Palace. Before long February had slipped away, and Rube began to prepare to leave for Texas and another spring training.

CHAPTER 12

"We Were Both Pretty Mad"

On March 6 several thousand cheering baseball fans, along with numerous newspaper reporters, photographers, and a motion picture cameraman, greeted the steamship *Lusitania* as it pulled into New York's Cunard Line dock. The ship's siren sounded in response, knifing through the sleet and snow, as her passengers shouted excitedly and waved tiny American flags from the outer rails of the deck. They included 67 major league ballplayers—almost all Giants and White Sox—led by John McGraw and Bill Klem; some wives were also aboard the ship. The players were returning from a five-month world tour during which they had played exhibitions before thrilled (if often confused) crowds in Toyko, Paris, Cairo, and other exotic locales. They had gambled in the casinos of Monte Carlo and been received by Pope Pius X at the Vatican, and had played their final game at the Chelsea Grounds outside London before King George V. Now they returned to the United States like soldiers returning victorious after a war. In recognition of their celebrity status, the usual customs procedures were waived, and on the strength of affidavit alone the players were allowed to check their baggage through with no delay. Fred Merkle had the honor of being the first player to descend the gangplank, and he was followed by two pairs of newlyweds, Larry Doyle with his new bride, and Jim Thorpe with his. Both couples had taken advantage of the trip by combining it with their honeymoon. McGraw and his wife Blanche exited the ship to great applause, and they slowly worked their way through the crowd toward a waiting taxi. "I never realized the great value of baseball until we made this trip," McGraw told reporters before he was driven away, adding that he was already making plans for another trip, perhaps to South America.[1] Later that night the party was honored with a command performance at the Palace Theater (there were no baseball acts on the bill, however), and within just a few days the Giants departed for what was left of spring training. Rube and Mathewson, who had declined to travel abroad with the group, had already been in camp over a week. (Rube, bored and restless while waiting for his teammates, exercised some exceedingly poor judgment and fired a pistol out of his hotel room for fun one day. The village dignitaries were not pleased and threatened to lock him up or, at the very least, escort him out of town; McGraw arrived just in time to smooth things over.)

There was at least one very notable absentee from Marlin Springs. The previous fall, after the defeat in the World Series, McGraw and Wilbert Robinson had a serious falling out. At a party hosted by McGraw, both men had been drinking heavily, and when the beer got the best of them they traded insults. McGraw criticized the way Robbie had handled third base coaching duties, and Robbie accused McGraw of making more mistakes than all his players combined, including relying too heavily on the hit-and-run and mishandling the pitching staff. The argument mounted until finally McGraw had enough. "This is my party," he hollered. "Get the hell out of here."[2] Robbie poured a beer over McGraw's head and left, and his subsequent apology was ignored. Robbie no longer had a job with the Giants (he became manager of Brooklyn), and it was 13 years before the two men spoke again.

Clearly Rube missed Wilbert Robinson's guidance and friendship in the early part of the season. By mid-July he still had not put together two victories in a row, although the Giants had climbed back into their accustomed first place position. On July 17, Rube's record stood at 6–8 when they arrived in Pittsburgh for a four-game set against the seventh place Pirates. In what one reporter termed "The most remarkable game of ball played in the National League this year," Rube was matched against Babe Adams, the Pirates' fine right-handed pitcher. Adams, 32 years old with 73 wins in the last five years, and on his way to a career record of 194–140 over 19 years, all with Pittsburgh, had established himself as one of the circuit's most consistent and successful pitchers. The effort he gave this day would earn him a place in baseball history, for he matched Rube nearly pitch for pitch for a full 21 innings.

In the bottom of the first, Rube plunked leadoff hitter Eddie Mensor in the ribs with his first pitch. Mike Mowrey sacrificed Mensor to second, and Wagner drove him home with a long triple to the center-field wall. The Giants tied the score in the third when Doyle drove in Bescher, and the score remained knotted for another 18 innings.

The Pirates' best chance came in the sixth. Wagner singled (his third hit of the day in nine at-bats) and took third on Jim Voix's base hit. But Honus overran the bag, and Bescher fired the ball to Milt Stock. In the scramble back to third, the ball popped out of Stock's glove, and as he and shortstop Fletcher searched frantically for it Wagner sprinted safely home, apparently with the lead run. He strolled toward the dugout, grinning broadly, until he was halted by umpire Bill Byron. The baseball, Byron discovered, was concealed underneath Honus' arm. He was called out for interference, and the score remained tied.

Rube pitched brilliantly the entire afternoon, although he admitted later that he lacked his best stuff. He gave up 15 hits, walked 4 men, and managed 2 strikeouts, but the defense was solid behind him and he craftily worked out of jams in nearly every inning. But Adams was just as tough, or maybe tougher. Heading into the 21st inning, he had allowed only eight hits and no walks and had struck out six Giants. Finally, in the last inning, with daylight quickly fading, Bescher singled with two out. Larry Doyle jumped on a fastball and slammed it over the fence in right. Rube retired the side in order in the bottom of the inning, and after 3 hours and 42 minutes the Giants had a 3–1 victory. "The champions went home to their hotel with tired bodies, but victorious hearts," said the *Times*, "a little sore, perhaps, but giving praise to the greatest team of ball players that has shown here this year."[3] The game was the longest in the history of the National League, breaking the record 20-inning contest between Chicago and Philadelphia in 1905, and only three innings shy of the major league mark. Even in the dead-ball era, where starting pitchers were expected to finish their games, Rube's and Adams' performances were amazing.

Accounts of the ballgame, however, were replaced by other news in national sporting pages just two days later, as the year-old Baseball Players' Fraternity (the directors of which included Ty Cobb and Jake Daubert) threatened to strike. At issue was the owners' treatment of a minor leaguer named Clarence "Big Boy" Kraft, whose contract had been purchased by Brooklyn from Nashville of the Southern League. Before he ever appeared in a game for the Robins, he was sold to Boston and then optioned to Newark. Finally Nashville claimed him again on a waiver technicality, and the National Commission upheld the claim. Before poor Kraft knew what had happened, the Fraternity (of which he was a member) filed a grievance, claiming that he had been shabbily treated. Further, the grievance stated that if he was sent back down to Nashville, the big leaguers would walk out.

The club owners and baseball establishment reacted with expected indignation. August Herrmann, speaking on behalf of both the Reds organization and the National Commission, argued that the Fraternity had no standing to make its threat, inasmuch as the rules governing player transactions and the contracts which bound players were the exclusive province of the league. The Fraternity itself was not even representative of all the players, Herrmann noted, since not all of them had bothered to join the organization. American League president Ban Johnson preferred to engage in some economic posturing. If the players carried out their threat, he said, the ballparks would be closed for the rest of the summer, the salaries of all players would be cut off, and the leaders of the rebellion would be heavily fined before they would ever be allowed to play again.

Some of those leaders, however, promised to back up their words. Roger Bresnahan, his managerial stint over and now finishing up his career with the Cubs, was all for a strike. "It will show whether the players can hang together," he said. "If they can, the club owners will be forced to change their methods."[4] Other stars, including Tommy Leach and Gavvy Cravath, also expressed their support. The Giants met as a team and agreed to disagree; many of the players, including the older ones with most of their playing days behind them, voted to strike, while the younger ones were skittish about the idea. Rube sympathized with Kraft and was ready to walk. Even Heinie Zimmerman of the Cubs, who had been expelled from the Fraternity for failure to pay his dues, was more or less in favor of a strike. "The Fraternity canned me," he said, "but if the others don't play I'll have to take a vacation also."[5]

In the end it was the owners, or more precisely one owner, who backed down. A strike was averted when Charles Ebbetts of Brooklyn again purchased Kraft for $2,500, assigned him to Newark, and awarded him five weeks' back salary, which made everyone happy. The Players' Fraternity was "jubilant over the victory,"[6] and its spokesman David Fultz proclaimed that the organization would continue to grow and vigorously assert the rights of its members. Ban Johnson could only note condescendingly that the union had seen "the chance to make a spectacular fuss, and made the most of it." He was glad, he said, that "the patient public had not been deprived of its favorite diversion."[7] John McGraw, always spoiling for a good fight, was actually disappointed that the issue had been settled amicably. "I would rather have seen the matter put through as planned," he said, "just to see if the players would go on a strike."[8] As for the player who caused the entire ruckus, "Big Boy" Kraft, he ended his major league career with a total of three at-bats in 1914.

It would seem logical for McGraw, after Rube's spectacular 21-inning effort, to proceed carefully and not risk his expensive left-handed arm. But on July 22, only five days after the record-setting game in Pittsburgh, Rube started against the Reds in Cincinnati and, amazingly, he was superb. He retired the first nine batters he faced, then in the fourth inning gave up a triple to Bert Daniels. His old friend Buck Herzog drove Daniels home with a ground ball for the only Cincinnati run of the day. The only other hit Rube allowed was a scratch single to Reds pitcher "Shufflin' Phil" Douglas in the sixth. With the 4–1 victory, Rube had evened his record at 8–8, and with two terrific outings in a row he felt sure he was on his way to another outstanding season.

As a team the Giants were also confident that they were in prime shape to secure a fourth straight pennant. "Well, it's this way," said McGraw on August 29. "We are not going to win in a walk. Perhaps we may not cop at all, but my point is that every club in the league is sending its men to night school to figure out ways and means to pull us off the top perch.... The umpires are not handing us anything. Even the crowds welcome my men as though they were Germans on French soil.... It's the league against New York. I feel like Kaiser Bill.... [Still] I really believe that next week will mark the beginning of our rapid march toward the pennant."[9] With a record now of 49–32, the Giants' hold on first place seemed comfortable enough. The Cubs trailed them by five games in the loss column, followed by St. Louis and its new manager Miller Huggins. No one seemed concerned that the Boston Braves had, since the Fourth of July, put together a modest win streak, climbing from last place to fourth.

12. "We Were Both Pretty Mad"

But the Braves kept on winning, managed by the profane George Stallings, a man who "could fly into a schizophrenic rage at the drop of a pop fly" and deliver colorful tirades that could embarrass even the most seasoned of veterans.[10] On the field the Braves were led by former Cub Johnny Evers and tiny shortstop Rabbit Maranville and by the pitching of unknowns Bill James, Dick Rudolph, and Lefty Tyler, who won 69 games between them. Boston surged forward in the standings, taking the league by storm and surprising everyone, including themselves. They began to draw so many fans at home that they arranged to play their home games down the stretch at Fenway Park, since the capacity at little South End Grounds, their usual home field, was only 7,000. By the end of August, they were challenging the Giants for first place, and with the seemingly invincible Philadelphia A's once again about to claim the American League pennant, headlines noted that at least fans might not have to endure yet another New York stumble in the World Series. "Macks Would Like Braves as Rivals," blared the *Sporting News*, "Beating Giants is Monotonous."[11]

The Braves won 68 of their final 87 games, and the Giants struggled to retain first place. Although they missed Herzog at third base, they did not suffer serious declines offensively. Their team batting average of .265 was second in the league, and they led the league in runs scored and, as usual, stolen bases. Mathewson and Tesreau accounted for 50 of the team's 84 victories; the major problem, it seemed was Rube. After the masterful outings against Pittsburgh and Cincinnati, Rube proceeded to lose his next 12 straight ballgames. Although he had clearly lost some zip on his fastball — his strikeout total fell to 92 — he did not pitch poorly. His ERA rose half a run to 3.06, still a respectable figure, but he received almost no support from his team. Of the 12 losses in August and September, the Giants were shut out five times, including a 1–0 loss to Alexander and the Phillies that took only one hour and 12 minutes to play.

On September 2, Rube was beaten by Brooklyn 6–2, and when Boston took two games from Philadelphia the Braves took sole possession of first place. Three days later Rube lost 4–1 to Brooklyn and ancient Nap Rucker, but he scored the only Giant run of the day when he singled and came home on Snodgrass' triple. McGraw became so desperate for good pitching that he picked up on waivers Marty O'Toole — the same pitcher the Pirates had purchased for $22,500 in 1909. O'Toole managed to split a pair of decisions in his only starts; they were the last appearances of his career.

New York traveled to Boston on Monday, September 7, for a four-game series; the teams were tied for first with identical 67–52 records. Over 73,000 Braves fans jammed Fenway, the Boston management taking the opportunity to charge admission for both games of the doubleheader. Mathewson blew a lead in the ninth inning of the first game, allowing two runs on two singles and a double and taking the 5–4 loss. The Giants cruised to an easy 10–1 victory in the second game, although the contest was marred by some remarkable behavior by Boston's leading citizen. In the sixth inning, the Giants scored three runs, and with two out Snodgrass came up. Lefty Tylor, upset at the turn of events, fired four fastballs at Snow's head, knocking him down each time. The last pitch, Snow recalled later, "hit the button of my cap."[12] He cursed loudly at Tyler before taking his base and then thumbed his nose at the pitcher. Tyler responded by tossing the ball in the air and dropping it, mocking Snodgrass' famous muff of 1912. The crowd loved it and booed Snodgrass heartily.

When the last out had been made, Snodgrass took center field, and when the fans who stood beyond the roped-off section of the outfield continued to holler he thumbed his nose at them as well. (At least one report has it that he threw a baseball into the crowd; if that was true, he was very fortunate no one was injured.) "Well, that *really* set them off," he said. "It was the signal for all the pop bottles and trash of any kind that people had to come flying out on the field, in my general direction. The place was in an uproar. And just then a fellow jumped out of his box seat near the home dugout, and marched onto the field, accompanied by a couple of high-helmeted policemen. He had on a long-tailed coat, spats, and a top hat, and he paraded over to the umpires. It was the Honorable James M. Curley, the mayor of Boston. He said I had insulted the good citizens of Boston and demanded that I be removed from the field immediately. It was just before election time, and he was making what you might call a grandstand play for votes."[13]

Umpire Klem shooed the mayor off the field and play continued. The next inning, however, McGraw took the sensible way out and replaced Snodgrass with Bescher, and there were no further incidents. Mayor Curley, however, was not satisfied. The next day he wrote a letter to John Tener, president of the National League, demanding that Snodgrass be punished for the "flagrant and unwarranted insult to the public"[14] and that Klem be censured for refusal to comply with the demand that Snodgrass be removed. There is no evidence that his letter received a response from the league office.

His Honor was presumably satisfied, however, with the results of that afternoon's game. Before over 17,000 Tuesday afternoon fans, the Braves hammered Rube for nine hits and six runs, driving him from the box after four innings and holding on for an 8–3 victory. For the second time in a week, the Braves had taken over first place because Rube had lost a ballgame, and this time they would hold it for good.

As if Rube didn't have enough trouble on the field, there began to be difficulties at home. Blossom grew restless with another summer off from the stage, and in August she began to rehearse a solo act. She was booked to appear at Keith's in mid-September, just as the Giants began their final road trip of the season. Rube was not terribly pleased that she chose not to wait until the season was over, but he had little choice in the matter. Late at night on August 14, as Rube rested in his hotel room in anticipation of his next day's start against the Phillies, he received a sad phone call: Blossom's mother had died suddenly of heart failure. He caught the earliest train to New York to console his wife. A few days later he was knocked out of the box after three innings by Chicago. The Cubs went on to win 6–0, and New York now trailed the Braves by three games and was fading fast. "The failure of Marquard to win," said the *Times*, "has been the biggest reason for the Giants' slip backwards."¹⁵ By the time Rube finally won a game, against the Pirates on August 28 (the game was called after six innings with New York in the lead 13–6), the Giants were seven games behind, with only nine left to play, and their season was for all purposes over.

As September drew to a close, the clubs played out their schedules. At the Polo Grounds on October 1, the Braves and Giants fought to a 5–5 tie through five innings. Then with two out in the bottom of the sixth back-up third baseman Eddie Grant was called out on a close play at the plate. (Four years later Grant was killed in the Argonne Forest of France, the first major leaguer killed in World War I.) Moments later Merkle was called out trying to steal third, and the jockeys on New York's bench began to harass Bill Klem. An inning later the abuse continued, and finally Klem walked over and ceremoniously ejected 24 Giants from the game. The only ones spared were the players in the game and, in some strange sort of irony, McGraw. "They lined up and walked across the Polo Grounds doing the lock-step," said the *Times*. "Matty was the drum major and led the parade. The boys were quite kittenish and smiled for the first time since they lost the well-known pennant."¹⁶ Fittingly, the Giants went on to lose the game 7–6.

While the "Miracle Braves" continued their run by sweeping the Athletics in the World Series, the Giants took on the Yankees in a series of poorly attended games for the "Gotham City Championship." In what he must have seen as the only appropriate end to the nightmare season, Rube was hit hard by the Yankees in his only appearance. For the year his record was 12–22. There was no talk that he had reverted from peach to lemon, but Rube still had to endure the embarrassment of being one of the few pitchers ever to win 20 games one season and lose 20 the next.

Rube received his share of negative press. The worst seemed to come from sportswriter Sam Crane of the New York *World*, who had been a ballplayer before the turn of the century. Marquard was never as important to the Giants as he believed, Crane wrote. His off-season touring and contract squabbles kept him from reporting to spring training in shape. His criticisms of other players during the 1913 World Series had cost him the full-fledged support of his teammates, and in fact McGraw had tried to trade him that fall. Ironically, a deal with Boston for Lefty Tyler had nearly been made; how fortunate for the Braves that they had decided against it.

There was no shortage of baseball acts on the vaudeville stage that fall, but after nearly three straight years of constant touring, either with Blossom or with the Giants, Rube was relieved to take a break from show business. He did, however, duly note the competition. He and Blossom were spotted at Hammerstein's taking in the performance of Boston Braves stars Hank Gowdy and Dick

Rudolph, and Rabbit Maranville a few weeks later. Rube's friend Mike Donlin resurrected both his personal and professional lives: he had married a showgirl named Rita Ross (Rube and Blossom happily attended the wedding in Asbury Park, New Jersey) and then appeared on stage with Yankee Marty McHale in a brand-new act. McHale was a truly gifted singer whose beautiful baritone tenor earned him the nickname "The Baseball Caruso." The double-entendre act, called "Right Off the Bat," featured a song called "It's a Long, Long Way from Home."

Blossom, still grieving over the death of her mother, postponed her solo tour until early November and then left for a swing through the Midwest. Rube hired a nanny to take care of young Richard, and in early December he made plans to meet his wife in Milwaukee for the holidays. But before he could leave, he received a significant visitor: his name was Robert B. Ward and he was the wealthy owner of a Brooklyn bakery famous for its Tip-Top Bread. ("No Hands But Yours Touch Tip-Top Bread" was its slogan.) Ward also happened to own that city's entry in the outlaw Federal Baseball League, and he wanted Rube on his club's roster.

While few genuine superstars were induced to jump to the Federal League in 1914 (Christy Mathewson, for example, turned down an offer of $65,000 for three years, with an advance of $15,000), many solid, established players, all fan favorites, signed lucrative contracts with the new league. They included Al Bridwell, Edd Roush, Hal Chase, Claude Hendrix, and the aging Three Finger Brown. Even a group of major league umpires jumped to the new league. Perhaps the most significant of all the big league defectors was Joe Tinker, who signed to manage and play for the Chicago Whales.

Tinker was supremely confident that the Federal League would prosper and endure. He was openly critical of organized baseball's long-established methods and boasted of the new, fairer guidelines of the Federals. Players would not be mere "slaves" or, pursuant to the reserve clause, forever be the property of their respective major league clubs. Instead, if their club did not automatically increase their salary by a minimum of five percent each year, they would become free agents, at liberty to test the market themselves. Neither would Federal clubs negotiate with minor league teams for the rights to a particular player, but would instead deal with the player directly, normally offering a signing bonus of $1,000 in addition to the salary agreed upon. The Federals would "break the spell" that organized baseball held on its employees, Tinker predicted, and players and fans alike would benefit from the new major league.[17]

The 1914 Federal League season was a successful one. The caliber of play was perhaps a notch below major league standards, but no more. Boosted by a tight pennant race — Indianapolis edged Chicago for the crown — fan attendance, helped considerably by late-season, ten-cent tickets, was moderately high. While the National Commission refused to acknowledge the Feds' challenge for a true World Series, matching Indianapolis versus the Boston Braves, major league owners could no longer ignore the possibility that the outlaw league was for real. In January 1915 the Federals filed an antitrust lawsuit in United States District Court,

12. "We Were Both Pretty Mad" 151

alleging that organized baseball's practices were monopolistic and adverse to free trade. The case was to be decided by a district judge named Kenesaw Mountain Landis, and a decision, it was hoped, would be rendered quickly. In the meantime more and more big-name players jumped to the Feds, including Chief Bender and Eddie Plank from the A's, Hugh Bedient from the Red Sox, and Ed Reulbach from the Dodgers. Walter Johnson even agreed to jump, although he later changed his mind and remained with Washington of the American League.

With that scenario Robert Ward came calling on Rube in early December. He rightly assumed that Rube would be interested in joining his Brooklyn club not only because of the money, but because fully seven Clevelanders were on the Tip-Top roster, including old-timers Jim Delahanty and Bill Bradley. (Bradley, in fact, had been the manager in 1914 but would give way to Lee Magee in 1915 and play with Kansas City.) Rube's old friend Hooks Wiltse would also be on the club, and Brooklyn boasted the best player in the league in Benny Kauff, an outstanding outfielder long coveted by McGraw for the Giants. Ward and Rube discussed financial terms, and although Rube was still bound to the Giants by virtue of the contract he had signed in San Francisco before the 1913 season, a contract which had been extended for another year before the previous season, he assured Ward that he was a free agent. The next day, December 7, Rube executed an affidavit swearing that the Giants had no hold on him or any right to his services, and Ward forwarded a copy of the document to the Federal League office in Chicago. There it was happily received by the League president, "Fighting Jim" Gilmore, a Spanish-American war hero and self-made millionaire from the coal business. Ward then signed Rube to a three-year contract beginning at $10,000 per year and escalating to $12,000 and then $15,000 annually. Rube accepted a $1,500 cash bonus from Ward and was advised to report to his new club's spring training camp at Browns Wells, Mississippi, in March.

As Rube left New York to join Blossom, the press learned of his signing and treated it as one of the major events of the winter. *Sporting Life* called it "the season's greatest shock,"[18] and, predictably, most New York publications were critical of his apparent jump to the outlaw league. The *Sporting News*' Joe Vila opined that he "could not understand what kind of wheels are located in the Rube's head. He must have lost his senses temporarily, for nobody ever believed that he would stoop to such petty business.... These contract jumpers — and I include Walter Johnson — are discrediting base ball in the estimation of the public." Vila sneered that "the Flap Jack League will gain nothing by tempting players to violate their legal and moral obligations to their employers.... A contract breaker will throw a game if there's enough money in it for him."[19]

Fred Lieb, while detailing Rube's lack of success for the Giants in 1914, wrote that Rube's move was probably the result of fear that he would be traded by McGraw. Lieb noted that Rube was clearly still under contract with New York and could easily be prevented from playing anywhere else should court action become necessary. He quoted the club president, Harry Hempstead: "We have him bound to us by a contract which could not possibly be broken, and any court in the land will uphold us.... He has not a leg to stand on."[20] For some reason St. Louis owner Schuyler Britton also waded into the fray with a personal comment. Rube was "a nut," he said, "a queer sort of person whom he wouldn't take as a gift."[21]

Sid Mercer labeled Rube an "errant pitcher" who had surely made a "sad mess of things."[22] By taking the $1,500 bonus, Rube had opened himself up to a criminal charge of obtaining money under false pretenses, Mercer wrote, and predicted that regardless of Judge Landis' forthcoming decision in the antitrust case, one Cornelius J. Sullivan, a member of the Giants' Board of Directors as well as their legal counsel, would bring suit to restrain Rube from reporting to the Tip-Tops. Another sportswriter, Harry Dix Cole, could not resist pursuing the show business angle in his story: "The F. L. Producing Co. presents Richard Marquard," he wrote, "the eminent actor-ballplayer, in his latest role entitled 'Hurdling an Iron-bound contract.' Little else is being discussed at metro fanning bees except the latest move of the Giants' elongated southpaw."[23]

Not even David Fultz of the Players' Fraternity supported Rube's decision. If Rube had signed with Brooklyn while still under contract to the Giants, "he will unquestionably be expelled from the Fraternity," Fultz said in a written statement, "as the directors absolutely will not countenance any such disregard of their obligations by its members."[24] And then the Tip-Top management backpedaled. Business manager John Montgomery Ward, himself an old baseball renegade (back in the 1890s, when he was a standout player, he had led the ill-fated players' revolt), commented that if Rube had sworn falsely in his affidavit, "he was the man who was guilty of misconduct in this case and I think he should be called to account."[25]

The press finally caught up with Rube in Milwaukee just after the first of the year, and he issued a statement outlining his position. "The Brooklyn Feds made me a swell offer some time ago, and after being convinced that I was not tied to the New York Giants for life, I decided to better myself and accept. The Wards, of Brooklyn, have treated me splendidly, and you may rest assured that I will play with the Feds unless it can be shown that I am still legally bound to New York. I had no complaint to make about the Giants whatever. Manager McGraw gave me fine treatment, but it was simply a case of looking out for my own interests."[26]

Rube repeated a familiar theme, one that had guided his thinking since the early days in Cleveland before he had signed his first professional contract. "A ballplayer is worth what he can get and no more, and he can play only a certain number of years, and there is no reason why he should not get the most obtainable, the same as an actor, while the going is good. You know the magnates themselves started the players jumping contracts, and have no one but themselves to blame. I don't blame any player for trying to better himself financially as long as he is not breaking his signed contract.... I am not letting sentiment bother me.

If the Giants can prove that they have a legal right to my services, why, I will be with them, but otherwise I will stick to the Feds."²⁷

The *Sporting News* poked fun at Rube in its January 14 issue with some anonymous poetry entitled "The Promise of the Rube":

> "Dear Friend Gilmore," wrote the Rube,
> You'll be glad to hear.
> That I'll still be true to you —
> Pitch for you next year."
>
> "I am through with Jawn McGraw,
> (He is through with me).
> 'Leven thousand dollar beauts
> Aren't what they used to be."
>
> "Let me tell you, furthermore,
> That, with the greatest ease.
> I can still lose thirteen straight —
> Twenty, if you please."
>
> "So, doubt not that I am yours,
> Can this Hempstead boob;
> I will pitch for only you,
> Yours, with love, the Rube."²⁸

A month later Rube returned to New York and was immediately summoned to the Giant offices. He sat down with Hempstead, secretary Foster, and McGraw, who explained to him that it was within their power to see that he sit out the entire season if he insisted on reporting to Brooklyn. They could easily gain an injunction preventing him from reporting to camp in Mississippi and would suspend him without pay from the Giants until the entire matter was resolved in court. Hempstead, with McGraw's blessing, offered to repay Brooklyn the $1,500 advance if they released any claim they might have. Brooklyn agreed, and the three-year contract was torn up. With the matter now behind him, Rube prepared to report to Marlin Springs.

The press, however, did not quickly forget the matter. *Sporting Life* in particular was not impressed with Rube's maneuvering, brandishing him a "double jumper." Although Rube was in fine shape financially, the magazine claimed that he had accepted the $1,500 advance only to "carry him through the winter." Further, he had "pulled a stunt that will eventually ride him out of baseball for good.... NL players have always contended that Marquard does not stand the gaff any too well and this a safe bet that even his fellow players have lost respect for him and he is due to have a mighty rough summer if he plays at all."²⁹

And once again the *Sporting News* (Rube must have hated to read that publication) had some fun at his expense in a poem that was probably written by Grantland Rice:

I am sick of my freedom already,
I am weary of pounding the pave,
I am sorry I took such a Brodie
And I want to get back as a slave.
 Now I know I was bulled by the tempter,
Why, I must have been hypnotized then,
And I won't be quite the same Marquard
Till I'm back with the Giants again.

When I need a small chunk of mazuma,
And I tell my sad tale to McGraw,
He returns me the stare of an iceberg
And my tears do not cause him to thaw.
 When I stand in the Ward office doorway,
And hint at a little advance,
Why, those cold, grasping Federal magnates
Say, "To you? Beat it, Rube. What a chance!"

Oh, it wasn't like that in the slave days,
I was always in right for a touch;
It is terribly hard on a southpaw
Who has put himself really in Dutch.
 And they're taking my case to the law sharks,
Though I surely have trouble enough;
I'm an orphan, a boob, and an outcast
And I'm cleaned, which again, boys, is tough.

Won't you open the gate for me, Muggsy?
Won't you toss out the life line to save?
I am sick of my freedom and Brooklyn
And I want to enroll as a slave.
 Have the jeweler make me some shackle,
I am waiting to hear you say when;
For I want to be somebody's southpaw
And get back to the Giants again.[30]

Rube did not have a productive spring camp. Since he had not toured all winter, show business could not be blamed for his slow start, but he seemed tired and the writers wondered whether he had lost the speed on his fastball for good. Rube assured McGraw, however, that he would come around when it counted. Even more concern was expressed over Mathewson; during most of training camp it seemed more of an effort than usual for him to find the plate. Still, while the team's once-dominant pitching staff suddenly showed signs of cracking, the Giants were favored to recapture the pennant, as the Braves' performance of 1914 was viewed by most as an aberration.

 Jeff Tesreau earned the honor of pitching on Opening Day, and he had little trouble handling Brooklyn at the Polo Grounds, 16–3. Larry Doyle was the hitting star, going five for five and driving in four runs in the rout. Newcomer Hans Lobert, who had been acquired from the Phillies and was a solid veteran of 10 major league seasons, took over third base duties and had three hits, and McGraw gave Jim Thorpe another chance to prove himself. He played well in right field but managed only a scratch single in five trips to the plate. When he struck out, noted the *Times*, he appeared to be in "mid-Summer form."[31]

An unexpected sad event interrupted Rube's preparation for his first start of the year. His grandmother Christina, the woman who had raised him after the premature death of his mother, passed away on April 13 at the age of 81. Rube hurried home and stood with his family as she was laid to rest alongside her beloved Ferdinand, who had passed away almost exactly three years earlier. There was no time to linger, however, as Rube was needed in New York.

On Thursday, April 15, Rube took the mound against the Robins, turning in one of the finest games of his career. "Long lean Rube Marquard, a good pitcher today and a bad one tomorrow," wrote W. W. Aulick, "promulgated a pitching masterpiece ... which brought back to the eccentric southpaw all the admirers he lost when he nibbled at the Federal League bait, jumped his contract, and vaulted back again."[32] Rube pitched a no-hit game, winning 2–0, the first and only one of his big league career and the first since his days with Indianapolis in 1908. He very nearly threw a perfect game, walking only two men and allowing one other baserunner on Fletcher's error. He struck out only three, but his sharp-breaking curveball had the hitters consistently driving the ball into the dirt, and 21 Robins grounded out. As with most pitchers who toss no-hitters, Rube was the beneficiary of plenty of good defense behind him — Lobert and Merkle in particular made outstanding plays — and some good fortune, too. Rube swung in desperation at an 0–2 pitch from Nap Rucker in the seventh inning, broke his bat, and still blooped a single to right, scoring Merkle with the Giants' second run. The game's closest call came in the top of the ninth. With one out, Robin center fielder Hy Myers sliced a shot over the first base bag. Merkle dove and knocked it down, then frantically scrambled on his hands and knees, just barely beating Myers to the bag for the out. Rube fanned the final hitter, the dangerous Zack Wheat, surprising him with a fastball at the letters. The crowd stood and cheered as Rube ran excitedly to the sidelines and accepted congratulations from his teammates. He had completely baffled a team that featured four of the league's top hitters in 1914, and it gave him no small measure of satisfaction that he had accomplished the feat in front of his old friend and tutor Wilbert Robinson. "The Rube may be an amateur actor and all that," proclaimed Aulick, "but by jiminy crickets, how he can pitch when he is fit!"[33]

Off to a 2–0 start, New York proceeded to lose its next seven games. Bill "Pol" Perritt, over from St. Louis, was beaten 5–3 by Brooklyn in his first start for the Giants, and then the visiting Phillies swept a four-game series, rocking Mathewson, Fromme, Tesreau, and Perritt. The last game of the set was particularly tough for McGraw to take: His club was beaten 6–1 on a two-hitter by

George Chalmers, a pitcher whom McGraw had unconditionally released only eight days before. On April 22 the Giants traveled across the river to Brooklyn for the Robins' home opener at Ebbetts Field, where again Rube took on Rucker. The cold weather kept the crowd down, and Rube lasted just six innings, wasting a three-run lead and losing 6–4. When Matty was roughed up the next day, 7–5, the Giants found themselves in last place.

Because the Federal League had bit into major league attendance — the Giants alone suffered a dropoff of nearly 300,000 fans in 1914 — the owners felt a severe financial strain, and it was agreed among the clubs that all rosters would be pared to 21 players by May 21. McGraw, facing the deadline and concerned about his club's listless play, nearly pulled off a one-sided coup in late April. It was announced that he had traded three disappointing players, Perritt, Jack Murray, and Dave Robertson, to Brooklyn for Zack Wheat. But the Robins wisely backed out of the deal at the last moment, and McGraw had to look elsewhere to reduce the size of his team. He received a short extension from the league and then reassigned several players, including Jim Thorpe, to the minors.

The Giants played sluggishly for two months, hovering around the .500 mark but rarely climbing above it. Snodgrass in particular had his problems at the plate, and when his batting slump carried over to other aspects of his game he heard about it from McGraw. On June 30 the Giants traveled to Brooklyn, with Rube matched against "Big Ed" Pfeffer, a hard-throwing right-hander who was coming into his own in 1914, on the way to 23 victories. After seven innings the Robins led 1–0, their run being unearned because of Merkle's error at first. But in the eighth, with two men on, Zack Wheat got hold of one of Rube's fastballs and drilled a shot to center. Snodgrass "must have thought that the ball was made of hot lead or something because after sticking out his hands in the direction of the ball, he suddenly withdrew them from the immediate vicinity. Then Snodgrass stood as if posing for a photograph, while the ball rolled to center field for a home run. Snodgrass did not even chase the ball."[34] Rube gave up a couple more hits, then watched as Chief Meyers threw the ball into center on an attempted double steal. The Giants managed only two hits off Pfeffer and were shut out 7–0.

Brooklyn won again the next day as Nap Rucker beat Tesreau 9–2, and again Snodgrass earned McGraw's wrath. In the second inning, he loafed on his way to first base, allowing the Robins to execute a double play and kill a potential Giant rally. McGraw dished out the ultimate embarrassment for any ballplayer and yanked him from the game; the two men had words in the dugout. Snodgrass eventually returned to the lineup, but continued to play listlessly; within a month he was given his unconditional release. (Strangely enough, Red Murray, Snow's replacement in the Brooklyn game and a longtime regular, was also released for reasons less clear, leaving the club seriously short in the outfield.)

Plugging the new holes in the outfield was not the only problem McGraw faced; the Giant pitching staff was struggling. Tesreau was on his way to a 19-win season, but Mathewson seemed to lose his edge almost overnight. Plagued by tendonitis, he appeared in only 27 games in 1915, winning 8 of 22 decisions in the only ineffective season he ever had as a Giant starter. Alex Schauer, born Dimitri Dimitrihoff in Russia and called, naturally, "Rube," was thrust into the rotation but was a huge disappointment, winning only 2 of 10 decisions. The real Rube, Marquard, was erratic, alternating fine outings with horrible ones. He was used occasionally in relief and could voice no complaints, for he knew as well as anyone that he was not the pitcher he had once been. Part of the problem may have been his age. While everyone assumed he was only 25 years old, he was actually 28, and his left arm had endured nearly 15 years of heavy use. He had become no better than a .500 pitcher on a mediocre team, and Rube and the Giants seemed powerless to overcome their predicament.

Chief Meyers placed at least part of the blame on reasons other than pitching. It seems that the players and coaches were not the only ones frustrated by the downslide; relations became strained among several of the wives. The women customarily sat together in the same section of box seats at the Polo Grounds, and some of them became a little too critical of certain players. "When hubby made an error, or hubby did something out there that wasn't right, Mrs. So-and-so would say something," recalled Meyers. "They were fighting up there among themselves, dissension.... Well, that stuff got down in the clubhouse, and some of the fellows that had wives sitting up in that box together, why, they wouldn't speak to one another." Chief remarked that the female species "is the deadlier of the two."[35]

Whatever the reason, the Giants remained in the cellar, or close to it, through July and most of August. On August 16, Rube appeared in relief of Tesreau in the tenth inning of a 1–1 game against Brooklyn. He struck out pinch-hitter Joe Schultz with the lead run on second base, then happily watched Meyers drive home Lobert with the winning run in the bottom of the frame. The win pulled New York to within one game of .500 at 50–51, and Rube's mark on the season stood at 9–7.

Speculation among the sporting crowd was that McGraw had tired of Rube's unpredictability, that he had never quite forgiven him over the lack of loyalty shown the Giants over the Federal League contract and was now shopping him around the league. On August 21, Rube started against St. Louis at the Polo Grounds, but he was routed for five hits and three runs in only an inning and a third. McGraw came out to the mound and took the ball from him, and Rube walked slowly off the field "with his head down, and visions of that waiver rumor dancing before his eyes."[36] The crowd game him a nice cheer despite his performance, perhaps in appreciation of past successes, and Rube managed to acknowledge his fans with a tip of his cap before he disappeared into the clubhouse. It was the last time he would appear in a New York Giant uniform.

Rube always claimed that he "traded himself" away from the Giants:

I didn't seem to be able to get going in 1915 after I pitched that no-hitter in early April, and late in the season McGraw started riding me. That was a very bad year for the Giants, you know. We were favored to win the pennant, and instead we wound up last. So McGraw wasn't very happy.

After I'd taken about as much riding as I could stand, I asked him to trade me if he thought I was so bad.

"Who would take you?" he said.

"What do you mean?" I said. "I can lick any club in the league." Heck, I wasn't twenty-six years old yet.

"Lick any club in the league?" McGraw said. "You couldn't lick a postage stamp."

"Give me a chance to trade myself, then," I said. "What would you sell me for?"

"$7,500," he answered.

"OK," I said, "can I use your phone?"

"Sure," he said. We were both pretty mad.

So I got hold of the operator and asked her to get me Wilbert Robinson, manager of the Brooklyn club. See, Robbie had been a coach with us for years before he became the Dodger manager in 1914. After a while she got Robbie on the phone.

"Hello," he says.

"How are you, Robbie?" I said.

"Fine," he said. "Who is this?"

"How would you like to have a good left-handed pitcher?"

"I'd love it," he said. "Who is this? Who's the man? Who are you going to recommend?"

"I'm going to recommend myself."

"Who are you?"

"Rube Marquard."

"Oh, what are you kidding around for, Rube" he said. "I have to go out on the field and I don't have time to fool around."

"No, I'm serious," I said. "McGraw is right here and he says he'll sell me for $7,500. Do you want to talk to him?"

"Of course I do," Robbie said. And right then and there I was traded from the Giants to the Dodgers."³⁷

Actually, the circumstances surrounding the transaction were not nearly so cut and dried. On August 25 the Giants were in last place, having lost seven of their last eight games. McGraw obtained from Cincinnati left-handed pitcher Rube Benton, a five-year veteran with a lifetime record of 54–62. To make room for Benton on the roster, the Giants offered Rube on waivers, but he was not claimed by any of the other major league clubs. Rather than give him his unconditional release, as he had Murray and Snodgrass, McGraw assigned Rube to Toronto of the International League, with the understanding that the Giants would secure future rights to a young pitcher named Fred Herbert. Toronto manager Jim Clymer was in New York and personally negotiated the deal with

McGraw. He had no luck, however, in dealing with Rube, who steadfastly refused to report to Toronto ("a bush town," he called it) or, for that matter, any minor league team. Rube said he would rather retire.

Rube was now in a sort of baseball limbo. He could no longer, of course, suit up with the Giants and could not even hang around the clubhouse while his fate was decided. He was the property of Toronto but would not go there. He was not a free agent and could not, technically, contact any of the major league teams. He frantically wired the Federal League office in Chicago but his inquiries were ignored. Even the outlaw league wanted nothing to do with him after the affidavit fiasco of the previous winter. Finally on August 29 he received McGraw's permission to call Wilbert Robinson. He convinced Robbie that there was still life in his arm and that the Robins, who were surprisingly hanging tough in a pennant race, could benefit from his experience and savvy. Robbie's chance to claim Rube on waivers had passed, but he offered to purchase Rube outright for $1,500. McGraw was willing to sell Rube, but only for the waiver price of $2,500. Robbie convinced Charles Ebbetts that Rube was worth that price, and the deal was struck. Toronto was paid an undisclosed sum to relinquish its claim to Rube, and Herbert did, in fact, appear in two games with the Giants in September — the only appearances of his major league career.

If he had to leave the Giants, there was no team Rube would rather have gone to than the Robins. Aside from the fact that he did not have to disrupt his family and move to a new city, he was relieved to be reunited with Robinson, who had seemingly found his niche in Brooklyn. It was the first team he had ever managed — Hughie Jennings of Detroit had been Ebbetts' first choice — but in just a year and a half Robbie had transformed the club into a contender. Heading into the stretch, they were in second place, only percentage points behind Philadelphia. With sluggers Jake Daubert, Zack Wheat, and Casey Stengel propelling the offense, it was the pitching staff that needed to be addressed if the Robins were to take the pennant. In addition to Rube, Robbie acquired standout Chicago spitballer Larry Cheney, and he immediately signed both men to three-year contracts. Rube was happy still to be in the league and did not argue over taking a $2,000 cut in salary. With a little luck, he figured, he might make up the difference with another World Series check.

There were other big-name transactions in baseball at almost the same time in late August. On the twentieth, Cleveland owner Charles Somers, his sixth-place Naps drawing poorly and in dire financial straits, traded Shoeless Joe Jackson to the White Sox for three players and $31,500 in cash. And on September 1, Connie Mack sold Home Run Baker, who had been holding out all year in a salary dispute, to the Yankees for $15,000. Both of these deals drew more media attention than the one involving Rube, who was widely perceived as over the hill.

But Robbie believed Rube's career could be resurrected. He quickly diagnosed Rube's problem as nothing more than a tired arm and thought that steady work was the last thing he needed. Instead his plan was to slowly, if at all, work

Rube into the starting rotation by choosing pitching assignments carefully — throw him in relief against certain teams and in certain situations in the hope that he would regain his confidence. If handled properly, Robbie believed, Rube would eventually come around and become productive, just as he had been rejuvenated back in 1911 after two years as "the lemon." Rube, eager to prove himself again, was in no position to question the advice of his mentor and cheerfully accepted his new, limited role with the club.

Both Cheney and Rube saw their first action in Brooklyn uniforms on August 31, against Pittsburgh at Ebbetts Field. Cheney started the second game of a doubleheader and pitched well for seven innings, leaving with the Robins down 2–1. Rube pitched the rest of the way, and when second baseman George Cutshaw doubled home Daubert and Stengel in the eighth, Rube received credit for the victory. A week later Rube again came on in relief of Cheney (former Athletic Jack Coombs, now 32 years old and several years removed from his glory days in Philadelphia, also threw in middle relief for Brooklyn), and Rube secured a 6–3 victory.

But the Robins could not quite hold on and faded in the last few weeks of September. Boston made another late charge and passed them in the standings, but neither club could catch the Phillies, who rode Grover Alexander's 31 wins and Gavvy Cravath's clutch hitting to the first pennant in their history. Rube did make two starts before the season ended, on September 14 against St. Louis (he was beaten 6–2) and again on October 6 against the Phillies (he had no decision in a 9–6 loss). But he pitched well enough in his scattered relief appearances to give Robbie reason to be hopeful. Even *Sporting Life* changed its tune and decided that Rube might make good again. "Marquard has surely had a meteoric career," wrote Harry Dix Cole, "but as he is a young man he should have quite a bit of good baseball left in him, if he can be induced to take the game seriously."[38] As for Rube, he believed that he had a future in Flatbush.

CHAPTER 13

The Boys from Across the Big Bridge

Judge Landis refused to issue a ruling in the antitrust litigation before him, fearful that a decision either way might "tear down the very foundation" of the game most revered as a "national institution."[1] He knew also that the longer he kept the matter under advisement, the greater the chance the parties would settle the case on their own. Finally a compromise, part buyout and part merger, was reached between the owners of all three leagues, and it was subsequently approved by Landis. The Federal League disbanded, club owners taking payments of some $600,000 plus varying amounts of stock in major league clubs in exchange for dismissing the suit. Two Federal owners, Harry Sinclair and Charles Wheegman of Chicago, took over the St. Louis Browns and the Chicago Cubs, respectively. The players were left out of the negotiations, a fact which must have chagrined Joe Tinker, and the Players' Fraternity fell apart. Major league owners were happy with the settlement and relieved that the Federal competition, which had staggered them at the turnstiles, was gone. They backed off of their threat and welcomed back those players who had jumped to the outlaw league. Things would get more or less back to normal in 1916, and the biggest sigh of relief came from Brooklyn.

Charles Hercules Ebbetts, called Colonel by his friends, had dedicated his life to major league baseball in Brooklyn. Beginning in 1883 he had performed any job that needed doing for the ballclub. He sold tickets, programs, and refreshments, assisted with the groundskeeping, and swept up the grandstand after ballgames. His loyalty to the team was such that he devoted virtually every waking hour to promoting it in one fashion or another, and eventually he was rewarded with the promotion to business manager. In 1902 majority shareholder Harry von der Horst fell ill and announced his intention to sell his shares. Manager Ned Hanlon was the likely buyer, and his controversial plan was to transfer the franchise to Baltimore, where he had once played, along with John McGraw and Wilbert Robinson, for the old Orioles.

Ebbetts could not bear the possibility that his beloved Brooklyn might lose its team, and he miraculously persuaded a wealthy furniture dealer named Henry Medicus to loan him the money to purchase the stock himself. He thus became principal owner of the club and began to operate it with a philosophy refreshingly different from that of any of his 15 counterparts: He believed that the interests of the fans were the paramount concern, and profit margin came second. His club was continually on the brink of economic collapse, but he was not driven by money alone. Once he refused to sell two of his best players when offered $30,000, insisting that "the Brooklyn fans deserve the best team I can give them."[2]

In large part Ebbetts held this belief because of the characteristics of the borough itself. Brooklyn, and particularly the Flatbush section, had a small-town feel to it not found, for example, across the bridge in Manhattan. Brooklyn fans took a special, personal interest in the players, one that might more usually be found in the minor leagues. After games the players often gathered at a neighborhood cigar store to mingle with fans, discuss the day's events, and make plans for tomorrow's game. Most married players lived in modest apartments along Parkside and Flatbush avenues, where they blended comfortably into the community. (Rube and Blossom, however, having just purchased a larger and fancier apartment on Riverside Drive, chose to remain in the big city.)

For many years home games were played at Washington Park, so named because it was built on the site where General George Washington had led the Continental Army into battle during the Revolutionary War. (The fact that the British had been victorious there did not diminish the historical significance of the area.) But by 1913 the old stadium was in serious disrepair. The team had finished in the second division for ten straight years, and what the franchise needed, and the loyal fans deserved, thought Ebbetts, was a new stadium. He personally walked the neighborhoods of Brooklyn in search of a suitable location and found one which, despite its unattractive state, seemed promising. It was a large field surrounded by shacks and tenements; nearby inhabitants disposed of their trash in the field and farmers allowed their swine to wallow there. The site was thus called Pigtown, and on it Ebbetts would build his monument.

Once again Ebbetts utilized his considerable personal charm to secure the necessary financing. He convinced a pair of wealthy Brooklyn contractors, brothers Edwin and Stephen McKeever, that the project was a sound one. On condition that they received a percentage of the club's ownership, they agreed to help him build it. The new stadium was a massive structure of steel, brick, and stone that was highlighted by a grand rotunda of Italian marble inside the main entrance and adorned by chandeliers shaped of crossed baseball bats. When it opened in 1913, Ebbetts Field was rightfully labeled as one of the spectacular wonders of the sporting world. It held 25,000 fans and soon became known as a comfortable park for player and fan alike.

Wilbert Robinson was hired as manager in 1914 and the club almost immediately turned around. Now called Uncle Robbie, a moniker given him by famed sportswriter Damon Runyon, he was a perfect fit for Brooklyn. His club finished fourth that year, and a strong third in 1915, and now with the Federal League and its Brooklyn franchise gone for good, Ebbetts rewarded Robbie with a new three-year contract. When the Robins assembled for training camp in Daytona Beach, Florida, in March of 1916, they were hopeful of again challenging for the pennant. Robinson preached that if he had "three good pitchers and four good hitters" he would produce a winner, and it seemed he had the pieces in place. Rube was particularly delighted to learn that Robbie had acquired Chief Meyers from the Giants to catch, at least on a part-time basis.

Robbie's ideas about spring training were nearly the exact opposite of McGraw's. He ran a loose and nearly carefree camp, allowing the men to get in shape at their own pace and in their own ways. He could be just as sarcastic and profane as McGraw, but his temper quickly cooled and his players learned to shrug off the criticism. They also came to appreciate the liberal manner in which he praised and encouraged their performance. There was always room for practical jokes, late-night hours, and good times at Robbie's camp. The players were allowed, even encouraged, to take advantage of the attractions the resort location offered, and they lounged on the beaches and in the nightclubs whenever possible.

One day a large group of ballplayers gathered at water's edge to witness a young airplane pilot and stuntwoman named Ruth Law perform on behalf of a local sporting goods company. She flew along the coast at a height of a thousand feet and dropped dozens of golf balls into the sand. Robinson bet some of his players that he could catch a baseball dropped from a plane, if it flew at a lower height of perhaps 400 feet. (Gabby Hartnett, the catcher for the Washington Senators, had once caught a ball dropped from the top of the Washington Monument, no doubt providing Robinson's inspiration.) The boys took Robbie up on his boast, and the next day the event was staged. But one of the players, probably Casey Stengel, substituted a grapefruit for a baseball. With a great crowd gathered around, the plane roared by above and the missile was dropped. Amazingly Robbie caught it, or at least came close. The grapefruit fell through his hands and exploded onto his chest, knocking him to the sand, where he began to scream in horror, thinking that the juice was his blood. As the players howled with laughter, he realized he had been had, and the episode went down as one of the great pranks in baseball history. (Ruth Law continued to make headlines with her flying. Two years later, while making trans–Atlantic flights on behalf of the Red Cross, she was suspected of spying for the Germans and was grounded for the duration of the war.)

After six weeks of fun, the regular season began, and Brooklyn hosted the Braves on Wednesday, April 12, in the opener. Robinson was presented with the traditional floral horseshoe for good luck, and as Shannon's Band, the local favorite, played "The Star-Spangled Banner," Stengel assisted in the raising of a huge American flag over the center-field bleachers. Just over 10,000 fans were on hand to see their heroes, oddly dressed in uniforms with a light plaid pattern, drop a 5–1 game. Larry Cheney contributed heavily to his loss by issuing four walks, uncorking a wild pitch, and committing a critical throwing error. The Braves also took the next two games of the initial series, beating Sherry Smith and then Nap Rucker, and the Robins were winless as they traveled to take on the Giants at the Polo Grounds.

Cold and wet weather canceled two games, although finally on April 19 the teams squeezed in a game between thunderstorms. Harry Smith defeated Tesreau 7–3, and Chief Meyers gained some measure of satisfaction on his first return to his old home by crashing an RBI double and playing well behind the plate. The next day, in Boston, marked Rube's first appearance of the year, but it was a forgettable one. Coombs started but was ineffective, giving up four runs in an inning and a third. Rube came on but fared no better, and by the time he left the game for a pinch hitter in the fifth the Robins were down 8–0, where the score remained.

A fine crowd of 28,000 came out to the Polo Grounds on Saturday, April 29, to see the Giants take on the Robins. "The boys from across the Big Bridge" beat their hosts 5–4 in 12 innings, Rube pitching part of the ninth inning and picking George Burns off base at a key moment, then giving way to Cheney, who finished and got credit for the victory. Although Giant fans went away disappointed in the result, they did witness something unusual: Fred Merkle slammed three doubles, the last of which sailed into the C. T. Silver sign in front of the left-field bleachers, entitling Fred to a free $2,000 automobile. It was the first time the feat had ever been accomplished, and it was considered "the most amazing hit ever made" at the Polo Grounds.[3]

After Sunday's off day, the two clubs met again on Tuesday, and the result was much the same. Rube pitched the eighth inning in relief of Nap Rucker and then gave way to Coombs, who wrapped up the 8–5 Robin win. Cuban Emilio Palmero started for the Giants but was hit hard and lasted only three innings, the big blast being Stengel's three-run homer. New York's eighth straight loss was difficult enough for McGraw to take, but he also had to suffer from the fact that Robbie's team had now taken possession of first place. The next day the Giants finally won, 2–1, as Tesreau pitched a three-hitter over Big Ed Pfeffer, but on Wednesday the Robins again used three pitchers and held off New York 6–4. They had taken three out of four from the Giants, on the road, and thought they belonged in first place.

Rube was given his first starting assignment on May 16 in St. Louis, but he lasted only an inning. He walked the first two hitters, then threw a wild pitch. Two singles and a sacrifice fly later he was behind by three runs and was pulled from the game. Wheezer Dell threw fine ball the rest of the way for Brooklyn, but they still lost 5–4. (The season was still very young, of course, yet famed sportswriter Grantland Rice wrote a nationally syndicated column stating that "the once Eminent Rube has lost his grip," and predicted that his future looked bleak at best.[4]) Rube felt some tenderness in his left elbow after the outing, and Robbie took no chances with him. He ordered a week of rest, then had Rube ease his arm slowly back into shape. While he probably could have pitched earlier, Rube did not appear again in a game until June 2. With his team holding onto first place, Rube was content, for the time being, to watch and cheer his new teammates and shake his head in amazement at his old ones; as terrible as the Giants had been in April, they were terrific in May, winning 17 in a row and creeping up on Brooklyn.

When Rube came back, he continued to pitch effectively out of the bullpen. On June 2 he threw four strong innings in a losing cause against Pittsburgh, then allowed only one hit in four innings against the Cardinals on the fourteenth, wrapping up the win for Jack Coombs. With Coombs, Rucker, Cheney, and Pfeffer all providing quality starts, Rube became an effective "closer," many years before the term came into common use. In June he racked up five saves for the Robins.

But as the summer wore on and Brooklyn remained in the pennant race, Robbie worked Rube into the starting rotation. On July 1, Rube took the mound in the second game of a doubleheader in Boston, the Robins having lost the first game 7–4. He surrendered six hits and lost 2–0, most of the damage coming from the bat of Sherwood Magee, who made seven consecutive hits on the day and figured in seven of the Braves' nine runs. While the sweep enabled Boston to pull within three games of Brooklyn, both Rube and Robbie were pleased with his effort.

Rube's next appearance came just three days later on the Fourth of July, before a tremendous crowd of 27,000 at the Polo Grounds. Cheney started the first of two games against the Giants but couldn't get through the first inning, allowing five hits and five runs before Rube took over. He went the rest of the way, giving up only seven hits and one unearned run in the seventh, and Brooklyn came back to win 7–6, knocking Perritt and then Mathewson all around the yard. They also won the second game, this time beating Tesreau 6–2 and overcoming the unwise baserunning of third baseman Harry Mowery, who tried to steal second base with the bases loaded in the fifth inning. Giant fans got a laugh out of the attempt but found no humor in the standings, for with two losses their club once again fell into the second division.

Rube seemed to be finding his groove again, though he seldom pitched more than once every week or ten days. He won his next three starts, then lost 4–1 to Boston's Dick Rudolph on August 15, Braves first baseman Ed Konetchy nailing him for two doubles and a triple. Another Boston pitcher was impressive on that day: Red Sox left-hander Babe Ruth outdueled Walter Johnson, finally winning 1–0 in 13 innings and solidifying the defending champions' hold on first place in the American League.

Rube won his sixth game of the year on August 19, shutting out the Pirates 1–0, no doubt benefitting from the absence of Honus Wagner from the lineup. On the twenty-fourth he dropped a 2–1 decision to Cincinnati although both runs were unearned. The Reds were now managed by Christy Mathewson, who had been traded by McGraw so that he could run his own team.

Heading into the stretch, Brooklyn hoped to stave off Philadelphia and Boston for the pennant, and Rube's clutch pitching more than lived up to Robbie's expectations. He lost 2–1 to St. Louis on September 18 but struck out seven Cardinals, his highest total in three years and evidence that the pop had returned to his fastball. On the twenty-second he threw again against St. Louis, this time winning 11–1 and striking out five. His battery mate, Chief Meyers, showed that he was still a threat with the bat: He singled twice and drove in two runs, and he was so feared by Cardinal pitchers that they walked him intentionally three times. Fred Merkle, who had been picked up off waivers, provided a key pinch hit. Then on September 30, Rube came up with one of the finest performances of his career in a game that had a huge impact on the race for the championship.

Philadelphia came to Brooklyn only percentage points behind the Robins. Eppa Jeptha Rixey, the Phillies' fine pitcher, beat Pfeffer 7–2 in the first of two games, and the Robins found themselves in second place for the first time in two months. The afternoon game matched Rube and Grover Alexander in yet another crucial contest between the two star pitchers. This day Rube was nearly perfect, allowing only three hits, fanning seven, and putting Brooklyn back in first place with the 6–1 win. Casey Stengel broke open a 1–1 game with a long home run in the fifth inning, beginning a steady stream of hits off of the shaken Alex. Rube gave up two hits and a run in the first, then did not allow another baserunner until the ninth, when he gave up a meaningless single. It was Rube's 13th win of the season against only 6 losses, and his ERA of 1.58 was second in the league, barely behind Alexander's 1.55. "Rube Marquard," said the *Times*, "at various times consigned to the scrap heap ... was in invincible form.... His fastball hopped and jumped like a cork in the sea." Even John McGraw, who witnessed the contest, commented that "when Rube gets the hop on his fast one he is unbeatable."[5]

McGraw's Giants had been unbeatable themselves, although their recent 26-game winning streak had come too late in their roller-coaster season to gain them the pennant. Wilbert Robinson congratulated McGraw on the streak, yet couldn't help but remind him that what really mattered was who came out on top. "We all have to take our hats off to McGraw," he said, "and I am as proud at this moment of his feat as of the standing of the Brooklyns in the National League."[6] For the Robins remained in first place and took the first pennant in their history, although the circumstances under which they claimed it led many to suspect the motives of their most-hated rivals, the Giants.

On October 3, Brooklyn beat the Giants 9–6 at the Polo Grounds and clinched the flag as Philadelphia dropped a doubleheader to Boston, eliminating both teams. After five innings McGraw became so disgusted with the Giant's play that he left the bench and later hinted strongly that his club had not given its best effort. "I do not say that my players did not try to win," he said that night, "but they refused to obey my orders, and they disregarded my signals.... I do not like indifferent playing of this kind after the hard work we have had this season."⁷ The *Times* noted that "there were many features of the Giants' play which were very unlike the tactics which the club pursued during its recent outburst of great playing. The Brooklyn batsmen hit many grounders to the infield which went as hits, although a dozen times during the last few weeks the same Giant infielders have fielded grounders which looked much more difficult."⁸ Perhaps the most glaring example came in the fifth inning, when Parritt twice took full windups with the bases full, allowing a crucial run and putting the Robins in the lead.

The *Times* speculated that the Giants were eager to see Brooklyn take the pennant because they still held a grudge against the Phillies, a feud that dated back to 1908 when "Coveleski the Giant-Killer" took them out of the race in the weeks following the Merkle incident. In more recent years, pointed out the *Times*, there had been several fistfights between Giants and Phillies, as well as the brawl between McGraw and Addie Brennan in 1912 which nearly resulted in a riot. Wilbert Robinson, however, discounted such theories. "Manager McGraw's suspicions in this matter are ridiculous," he told the press. "His statement is very unsportsmanlike, and I am greatly surprised that he would say such a thing. It looks to me like an alibi for the wretched playing of his club, which seems to have gone to pieces under the strain of their record-breaking winning streak."⁹ Off the record Robbie was less polite. "Tell McGraw to stop pissing on my pennant," he said.¹⁰

The National Commission was sufficiently concerned over McGraw's remarks to launch an investigation into the affair, although it ultimately took no action. McGraw refused to manage the final two games against Brooklyn, retiring instead to the safety of a Maryland racetrack; he later refused his players' gift of a leather-bound set of the works of William Shakespeare. Not one of his players showed up at a season-ending party at the Rialto Theater. As the Giants were in turmoil, Rube and his teammates prepared to face Boston in the 1916 World Series.

The champion Robins were the idols of Brooklyn. On Friday morning, October 6, they gathered at Ebbets Field, where they received final instructions from Robbie in preparation for the trip to Boston. At 11 o'clock they left the clubhouse and were serenaded by a brass band and surrounded by a legion of supporters "usually accorded a Presidential nominee."¹¹ Then the players and coaches crowded into 18 touring cars and embarked on a carefully orchestrated procession through the fan-lined streets of Brooklyn. At each stop along the route they were cheered, and at the YMCA on Bedford Avenue they accepted the congratulations of Borough president L. H. Pounds, who admonished them to "bring home the highest laurel of the baseball world — a world's championship." They received the final sendoff from 5,000 supporters at Grand Central Station, and, as usual, Rube was one of the most popular players. His emergence from a car "brought forth a stirring ovation, while the big southpaw just grinned his appreciation."[12] Later that evening they arrived in Boston, along with a contingent of 600 Brooklyn boosters (most of whom did not have tickets to the games but were along for the party), and checked into the Hotel Brunswick. Ironically, the club's biggest fan, Charles Ebbetts himself, was not along on the trip; he was hospitalized in New York with an ear infection and would miss the first two games of the Series.

The Red Sox, managed by Bill Carrigan, were defending world champs, having defeated the Phillies in the 1915 World Series. The club had undergone some significant changes since beating the Giants in the turbulent 1912 Series. Tris Speaker had been traded to Cleveland in April, just as the season was about to begin (undaunted, he led the league in hitting with a .386 average, dethroning Ty Cobb for the first time since 1906), and Smoky Joe Wood and Jake Stahl were also gone. Harry Hooper remained, however, as did Duffy Lewis and Larry Gardner, among others. The most significant addition was young Babe Ruth, only 21 years old but already one of the best pitchers in baseball, with 43 wins in just over two full years in the league. His ERA of 1.75 was the lowest in the league, and his nine shutouts set a new record. Ernie Shore, Dutch Leonard, and submariner Carl Mays rounded out the fine staff, one that oddsmakers believed was capable of stifling Brooklyn's heavy hitters.

In fact most baseball insiders picked the Red Sox to win. Ty Cobb, Ring Lardner, and Hugh Fullerton all predicted a Boston Series victory, in five games or six at the most. They agreed on something else: Rube Marquard remained a terrific pitcher. Recalling that Rube had beaten the Sox twice in 1912, Cobb said: "Just now Rube is going about as well as he ever did in his life. With the speed he has Marquard will look awfully good out there on a dark day."[13] Former Athletic Jack Barry, now the regular Boston second baseman, was sitting out the Series with a broken hand and was wary of Rube's talents in his Boston *Post* column. "Rube Marquard, with his fastball shoots and his southpaw slants ... will have to be reckoned with."[14] Another celebrity author, Grover Alexander, noted that he "never saw Marquard look better than he did in the last series against us in Brooklyn.... The southpaw has a better curveball than he had back in 1912. The Red Sox may beat him but if they get more than a pair of runs off him I miss my guess."[15] Wilbert Robinson agreed. He had every confidence in "the eccentric Rube" and named him to start game one, to face 13-game winner Ernie Shore.

Over 36,000 fans, including the familiar Royal Rooters, filled Fenway Park on Saturday, October 7. The Sox reached Rube for the game's first run in the third inning, when Dick Hoblitzell tripled and Lewis doubled. Two innings later they scored again when Hooper doubled and Otto Walker tripled. In the seventh, Harold Janvrin, playing for Barry, doubled, and the Brooklyn defense proceeded to fall apart. Olson and Cutshaw booted ground balls, and Chief Meyers had a passed ball. Two hits and a sacrifice fly produced three runs, and when an inning later Stengel's throwing error allowed another, Boston led 6–1.

Conversely, the Red Sox defense was superb. They executed four double plays and bailed Shore, who allowed nine base hits, out of jams in nearly every inning. Harry Hooper made a customary clutch play in the fourth. After Zack Wheat tripled in Stengel with the first Brooklyn run, Cutshaw sliced a drive to right. Hooper sprinted toward the foul line and made a diving grab, then from his knees fired a strike to catcher Forrest Cady, just in time to nip the sliding Wheat. The San Francisco *Chronicle* noted that Hooper, a native Californian, "has long since developed the world series habit of making impossible plays," and this one was "never equalled."[16] Smoky Joe Wood said that when the chips were down, "that guy played like wildfire."[17]

But in the ninth inning, Shore finally weakened. A cluster of hits and an error by Janvrin (the only Sox miscue of the day) led to four runs, and suddenly the Sox lead was just one at 6–5. With two out and the bases loaded, Carrigan lifted Shore and summoned Mays to pitch to Zack Wheat. Hitless in his first four at-bats with a pair of strikeouts, a base hit was now Wheat's chance to "even up the day's count and displace the crown of thorns upon his brow with the olive wreath."[18] He drilled a sharp grounder just past the reach of Gardner at third and into the hole at short. As the crowd screamed, Janvrin rushed over and snagged it with his backhand on the shallow outfield grass, planted, and threw to Hoblitzell just ahead of the streaking Wheat, and the game was over. There might have been better World Series games played, said the Boston *Herald*, but "no Bostonian can ever recall a more nerve-wracking finish."[19]

Brooklyn fans blamed the loss on the shoddy Robin defense, but Rube offered a different explanation. The home plate umpire was American Leaguer Tommy Connolly, who warned Rube repeatedly that his motion with men on base was close to a balk, and this warning upset Rube's rhythm and his concentration. "The Red Sox fans didn't get my goat but Connolly did," Rube told Nate Cook of the Cleveland *Press*. Rube was counting on pitching again in the Series and predicted victory. Not only had he learned a great deal about the Boston hitters in the first game, but his teammates "will have recovered from some of the stage fright which they underwent." And he had an extra incentive to pitch better next time: "My wife is making a special trip east," he said, "having received a leave of absence from the theatrical company she is with, to attend the rest of the series."[20]

After a day off, game two was played on Monday, also in Boston, with surprise starter Sherrod Smith going against Babe Ruth. The Babe had not been given the chance to pitch in the 1915 World Series, although he had desperately wanted too, and he was not in the least bit nervous this time. "It makes no difference to me which game I pitch or where," he said nonchalantly. "If the big boss says the word I will be there, for I never felt better in my life."[21]

But the Robins struck right away in the first. Hi Myers slammed a towering drive off the center-field wall, and as the ball bounced crazily off the fence's angles he legged it all the way around the bases for a home run. Boston tied it in the third when shortstop Everett Scott tripled and scored when Cutshaw booted Ruth's grounder. The game remained deadlocked at one until the bottom of the 14th inning, both pitchers going the entire way. Then Hoblitzell walked for the fourth time in the game. Lewis bunted him to second, where he was replaced by pinch-runner Mike McNally. Del Gainor hit for Gardner who, although he had hit .308 on the year, was just one for nine in two Series games. As twilight quickly faded Gainor took a ball, swung and missed for strike one, and then poked a fastball to leftfield. A "report like that of a rifle shot echoed through" the park, and over 41,000 people rose to their feet as the ball fell safely in front of Wheat.[22] He grabbed it on one hop and fired a throw to catcher Miller, but the speedy McNally slid in just ahead of the ball, and the Red Sox had a 2–1 victory. The game was the longest in World Series history, and Boston now had a two-game advantage.

Brooklyn won game three behind Jack Coombs the next day at Ebbetts Field. Unusually cold weather kept the crowd down to 21,000, but those who braved the chill were treated to the first-ever Brooklyn victory in a World Series game. Leadoff hitter Hooper smashed the first pitch of the game over the wall in right, but the wind blew it just foul, and Harry subsequently flew out. Good fortune stayed with the Robins as they roughed up Mays for seven hits and four runs, taking the 4–0 lead into the sixth inning. Then Hooper drove in a run with a triple, again barely missing a home run, and he later scored on Chick Shorten's single. In the seventh, Gardner blasted a homer, and with the Brooklyn lead cut to 4–3 Pfeffer relieved Coombs. Big Ed went the rest of the way, retiring eight straight and earning the save. Counting the four wins he had earned with the A's, the win pushed Coombs' career Series record to 5–0.

On Thursday, Rube got the call again, this time going against Dutch Leonard. He started well, causing Hooper to bounce back to the mound and then fanning Janvrin and Walker. Members of the crowd sensed that Rube had his best stuff and rose to their feet, Blossom among them. They "rent the air with shrieks and stentorian cachinnations such as no theatrical noise creator ever dreamed of in his most strenuous efforts, accompanying them with such demonstrations of uncontrollable joy as must have warmed the hearts of the Superbas to their task."[23]

Brooklyn struck in the bottom of the inning. Jimmy Johnston stroked a triple to the gap in right center field and scored on Myers' single. Myers later scored when Janvrin kicked a groundball, and Rube was working with a two-run lead. But he inexplicably walked Hoblitzell to start the second, and Lewis drove a fly to deep right field. Johnston ran back for it and managed to get his glove on the ball before he crashed into the wall, the ball popping loose in the process. Hoblitzell had held up, unsure if the ball would be caught, and made it only as far as third base, Lewis pulling into second. The Brooklyn infield played in, hoping to cut off the run at the plate. With Gardner up, Chief Meyers suspected a squeeze, so Rube kept the ball high, hoping to frustrate the effort. But Gardner wouldn't bite and took three pitches for balls. Finally he took a called strike, fouled off two more pitches, and drove a fastball to the wall in deep center. He sprinted all the way around the bases, sliding in safely ahead of the relay throw, and the Sox took a 3–2 lead. The Royal Rooters "yelled like maniacs in the third-base section, and the scene in the Boston dugout rivaled that of Dante's inferno."[24] The Sox scored again in the fourth, and Robbie, who could wait no longer, pulled the disappointed Rube from the game. Cheney and then Rucker finished up, but the Robins could manage only one more hit off Leonard the rest of the way, and Boston won 6–2 to take a commanding lead in the Series at three games to one.

Before the fifth game, Bill Carrigan startled Red Sox fans by announcing that he would retire from baseball after the Series, no matter the outcome. He was interested in politics and would run for mayor of his hometown, Lewiston, Maine, on the Democratic ticket.[25] In true fashion the Red Sox "won one for the old man," Ernie Shore holding the Robins to three hits for the second game in a row in the 4–1 victory. When the last out was made, Rube watched a painfully familiar scene as the Royal Rooters, dressed in crimson suits and top hats, blowing horns and shaking tambourines, paraded around the field in celebration. The Red Sox had won their third championship in five years.

While Rube was happy to see Blossom for a few days during the Series, the reunion was short-lived, for she immediately went back out on the road. Her show, "Seeley's Syncopated Studio," was filling theaters nationwide. Accompanied by pianist/saxophone player Bill Bailey and banjoist Lynn Cowan, Blossom's 20-minute set included such numbers as "Coal Black Rose," "Amazon," and a Hawaiian song called "Cherry Blossoms." Said *Variety* in December 1916, "Miss Seeley is displaying considerable grace in her customary high class fashion.... The vehicle should prove acceptable for a long time to come."[26] Blossom insisted on performing only in front of velvet red and black curtains scented with her favorite perfume, lending a unique and fairly enchanting aura to the performance. Many audiences came back to the same theater night after night to see her.

Rube sometimes traveled to meet Blossom, bringing Richard, Jr., along, but more often he left him for a few days in the care of the full-time nanny he had hired. He marveled at Blossom's enormous popularity and her limitless energy on stage, and he remained very proud to be her husband. Occasionally Blossom called Rube out on stage to take a bow, and sometimes he could be coaxed into joining her in one of the old numbers they had first performed at Hammerstein's and the Palace several years before. The nimble Rube still moved as gracefully in a top hat and tails as he did on the ballfield.

Sometimes, to pass the time in a strange city, he borrowed an idea from Wilbert Robinson and performed an "astounding baseball maneuver" in the middle of a busy street. Dressed in a fine suit of clothes and surrounded by security guards, he proceeded to catch baseballs thrown off of high buildings, to the to the amazement of thrilled (and paying) customers. And he took another shot at the vaudeville stage, teaming with a comedian named William Dooley to mediocre reviews at the Palace. The paychecks were nice, but his heart was no longer in it.

Inevitably the conversations between Rube and Blossom turned to their future, for as much as he appreciated her continuing success he wanted her to come home to New York and settle down for good. He asked her to quit the stage, or at least call a halt to the constant touring. Blossom was not nearly ready to do that, but they settled on a compromise: Blossom would remain, whenever possible, in New York during the summer months, and would only travel in the fall and winter.

For the last two weeks in March and the first week in April 1917, the defending National League champion Robins and world champion Red Sox traveled around the South and Midwest, playing a series of 10 exhibition games. Inclement weather caused the cancellation of most of those games, however, disappointing large crowds in Arkansas, Iowa, and Missouri. In Peoria, Boston owner Harry Frazee hosted a lavish dinner at his home for the players and coaches of both teams, and Rube and Robbie were happy to attend, laughing that such an event would never take place on a John McGraw club. Despite the fairly constant rain, Rube enjoyed himself on the tour and managed to strike up friendships with several Red Sox players, including the soft-spoken Harry Hooper and the gregarious Babe Ruth. The Babe loved to hear Rube talk about his vaudeville days (particularly the money that could be made on stage), and the two agreed that they would get together next spring in Florida and play some golf.

Opening Day festivities at Ebbetts Field took place on April 11, with Philadelphia in town. As the war in Europe continued, most fans were in a patriotic mood, and precisely at 3:30 P.M. both clubs marched solemnly across the outfield grass to the flagpole as the crowd stood at attention. As a detachment of 400 sailors from the Brooklyn Navy Yard stood by, a Naval Battalion band played the "Star-Spangled Banner" as the flag was raised. The Honorable Judge George Frefield, past grand master of the New York Masons, gave a short speech and then threw out the first ball; the new season was underway.

Robbie had every reason to believe his club would challenge for a second straight pennant in 1917. The Robins were healthy and confident, with the exception of an unsettled infield. (Third baseman Mike Mowrey was a salary holdout, and 29-year-old Albert La Vern Fabrique, called "Bunny" by his teammates, was handed the shortstop job, despite having only two big league games under his belt.) Wheezer Dell could not hold the Phillies in check, however, and dropped a 6–5 decision to Grover Alexander. Three days later Sherrod Smith was pounded 11–3, and Brooklyn was off to a poor start.

The rain and cold weather hindered Rube's ability to get his arm loose, and Robbie held him out of action until April 25. Then he threw five innings against

Boston before his shoulder tightened, and as in years past Robbie took no chances with his expensive veteran, waiting three weeks before calling on Rube again. With most of the hitters slumping miserably, Brooklyn had lost seven straight games by May 15, and Cheney struggled early against the Reds, giving up four hits, two hit batsmen, and heaving a wild pitch. With the Robins down 2–0, Rube entered the ballgame and went the rest of the way, allowing no runs. He banged out two singles himself and scored two runs, and assisted by Stengel's three-run homer, the Robins came back to win 6–2. From that date on, Rube was back in the regular rotation, on his way to another excellent season.

The year was steadily marked by some of the most outstanding performances of Rube's career, particularly in June and July. Robbie regularly matched him against the opposition's top hurler, an honor of sorts and a challenge Rube truly enjoyed. On June 21 he continued his remarkable mastery over Alexander with a 4–2 win (no small feat considering Alex was on his way to a third consecutive 30-win season in 1917), and four days later he defeated Boston and Dick Rudolph 3–2. He beat Philly again, 5–3, three days later, this time against Eppa Jeptha Rixey. Only Olson's error, which paved the way for all three runs, cost him a shutout. Rube got that shutout on July 14, two-hitting Pittsburgh and Bullet Miller 1–0 on the strength of Cutshaw's RBI single in the second inning.

Although Brooklyn hovered around the .500 mark for much of the season, it remained only nine or ten games behind league-leading New York, and the Robins believed they could make a run for the flag if things fell into place. In late July they began a modest seven game winning streak, topped off by Rube's 3–2 win over the Cardinals in St. Louis, but the Giants, too, kept winning, and refused to yield any ground.

Even in defeat that summer Rube was often spectacular, particularly against Jim "Hippo" Vaughn and Chicago. On July 10 at Ebbetts Field, the Cubs won 1–0, each pitcher throwing a four-hitter, as one of Rube's old teammates from the Giants did most of the damage. Larry Doyle singled and was sacrificed to second by Fred Merkle, and moments later he scored the only run of the game as Hi Myers dropped a fly ball and then threw wildly to the plate. Three weeks later on August 8, this time at Chicago's Weeghman Park (the place was not renamed Wrigley Field until several years later), Vaughn again shut out Rube and the Robins, this time on a two-hitter, 2–0. Vaughn, on his way to 23 wins in 1917, retired 26 in a row until the ninth inning, and Rube allowed only seven hits himself. On August 20, Rube lost 1–0 to the Pirates. Fittingly, his old nemesis Hans Wagner, now 43 years old and in the final year of a glorious career, led off the top of the 10th inning with a screaming double off the left-field wall, then scored on the ensuing sacrifice when Cutshaw threw over Daubert's head at first.

Late August saw an amazing string of extra-inning ballgames. On the twentieth, Pittsburgh beat Rube 1–0 in 10 innings. The next day the Robins and Pirates battled to a 3–3 tie, the game being called because of darkness after 13 innings. Then on the twenty-second the same two teams played for 22 innings,

Pittsburgh finally scoring the winning run, unearned, off Rube, who was the third Brooklyn pitcher of the day. The contest broke the National League record for longest game; the old record, of course, was the 1914 game in which Rube and Babe Adams had each gone the distance. In the three-game series, Pittsburgh and Brooklyn had played 45 innings of baseball.

Sunday baseball came to Brooklyn, at least temporarily, on July 1. The game between the Robins and Phillies was preceded by a concert and patriotic demonstration put on for the benefit of the "Militia of Mercy and kindred wartime societies."[27] After the show Ebbets ordered that the sale of tickets be halted and spectators be allowed to watch the ballgame for free, so that the borough's ban against professional sporting events on Sundays would not be violated. Patriotic fervor had its limits, perhaps; only 2,000 fans stuck around after the concert to watch the game.

Despite the lack of a close pennant race, a nice crowd turned out at the Polo Grounds on Tuesday, August 14, to see a doubleheader between the Giants and Robins. Ferdie Schupp beat Brooklyn 5–4 in the first game, but Rube was too tough in the second, allowing only five hits and winning 3–1. He struck out six and gave up only a ninth inning homer to ex–Cub Heinie Zimmerman in gaining his 15th win of the season. In the sixth, Stengel stroked a single off Tesreau, and when he tried to steal second his spikes came up near Fletcher's thigh. The two men began to swing at each other, and both benches emptied. Soon fights broke out between Giant and Robins fans in different sections of the grandstand, and it was 20 minutes before the "pugilistic conflagration" was brought under control in all corners.[28] To Rube it seemed that, in New York at least, some things never changed.

On August 25 the Cardinals came to Ebbets Field for a Saturday doubleheader, and Pfeffer and Rube each threw shutouts by scores of 12–0 and 4–0, allowing only seven hits between them. On Labor Day, Grover Alexander did them one better; he threw shutouts in *both* games, and the defeats all but eclipsed any hopes Brooklyn might have had of finishing in the first division, much less challenging for the pennant.

The Robins struggled offensively in 1917. Daubert was particularly disappointing, dropping 55 points from his previous year's batting average of .316. Fabrique failed miserably at shortstop, managing only a .205 average before being released to Toledo, never again to appear in the majors. George Cutshaw broke a rib in August and was gone for the rest of the year. Stengel hit .257, although he did lead the club in several categories. His erratic behavior both on and off the field grew too much for even Robinson to take, and after the season both he and Cutshaw were traded to Pittsburgh. At season's end the Robins found themselves with a record of 70 and 81 and in seventh place, 26½ games behind the Giants, who went on to lose the World Series to the White Sox.

In December, Robbie acquired pitchers Burleigh Grimes and Al Mamaux, along with shortstop Chuck Ward, in the Stengel deal. Since Robbie had twice resurrected Rube's career and had also salvaged Nap Rucker, he hoped to do the same for Grimes and Mamaux, who had a combined record of 5–27 in 1917. The *Sporting News* agreed. "Fans remember how Rube Marquard came to the Superbas late in 1915 and was as worthless a piece of junk as ever littered up a payroll. Aye, until nearly July 1, 1916, Marquard was as bad as in 1915, but Uncle Wilbert would get up in the middle of the night to assure perfect strangers that there was nothing the matter with Rube except his belief that he was hoodooed, and that if he ever won a good game he would be a star again. It fell out exactly that way.... He has been about as valuable a pitcher as the National League could show."[29] Robbie's efforts would prove to be successful again, particularly with Grimes. For the next 15 years, "Ol' Stubblebeard" would be one of the league's best pitchers, beginning with an 18-win season in 1918. Grimes was a master of the spitball; he was one of only a few who were "grandfathered" and allowed to continue throwing the pitch after "freak pitches" were banned. Mamaux, however, would not produce immediate dividends; he suffered a variety of health problems and appeared in only two games for Brooklyn that year, losing his only decision.

Rube had no desire to get into another salary dispute and was, along with rookie pitcher John Armstrong Russell, the very first player to sign a contract, agreeing to terms in mid–January. The National Commission had adopted a new form for contracts because of the war. They were to run for the scheduled season, however long it might be, instead of the former six months. If the schedules were curtailed as expected, the player's incomes were to be cut automatically in like proportion. The new contracts also expressly eliminated any reference to the Players' Fraternity; there was no new talk of forming another union.

But the bolstered pitching staff could not help an anemic offense, and the changes did little to improve Brooklyn's mark in 1918. The Robins got off to a horrible start at the Polo Grounds when Rube was shellacked for four hits and three runs and didn't last the first inning. The Giants won 6–4, then took the next three games to sweep the series. The Robins then dropped three games to Boston and two more to New York before Larry Cheney finally earned a victory against the Giants on April 27. But in losing their first nine games, the Robins had established a new league record and never recovered.

One highlight of an otherwise dismal season occurred on June 18 when the Pirates came to town. Brooklyn was in last place with a record of 15 and 27, Pittsburgh in fourth but 10 games out, and barely 1,000 fans turned out for the first game of the series. The *Times* noted that "the contest was sort of a family reunion, for it gave Brooklyn fans an opportunity to greet two of their erstwhile favorites, George Cutshaw and the ever-nonchalant Casey Stengel."[30] In the bottom of the first inning, Stengel took his position in right field, talking with his old buddy Cadore, who was watching the game from the Robin bullpen. Suddenly a small bird flew into the wall and fell stunned to the ground, and Stengel, unable to think of anything else to do, put the bird under his cap. When the inning was over, he jogged to the bench, having forgotten about his new friend. He was the first batter up and received a nice cheer from the crowd as he stepped into the box to face Rube. But suddenly, Stengel said later, "the bird commenced wiggling and I had to get rid of it."[31] He called time and stepped out. When he lifted his cap, the sparrow flew away as the fans laughed and cheered. Rube was as amused as anyone, but quickly induced Stengel to ground out to short. The Robins went on to win 1–0, Rube allowing only three hits and striking out five, including two pinch hitters in the top of the ninth.

But not many days went Rube's way in 1918. He thought that he was "bitten by the hoodoo jinx" all year long. Statistically at least, in terms of innings pitched, runs allowed, and strikeouts, his season virtually mirrored 1917. But he received very little offensive support, and his won-loss record plummeted to a disastrous 9–18 (four of his victories came on shutouts). Those losses, embarrassingly enough, led the league.

World War I took its toll on the Brooklyn club. Pitchers Sherrod Smith, Leon Cadore, Johnny Miljus, and recent acquisition Chuck Ward enlisted, and Ed Pfeffer was drafted. By June 20 only 16 players were on the roster. There was some talk among league officials of consolidating both major leagues into one circuit, or perhaps canceling the season altogether. While President Woodrow Wilson decreed in July that there was "no necessity at all for stopping or curtailing the baseball schedule," Secretary of War Newton Baker recommended the season be at least shortened, and the owners voted to do just that. It was agreed that the regular season would end on the first of September and the World Series would begin immediately thereafter. Ebbetts made plans to convert his ballpark into a storage facility for the army if the war continued into the fall and winter, and other owners made similar plans for their stadiums. If that happened, there would be no major league baseball at all in 1919.

In the summer of 1918 Rube was listed as 28 years old, although he was actually 31, and while he was not likely to be drafted, he felt the call to do his part in the war effort. (The government had also issued a "work or fight" order, giving "nonessential" individuals, such as ballplayers, until July 1 to find defense-related work or be subject to induction.) On July 20, while with the Robins in Chicago, Rube enlisted in the United States Naval Reserve Forces as a machinist's mate, first class, for a three-year hitch. When the season was over, he reported for active duty and training at the Mine Sweep Division at Tompkinsville, New York. He was released from active duty three months later, just after the war ended, but fulfilled his obligation in the reserves. He earned an honorable discharge on September 30, 1921, and he was proud of his military service for the rest of his life.

Chapter 14

"I Guess I'm the Fall Guy"

By winning seven of its first eight games in 1919, Brooklyn surprised everyone, but the biggest news in the city was that its aldermen passed an ordinance repealing Sunday "blue laws" by a vote of 64 to 0. Beginning May 4, professional baseball would be played on the Sabbath, provided the games started no later than 2 P.M. and were conducted in an appropriate manner, free from rowdyism or excessive revelry. "I am going to add a commandment to the ten, making it eleven, and here it is," said Brooklyn borough president Frank Dowling. "Thou shalt play ball on Sunday but thou shalt not be disorderly."[1]

Rube was given the honor of taking the mound on May 4 before an overflow crowd of 25,000 Brooklyn fans, and he came through with an outstanding performance, beating Boston 6–2. The Braves scored their runs in the bottom of the first when Robin third baseman Jack Sheehan allowed Buck Herzog's grounder to go through his legs, plating two, but Rube allowed only five hits after that, no runner getting past second base. He helped out offensively as well, cracking two singles and driving in two runs.

A week later Rube threw against the Giants at the Polo Grounds, leaving after seven innings with the score tied at two. Although the Giants eventually won the game on Larry Doyle's home run, Rube always took great satisfaction in pitching well against his old club and the manager who had let him go. He continued to exhibit good stuff for his next six starts, compiling a 3–3 record with a fine ERA just over 2.25. But Brooklyn played mediocre baseball, going into the June 10 game at Cincinnati with a record of just one game over .500.

Rube was matched that unusually warm day against his old foe Slim Sallee. Reds leadoff hitter Morris Rath, at 5'8" one of the tiniest men in the league, greeted Rube with a homer, one of only four in his career. The Robins tied the score in the fourth when Konetchy singled in new outfielder Tommy Griffith, but in the bottom of the inning the Reds erupted for three runs. Heinie Groh and Edd Roush singled, Greasy Neale doubled, and when Ivan Olson booted Rube Bressler's grounder Cincinnati led 4–1.

Rube led off the top of the fifth inning by drilling a long drive to the gap in right center field. He rounded second at top speed, intent on trying for third, but his spikes caught on the bag and threw him off balance. He fell to the ground awkwardly, breaking his left leg. He was in severe pain as players from both teams gathered around him. Finally an ambulance came through the outfield gate, and he was lifted onto a stretcher. He was taken to the hospital, where his leg was set, but he was lost for the season.

Within the week the Robins continued their western trip while Rube returned to New York, but the news there was not good, either. Rube had hoped that, with his injury, he and Blossom could at least spend the rest of the summer together, but she began to make plans to tour again instead.

"I asked her to quit the stage," Rube said many years later. "I told her I could give her anything she wanted."

"No," she said. "Show business is show business."

"Well," I said, "baseball is mine."[2]

The quarreling increased, and each side made hurtful, and probably unfounded, accusations. By July they had separated for good.

Rube bided his time. He invested for a while in a cafe in Brooklyn, but he had no interest in the business's day-to-day operations and soon sold out. On crutches, he took to visiting local racetracks, where he enjoyed watching the horses run. He was not necessarily a heavy gambler, but he liked the excitement, the crowds, the atmosphere. He became friends with owners of several tracks, often exchanging ballgame tickets for passes to the private clubs frequented by owners, jockeys, trainers and track officials. He was no longer a Broadway star, and his baseball career was temporarily on hold, but he still possessed considerable celebrity status and very much enjoyed it.

Meanwhile the Robins floundered, leading the league in errors and finishing the season with a record of 69–71. Their fifth place finish marked the third year in a row, since the pennant of 1916, that they wound up in the second division. The Reds, led by the batting champion Roush, took the pennant by nine games over New York and prepared to face the mighty White Sox in the 1919 World Series.

That Series of course was clouded from the start. Rumors circulated freely that gamblers had convinced the Sox (and perhaps some of the Reds, as well) to throw at least a few games, but details would not come forth for nearly a year. Rube did not attend the Series. But the following story appeared later in Joe Williams' column in the *Sporting News*:

> Landis, if he were alive, wouldn't like this and perhaps Chandler, the new Landis, won't like it either, but I feel disposed to tell you a baseball story that has a race track background. It is a story that comes to me from Joe

14. "I Guess I'm the Fall Guy"

Judge, one of Washington's coaches, and it reaches back to the crooked world series, 1919, when the White Sox sold out to the gamblers. Judge told me the story in the Washington dressing room the other day.

"I'm out to the track, Jamaica, I think it was, in the fall of that year, with Rube Marquard, the old left-handed pitcher. We both like to play the horses and we are going about our business in a casual, simple sort of way when all of a sudden a fellow stops Rube and says: 'Bet all you can on Cincinnati to win the first two games.' You see, Cincinnati is playing the White Sox in this series. And then he says: 'Take all you win on the first two games and bet it back on Cincinnati to win the series.'

"Well, I am speechless. I know the White Sox. I see 'em play all season. I never see a better ball club. And I never hear a fellow talk with so much confidence. I mean, like saying Cincinnati can't miss winning the first two games. So I say to Rube, I say, that guy's practically telling you the series is fixed. And Rube says to me that's exactly what he's telling me, and do you know who he is?

"Well, it turned out to be Arnold Rothstein, notorious gambler who later was pistoled to death because he welched on a bet, the man who definitely fixed the series, no matter what anybody tells you to the contrary.

"So when I hear this," Judge says to me, "I go to Griff [Clark Griffith, owner of the Washington ballclub] and tell him. Griff laughs in my face. The series opens the next day. He sees the opening game, comes back overnight, calls me in. 'You were right,' he says, 'the series is fixed.' I'm not sure but I think he started the investigation which led to the blow-off. And even to this day I don't think I would have any doubts about that series if I hadn't been to the track with Rube and met the man who was later identified as Rothstein."[3]

Whether this exchange between Rube, Rothstein, and Judge actually took place is impossible to say. Yet Rothstein was no stranger in baseball circles and at one point was a partner with John McGraw in a New York poolhall. And Judge, a fine player with the Senators for most of his 20-year major league career, was born in Brooklyn and was a frequent visitor to metropolitan racetracks. If Rube was told of the fix, he obviously kept the information to himself.

Wilbert Robinson believed that his team needed a change of scenery and a fresh start in 1920. He took the Robins to New Orleans rather than Florida for spring training, and while most experts counted them out of the pennant race before the season began, Robbie was quietly optimistic. He expected good things from 27-year-old newcomer Pete Kilduff at second base. Wheat, Myers, and Griffith still formed a solid, hard-hitting outfield. And as always, the key was the pitching. Burleigh Grimes was the ace, and Pfeffer, Mamaux, and Cadore seemed ready to fulfill their promise. There was no reason, Robbie knew, why Rube could not return to form. Rube had never been seriously injured before, though, and the uncertainty of his recovery compounded by an unstable home life caused Robbie to again bring Rube along slowly. Rube was not the stopper he once was; he was, however, a committed team player who, if nothing else, understood his role. As the club's fourth or fifth starter, he was no longer expected to pitch 250 innings. But he would be called upon every week or so and was expected to provide consistent, quality outings if the club was to compete. And Robbie, like McGraw and other managers, looked for every possible advantage for his club. He persuaded Eddie Bennett, the humpbacked mascot of the White Sox, to relocate to Brooklyn, in hopes that the good luck he seemed to possess would transfer as well.

For the strategy to work, Brooklyn needed some help, and it got it. Cincinnati got off to a sluggish start and never fully righted, winning 14 fewer games than the year before (even though the schedule was expanded back to 154 games). The Giants, led by new star Ross Youngs but missing Frankie Frisch, out significantly with appendicitis, had a good club but were a year or so away from excellence. Chicago and Pittsburgh had their troubles as well and did not challenge as expected. Brooklyn took first place on June 1, lost it a day later, and regained it a month after that. The Robins battled throughout July and August, finally moving into the top for good on September 9. By the end of the month, they were within striking distance of the flag, and on the twenty-sixth, Rube shut out the Giants (his only whitewash of the year). The Robins clinched the flag a day later. Expected by most observers to finish near the bottom of the standings again, they had instead won the pennant "when no one was looking."

Rube appeared in 28 ballgames, finishing with a record of 10–7. He pitched 189 innings, 100 or so less than in his workhorse days with the Giants. His ERA was up slightly at 3.23, but he struck out 89 hitters, and his strikeouts-per-game ratio of 4.22 was fourth best in the league. His control was once again outstanding; he walked only 50 men all year long, fifth lowest among NL starters, and, as in years past, he saved his best stuff for the stretch, winning three straight in September. He was delighted to play in another World Series, and he was thrilled that the opponents would be the Indians of his hometown of Cleveland.

The Indians' triumphant season had been marred by the highest tragedy. On August 16, in the fifth inning of a game against the Yankees in New York, 29-year-old shortstop Ray Chapman was hit in the head by a submarine fastball from Carl Mays. He died the next day. Chapman's replacement was Harry Lunte, but Lunte was himself injured in early September, and minor leaguer Joe Sewell, an Alabaman only 21 years of age, was brought up to play shortstop. Sewell had fewer than 100 professional games under his belt but hit .329 for the Indians down the stretch, although no one could make Cleveland fans forget the popular Chapman. Technically, Sewell did not qualify for the World Series, since he was not on the roster by September 1, but Charles Ebbetts waived any objection and Sewell was allowed to play.

While it was the first World Series for Cleveland in the modern era, they were not short on championship experience. They were led by player-manager Tris Speaker, who hit .388 in 1920, and third baseman Larry Gardner, both of whom played for the old Red Sox. (Smoky Joe Wood was also a platoon outfielder with the club.) The Indians boasted no fewer than eight .300 hitters, including outfielders Elmer Smith and Charlie Jamieson and catcher Steve O'Neill, and their team batting average of .303 was nearly 30 points higher than Brooklyn's. Right-handed pitcher Jim Bagby led the staff with 31 wins, and Stan Coveleski and Ray Caldwell won 24 and 20 games respectively. Cleveland had won the pennant when Chicago faltered, due in large part to the fact that key Sox players were busy testifying before the Grand Jury about the previous year's Series, and the Indian pennant was seen as "a triumph for honest ball and hailed with satisfaction everywhere."[4] Cleveland was thus the sentimental favorite, and the oddsmakers installed them as 6–5 favorites.

For the second year in a row, the Series was a best of nine affair, and the Robins were fortunate that the first three games would take place in Brooklyn. Cleveland was supposed to have them, but construction of additional bleachers at League Park was delayed, and the schedule was switched. The first game was set for October 5, and Speaker took the unusual step of having his club travel to Brooklyn on the night train, arriving at 8:00 A.M. and then proceeding directly to the ballpark. There they changed into new blue uniforms with black crepe armbands, in memory of Chapman, and took batting practice in a stiff, cold wind. The weather was "much too cold for baseball," wrote Damon Runyon, one of 400 press corps members, and caused the players "to move sluggishly, like ants."[5] The capacity crowd, however, was primed for the game, and cheered heartily when it was announced that Rube would pitch for their Robins, facing Coveleski. One lady in the crowd cheered especially hard for Rube: his new ladyfriend, a stunningly beautiful woman named Naomi Malone, who was wrapped in a mink stole, hat, and stylish white gloves. She was seated in a special box section reserved for players' wives, where she was photographed for the papers.

Joe Evans led off for Cleveland and grounded to short. Second baseman Bill Wambsganss, routinely referred to by his friends and in the boxscores as "Wamby," lined out to Wheat in left field, and the Rube caught Speaker looking at strike three with a wicked curveball. In the second inning, however, the Indians broke through. "Tioga George" Burns (no relation to the Giant of the same name), dropped a Texas leaguer between Kilduff and Konetchy, the wind blowing the ball just out of the reach of both, and when Koney finally retrieved it he threw wildly to Olson at second. For some reason Wheat, in left field, failed to back up the throw, and when it sailed over Olson's head Burns raced all the way around to score. Gardner grounded out but Joe Wood worked Rube for a walk, then took third on Sewell's single. O'Neill then slapped a grounder just over the bag at third for a double, scoring Wood. Coveleski hit into a double play to end the inning, but the Indians led 2–0.

They scored again in the fourth. Wood doubled but Sewell grounded out, and with first base open most expected Rube to walk O'Neill to bring up the

Rube and Naomi Wigley Marquard. Photo courtesy Charles Guggenheimer collection.

weak-hitting Coveleski. But Robbie allowed Rube to pitch to O'Neill, and the gamble backfired. On a 2–1 pitch O'Neill stroked a double to the wall in right, and the Cleveland lead was now three. Rube was lifted for a pinch-hitter two innings later, but Coveleski was too tough for Brooklyn. He allowed a meaningless run in the eighth, cruising to the 3–1 victory. Rube had pitched well, allowing only five hits and two earned runs, but Covey was better, allowing only five hits himself and going the distance.

"I have no alibi to make," said Rube after the game. I was pitching good ball, but so was Coveleski.... Their hits happened to come at the moments when they meant runs."[6] World Series columnist Babe Ruth, now with the Yankees, predicted that Cleveland would go on to win the championship. "If Brooklyn cannot win with Marquard on the slab," he wrote, "Brooklyn cannot win the series."[7] Robbie was philosophical. "We did not get a single break in the entire game," he said. "This first blow hasn't disheartened us a bit, and we will go back at them just as confident as if we had won."[8] And come back they did, winning the second game 3–0 behind Grimes, and the third 2–1 behind Sherry Smith. Brooklyn led the Series two games to one as the teams boarded the train for

Cleveland (minus mascot Bennett, an oversight which some players viewed as a bad omen) and Rube anxiously awaited playing in front of his family and friends for the first time since he had left the sandlots 14 years before. His return, however, was less than triumphant. In fact, it was humiliating, but had nothing to do with his pitching performance.

On Saturday morning, October 9, Rube walked into the lobby of the Hotel Winton, where the Robins were staying. He was to meet his brother Herbert before he headed for the ballpark and pregame practice. While waiting, he had a conversation with a Brooklyn acquaintance who needed extra tickets for the games. The discussion was overheard by a plain-clothed Cleveland city detective named Soukoup, who promptly arrested Rube on charges of ticket scalping. Rube was taken into custody and transported to the police station, and while police court prosecutor Stanton filled out an application for a formal warrant Rube was allowed to appeal to police chief Frank W. Smith for his release. Smith agreed, issuing this statement to the crowd of reporters who had gotten wind of the story: "Under the circumstances we could not delay Marquard from reporting at the ball park. That would hardly have been sportsmanlike."[9] He approved the application but delayed serving the warrant until Monday morning, when Rube promised to appear for arraignment. Rube was hardly the only person in trouble; at least seven other people, including the former mayor of Somerset, were also arrested in Cleveland hotels by undercover detectives that morning as part of a crackdown on scalping of World Series tickets. The effort was the brainchild of E. S. Barnard, business manager of the Indians, who desired no irregularities in the wake of the 1919 fiasco. Rube made it to the park in time for 12:30 batting practice, where he had to advise Robbie of the morning's events. (Charles Ebbetts, NL president John Heydler, and Judge Landis, all in town for the Series, sat by grimly and only said that they would allow the legal system to run its course and would monitor the situation as it developed.) The manager was not pleased, but naturally turned his attention to the upcoming ballgame.

The entire city of Cleveland was excited about its team. "The first world's series game ever played in Cleveland ... means a lot to us who think the Fifth City is the greatest city in the world," wrote longtime local sportswriter Henry P. Edwards. "There is no city in all America that owns more red blooded citizens than this, the Fifth City, and it has been a source of deep regret for all of us that since 1879, when Cleveland went into organized baseball, we could not win a pennant."[10] Mayor FitzGerald issued a proclamation honoring the club, and directed that at precisely 12 noon, just before the teams took the field, automobile sirens and factory whistles be sounded in unison as a show of support. Indian fans from throughout Ohio were present for the Series; it was estimated that 7,000 out-of-towners had arrived.

The next four games of the Series would be played in Cleveland. Fans whose names were selected randomly had to purchase two grandstand tickets for all four games, at prices ranging from $26.40 to $52.30. The brand new bleacher section, in right field and running along Lexington Avenue, provided 2,000 additional seats which went on sale at eight windows the morning of each game. Lines for the precious tickets were very long, and only those willing to spend the night were able to buy them, although the warm weather made the task bearable for most. Hundreds of disappointed fans who could not see the game hung around the park all day anyway, listening to the crowd and calling to fans inside who might relay information down as to the progress of the game. One man watched the action from the topmost ledge of the nearby East Ohio building, dangling his legs over the side of a 100-foot precipice and making those who noticed him very nervous. And many fans gathered in area hotels or taller apartment buildings, and even on the fire escape of the Masonic Temple, just to get a view of the park's scoreboard.

Coveleski started his second game of the Series, opposed by Cadore. The Robins went down in order in the first, but the Indians punched across two runs on three hits in their half of the inning. When the first two Tribe hitters in the second inning also reached base, Robbie pulled Cadore and called on Mamaux, who got out of the inning. But in the third, Wambsganss and Speaker lined singles, and Robbie brought in Rube. He walked to "the hill under trying conditions, granting that he has any sensibilities," noted the *Plain Dealer*. "He was laboring under what surely must have meant some mental distress, due to the fact that he had been taken into custody for scalping tickets."[11] Perhaps it was true, for Burns greeted him with a single to left and both runners scored, and the Indians led 4–0. Rube pitched another two innings, allowing only one more hit and no runs, but Brooklyn's bats were quiet, and they fell by a final score of 5–1. The Series was now tied at two games apiece.

The next morning Rube was arraigned in police court in front of Judge Silbert. Standing in front of the bench alongside an attorney named Nate Becherman, he entered a plea of not guilty. The case was initially set for trial in five days, but when the judge was informed that the baseball teams might be back in Brooklyn, he moved it up to the very next day. Rube had no comment for the press, but John Heydler (who was also in court as an interested observer) stated that Rube's share of the Series gate receipts would be withheld until after the case was settled and that "if he is found guilty the league itself will take action."[12] What that meant was unclear, but the rumor was that Rube faced expulsion from the National League and possible banishment from baseball.

That afternoon's game was notable, not just because Cleveland won again, this time by a score of 8–1 behind "Sarge" Bagby, but because of the three remarkable records the club set in the process. Burleigh Grimes started for the Robins and had a rough first inning. Charlie Jamieson poked a single off Konetchy's glove at first. Wambsganss tried to bunt but fouled it off, then trickled one to short for an infield hit. Speaker bunted down the third-base line, but Grimes fell as he picked it up and could make no play, and the bases were loaded for cleanup hitter Elmer Smith. Smith swung and missed at two sharp spitters, and Grimes then threw low for ball one. He came back with a fastball, belt-high and over the plate, and Smith deposited it over the wall in right field (in fact, all the way over Lexington Avenue) for the first grand slam home run in World Series history.

There was more cause for Cleveland celebration in the fourth inning. Doc Johnston (brother of Brooklyn player Jimmy) singled up the middle, Grimes nearly getting beaned in the head by the drive. Sewell grounded out, Johnston moving to second, and O'Neill was walked intentionally to get to the pitcher Bagby. He lifted a fly ball to right field, ordinarily an easy out. But the ball carried just far enough to reach the first row of the temporary bleachers. It was the first Series homer hit by a pitcher, and the Tribe led 7–0. The badly shaken Grimes gave up a single to Jamieson and was pulled in favor of Clarence Mitchell, who retired the side.

If anyone had any doubts about things going Cleveland's way, they were put to rest in the top of the next inning. Kilduff and Miller singled, and when Speaker fired his throw to third base the runners held at first and second. Up came Mitchell, to the surprise of most, who figured Robbie would pinch hit for him. But Mitchell could handle the bat fairly well, a fact not lost on Cleveland, who played him to pull to right. With a full count the baserunners took off, and Mitchell lined a drive toward right center, just to the right of Wambsganss. It looked like a sure hit, but Wamby took a quick couple of steps and snared the ball. He kept running toward second and doubled off Kilduff, now nearing third base. Shortstop Sewell saw Miller still running toward second and hollered "Tag him, Bill! Tag him!"[13] As Wamby turned around, Miller stopped and stood open-mouthed, as if in a daze of disbelief, as Wamby tagged him with the baseball for the third out. Wamby knew immediately, of course, that he had completed an unassisted triple play and ran off the field to the dugout. It took most fans a second or two to realize what had happened, Wamby recalled later, but finally "the cheering started and quickly got louder and louder and louder. By the time I got to the bench it was bedlam, straw hats flying onto the field, people yelling themselves hoarse, my teammates pounding me on the back."[14] Cleveland went on to win 8–1, and the crowd of over 26,000 "could well congratulate themselves on their good fortune in having witnessed the three most notable achievements ever displayed in a single ballgame."[15]

With Brooklyn now trailing 3–2 in the Series and two more games scheduled in Cleveland, things looked bleak for the Robins. Rube had little time to worry about that, however; his case went to trial the next morning. Now represented by National League attorney Heintzman, Rube arrived early and nodded toward John Heydler, who sat tersely in the back of the courtroom. Prosecutor Stanton called Detective Soukoup as his first witness, and Soukoup testified:

> I was standing in the lobby of the Hotel Winton, when I heard someone say, 'Hello Rube, can you fix me up with some tickets?'

Rube said, "Yes, I've got a series of box seats which you can have for $350." He pulled out six tickets from his pocket and held them up to the man who approached him. The man said he did not want them at that price, and walked away. Marquard walked over to the cigar counter and another man walked over to him. I saw Marquard pull out the tickets, but at that time the cigar clerk tipped Marquard off that I was there, and Marquard put the tickets back in his pocket. I walked over to Rube and said, "You're the biggest rube in this hotel." I then asked him to come to the office, meaning the police station.[16]

Soukup further testified that at the station Rube told him, "I guess I'm the fall guy" and said that he had purchased the tickets for $275 and intended to make $75 on the deal. Soukup admitted under Heintzman's cross-examination that Rube had not offered the tickets for sale until he was approached by the man in the lobby and that the police had not specifically targeted Rube as a potential ticket scalper before the incident that morning.[17] Rube took the stand in his own defense. "I was waiting in the lobby for my brother," he testified. "He was coming from Youngstown and he asked me to get him some tickets for the game. While I was standing there, a Brooklyn man whom I knew well came up and said, 'Rube, have you got any tickets?' I replied in a joking way, 'Yes, here's six you can have for $50.' I pulled the tickets from my pocket, but immediately replaced them. I didn't try to profiteer at all."[18]

Judge Silbert did not buy Rube's explanation and found him guilty as charged. "I agree with Soukoup's statements," he said, "and feel that Rube has indeed been a rube, but think that hereafter he will stick to the game and try to keep it clean.... I am satisfied that Marquard violated the law and the spirit of the law, but I believe that he has been punished enough by being written up more than any presidential candidate, and feel that this has been a lesson to him."[19] He fined him one dollar and imposed costs of $3.80, which Rube immediately paid.

Outside the courthouse Rube laughed off the conviction, still insisting he had only been joking about selling tickets and that the minuscule penalty handed down "completely exonerated him."[20] But Charles Ebbetts and John Heydler grimly announced that team and league officials would decide upon any disciplinary action in the near future. They quietly informed Robbie that Rube was not to pitch again in the Series.

The Indians were now bursting with confidence. Walter "The Great" Mails shut out the Robins that afternoon 1–0 on a three-hitter, Cleveland scoring the game's lone run on a Speaker single and Burns RBI double in the sixth. They wrapped it up the next day, winning 3–0 behind Coveleski's third victory (and third five-hitter) of the Series. While the city of Cleveland went wild with celebration and their champions were showered with honors — Wambsganss, Speaker, and Coveleski in particular were rewarded with sets of diamond cufflinks and gold watches — Charles Ebbetts made an announcement. "I'm through with

Marquard absolutely," he said. "If anyone else wants him, they can have him. But Marquard will never again put on a Brooklyn uniform."[21] John Heydler stated that Rube's share of Series proceeds, $3,951, would be withheld and that league officials would meet to determine if any further action might be warranted, including possible banishment from baseball.

CHAPTER 15

Baseball's Most Picturesque Figure

Rube did not contest Blossom's petition for divorce in the fall of 1920. She was granted custody of Richard, Jr., now seven years old, although it was understood that the boy would spend much of his time with Rube's sister Hattie, who still lived in Ohio, when his famous parents were on the road. Blossom formed a stage partnership with a charismatic singer from Milwaukee named Benny Fields and continued to tour steadily. Rube and Naomi announced their engagement, although wedding plans were put on hold until the league powers decided whether Rube still had a baseball career.

It was a rough time for ballplayers in trouble. On October 22, just 10 days after the World Series ended, a Cook County grand jury handed down indictments of the eight White Sox involved in the 1919 scandal. On November 12 the owners comprising the National Commission decided that they needed help in policing the game and named Judge Landis their commissioner. They gave him a seven-year contract at $50,000 per year and reluctantly delegated to him absolute authority to act in "the best interests of baseball." While Landis did not formally take office until after the first of the year, his influence was felt immediately. He made no secret that he would deal, and deal harshly, with any disciplinary matters that were not resolved by the owners. In fact, the next spring he acted quickly and suspended the eight White Sox awaiting trial. Phillies infielder Eugene Paulette (who was suspected of dealing with gamblers in St. Louis) and Giant star Benny Kauff (who was charged, but not convicted, of auto theft) were also banned.

In view of Landis' drive to "clean up baseball" by eliminating undesirables, or even those who were merely suspected of an offense, it seems reasonable to assume that Rube would have faced a similar fate had the National Commission not acted. It decided that the loss of the World Series proceeds, in addition to the personal embarrassment Rube had suffered in his hometown, was enough punishment and elected not to forward the case to Landis. But on December 15, Ebbetts made good on his vow that Rube was through with the Robins and traded him to Cincinnati for pitcher Walter "Dutch" Ruether. But, as was often the case when Rube was in the news, there was controversy.

Ruether, from Alameda, California, was 27 years old and a veteran of three big league seasons. In the Reds' championship season of 1919, he had 19 victories, and he had one more in the Series. His record of 16–12 in 1920 included five shutouts, and he was regarded by most as a star on the rise. He had problems with his temper, however, and had been suspended by manager Pat Moran during the season for ignoring team rules. When the Reds, on top of the league on September 1, slumped and finished in third place, he became available. Still, the Cincinnati fans believed that Ruether would mature as he grew older and become a big winner, and they were unhappy with the trade. They voiced their opinions in letters to Cincinnati newspapers and calls to the Reds' front office, but once done, of course, the deal was final.

National baseball publications were of the opinion that the Reds had been taken. Although Rube was "baseball's most picturesque figure," said *Baseball* magazine, "on the face of it this trade would seem to favor Brooklyn, for Ruether is in his prime while Marquard is unquestionably on the down grade."[1] *The Sporting News* called Rube "one of the most likable fellows in the game," but said "the odds were against" his returning to form. "For the Rube has been in the big show a dozen years, and he has lived, too, as he went along, and he is not the enduring, steel-armed youth who pitched so many winners in a row, or pitched so many extra-inning triumphs in his prime." It took note of the public outcry, as well, noting that "Rube will be about as welcome in Cincinnati as a prohibition enforcement agent."[2]

Despite fan reaction to the trade, Rube looked forward to a new start in Cincinnati, both on the field and off. He knew from his early days in New York that the only way to please the paying customers was to come through on the mound, and when Moran assured him that he was expected to play an important role on the Reds' staff, he worked harder than ever to prepare himself physically for the season. Then just as the 1921 season began, he and Naomi were married in Cincinnati.

It was not the smoothest of events. The ceremony was originally scheduled for April 22 in Pittsburgh, but the clerk of court turned the couple away because Rube could not produce a certified copy of his divorce decree from Blossom. Then Naomi's mother fell ill, and she returned to Baltimore to care for her. Finally the vows were exchanged in front of Mayor John Harper of Loveland, Ohio, on April 26, as the Reds began the first home stand of the season. Naomi's photograph and the unusual events surrounding the "rather turbulent conjugal voyage of Rube Marquard" were featured in the Baltimore *Sun*.[3]

Naomi provided Rube the constant, reassuring presence that he needed. She never missed a home game and was waiting for him when he returned home. As much as he had loved Blossom, he hated the fact that she would not compromise

Mary and Wilbert Robinson, Naomi and Rube Marquard. Photo courtesy Charles Guggenheimer collection.

her career for a stable home life, even after the baby arrived. Naomi adored her new husband and was devoted to him totally. They were constant companions and the best of friends, and while the marriage produced no children, they remained happily married until her death in 1954.

Rube's new manager with the Reds had some impressive credentials. Moran had played 14 years in the big leagues, his intelligence and hustle overcoming a mediocre bat. He led Philadelphia to the 1915 title in his first year as manager and did the same thing four years later in Cincinnati. (Mathewson had managed only through 1918, when he went off to the war in France.) Moran was a disciplinarian of sorts, although almost anyone would be when compared to Wilbert Robinson. Moran expected his players to work hard, follow the rules, and conduct themselves as professionals. Rube had no problems with a little discipline and looked forward to the challenges Moran would give him.

The effort paid off, for Rube enjoyed a very productive year in 1921, winning 17 while losing 14. He appeared in 39 ballgames and threw 266 innings, the highest totals since 1914, his last year with the Giants. Since the recent emergence of Babe Ruth as a full-time slugger and the introduction of the new jackrabbit baseball, the game was quickly changing to power contests that the fans craved and came to demand. Earned run averages, of course, suffered because of it; still,

Rube's ERA of 3.39 was excellent and less than a run higher than the 2.59 mark of the leagues' leader, "Spittin' Bill" Doak of the Cardinals.

Rube was part of a staff that included 19-game-winner Eppa Rixey and Dolf "The Pride of Havana" Luque, who won 17. But although the club had some fine hitters — outfielders Rube Bressler, Pat Duncan, and popular Edd Roush among them — the overall offensive production was weak. Cincinnati's team batting average of .278 was lowest in the NL, and not one Red finished among the leaders in any offensive category. (Roush hit .352, his first of three straight years over .350, but appeared in only 112 games and did not qualify for individual batting honors.) The Reds scored only 618 runs on the year, an average of just four per game, and somehow managed to hit only 20 home runs. The Reds finished in sixth place with a record of 70 and 83, ahead of Chicago and Philadelphia.

When the season ended, Rube and Naomi returned to New York to watch the Giants defeat Babe Ruth and the Yankees in the World Series, every game being played at the Polo Grounds. Rube was pleasantly surprised at the fans' reaction to his appearance and happily signed autographs as in the old days. He was even more delighted to be invited by McGraw into the clubhouse to converse with the players. Despite the tempestuous parting some six years earlier, Rube and McGraw maintained a genuine affection for each other, and for a while during Rube's Brooklyn years, McGraw had unsuccessfully attempted to reacquire his former phenom.

Rube thought that he would finish his career in Cincinnati. He liked Moran — the feeling was mutual — and the fans warmed to him as well. The team was close-knit and, with the absence of Ruether and the cooperation of Rube, free from malcontents or troublemakers of any kind. Rube roomed on the road with his old friend from Brooklyn, Jake Daubert, who played first base for the Reds, and often he and Naomi enjoyed dinner at the Dauberts' during home stands. The nightlife of Cincinnati, of course, could not compare with the Broadway scene Rube had once been part of, but he liked the town and seemed content to settle down. (Cincinnati was known for its charm, and a good many Reds players decided to make it their permanent home when they retired.) Rube appreciated the fact that his father could travel down from Cleveland and see him play more often, and the newspapers never tired of reminding readers that Rube was another Ohio boy who had made good in the majors, like Tommy Leach, Cy Young, Ed Dalahanty, and others before him.

The embarrassment of the previous year's ticket scalping incident faded, and Rube was optimistic that Moran could lead the Reds back to glory if he got some batting production. Now a veteran of 13 full seasons, Rube had been fortunate enough to play in five World Series but had never been a world champion, and that was the incentive that continued to drive his career. In December, Moran made a move to improve the club offensively, acquiring George Burns and promising catcher Mike Gonzalez from the Giants, and rumors flew that more deals were imminent. Much to Rube's surprise and disappointment, however, he was one of the players involved.

On February 20, 1922, the Reds sent Rube and $500 to the Boston Braves for pitcher Jack Scott and shortstop Bill Koph. The Braves, owned by George W. Grant and managed by Fred Mitchell, were undoubtedly the league's poorest team. Since the miracle championship of 1914, the club had steadily declined, finishing second in 1915, third in 1916, and settling into the second division four years in a row. In 1921, the Boston Braves managed to win as many games as they lost and reached fourth place in the standings, but it would prove to be only a temporary ascent.

While Rube had no hopes that the Braves would seriously challenge for a championship in the near future, he was determined to prove that there was still plenty of life left in his arm. He reported to Florida on time and in shape, and, in what was now a familiar task, set about proving to his manager that he could be counted on for the upcoming season. Naomi was with him, of course, and he took pride in introducing her around; after all these years in the league he knew most of the players on sight. He especially enjoyed hooking up again with Babe Ruth, whose Yankees trained nearby. The Babe had signed a new three-year contract in March at $50,000 per year (although technically he was still under suspension for illegal barnstorming the previous fall) and was in his boisterous, outrageous prime. He had very little interest in training, and while he could not convince Rube to join him on any of his late-night excursions, he met him regularly on the golf course. The Babe insisted on playing for $50 per hole, and while that was a substantial amount of money to Rube, he was too prideful to turn his friend down, and the two played friendly, if expensive, matches all spring. In later years Rube loved to recall that he enjoyed setting up the Babe during exhibition games by telling him what pitch was coming — and then throwing the opposite. "That really burned him up," Rube said, smiling.[4]

Rube was given every opportunity with the Braves to assume the role of ace of the staff. In 1922 he took his regular turn on the mound, starting 24 games and appearing in 15 more. But the results were far less than he or Mitchell expected. His ERA ballooned to over 5 runs per game, by far the highest figure of his career. He allowed 12 home runs, the most ever, and for the first time he walked more hitters (66) than he struck out (57). He managed to win 11 games, but the club sunk to last place; the Braves won only 53 games and were the only major league team to lose 100.

But there came some unexpected good news during the off-season when it was announced that new owners had taken control of the Braves, a group that included none other than Christy Mathewson. Matty had been in extremely poor health since his return from France, suffering from the effects of a form of tuberculosis, and had been for the most part confined to his home at Saranac Lake in northern New York. There he partook of the "Adirondack cottage cure," an experimental nondrug treatment program consisting largely of bed rest, relaxation, and plenty of crisp mountain air. Matty was an excellent and conscientious patient but soon grew bored and restless with the inactivity. He belonged in baseball, a fact not lost on his friend John McGraw. He was free to come back to the Giants and assume coaching duties at any time, but because of the constant travel and the added stress of a pennant race (the Giants were in the process of winning four pennants in a row), his doctors advised against it. Now in February one Emil E. Fuchs, a former deputy attorney general, legal counsel to the Giants, and magistrate criminal court judge, purchased the Braves along with banker James McDonough, sportsman and entrepreneur Charles Levine, and, at the urging of McGraw, Mathewson.

In the subsequent front-office reorganization, Matty was installed as president and guaranteed as much or as little responsibility as his health would allow. He was ecstatic with his new role. "I never thought when I saw my first big league game in Boston back in 1899, when I paid 75 cents to see Kid Nichols pitch against Cy Young at the Old Walpole Street Grounds, that I'd one day be President of the Braves," he said. "For two years I've been trying to come back to baseball, living for the day, dreaming about it constantly. So when Judge Fuchs, whom I have known as someone who loves the game, gave me this opportunity, I grasped it."5

Rube was thrilled to learn that Matty was now associated with the franchise, but at Opening Day festivities in April 1923, he was shocked to see how his hero had weakened physically. Once tall and handsome and blessed with nearly unparalleled athletic abilities, Matty was now stooped and pale and 40 pounds lighter than in his playing days. Most of the younger players on the club could scarcely believe that this man was regarded as one of the greatest pitchers of all time — some said the greatest. He had lost none of his competitive nature, however, and Rube laughed as Matty amazed the unsuspecting with his skillful demonstrations of chess, checkers, and poker, taking their money in the process.

But Mathewson could do little about the terrible ballclub he had purchased. The Braves lost 100 games for the second straight year, although they escaped the cellar when Philadelphia managed to lose 104. Undoubtedly inspired by the presence of Mathewson, Rube personally rebounded with a better year. He started 28 times and threw 11 complete games. While again he only totaled 11 victories, his ERA fell to a very respectable 3.73, a figure boosted by three shutouts.

The addition of a new manager (Dave Bancroft) and some new players (most notably Casey Stengel, now in his 13th year) did nothing to improve the Braves' record the next year, 1924. Amazingly, they lost an even 100 games for the third year in a row, setting a record for futility that will never be matched. Stengel led the team with an unspectacular batting average of .280, and as a team they hit only .256, nearly 30 points less than the NL average. Their total of 520 runs scored was an abomination, fully 337 runs behind the first-place Giants. The pitching was not much better; their best hurler, Jesse Barnes, won 15 games but lost 20. Rube suffered from appendicitis so severe that for a time doctors feared

Above: Rube Marquard Day in Providence, and Rube and Naomi are very pleased with the presentation. *Opposite:* Manager Marquard (back row, fourth from left) and the 1926 Eastern League champions Providence Grays. Photos courtesy Charles Guggenheimer collection.

he might not live; he pulled through but was left too weak to contribute much to the team. He appeared in only six games all year and won just one.

Despite his unexpected health problems and the unpleasantness of pitching for a poor ballclub, Rube had found a nice measure of contentment off the field. He and Naomi kept a small apartment in Boston during the season, and during the winter, when not vacationing at Florida resorts, they returned to New York or stayed with her parents in Baltimore. They speculated in real estate, and one newspaper reported that they earned a profit of $50,000 in just one winter.[6] They lived well, dined out more often than not, and spent lots of money on jewelry and clothes. Naomi was partial to furs, ornately flowered dresses, and long white gloves, wearing them even at the ballpark or racetrack, and she was never seen in public without a beautifully plumed hat. Rube cultivated his Broadway image as a sharp dresser, favoring the day's popular plaid knickers, silk stockings, and black-and-white spats. He parted his hair in the middle, prompting Florida papers to note the comparison with F. Scott Fitzgerald.

Rube tried to be a good father to his son, but time and distance made it difficult. It didn't help matters that he and Blossom could not be friends, and the only communication between the two was through Rube's sister Hattie. And even then there were problems. On one occasion Rube and Naomi dropped in unannounced to pick up young Richard and bring him back to New York with them for a few days. Rube apparently wasn't clear with his sister as to his plans, and in the confusion Blossom panicked when she learned that Hattie had let him take the boy. A few days later Rube and his wife decided to attend one of Blossom's shows, Richard being home safe with a nanny, and they ventured to the theater, where they settled into front-row seats. Midway through the performance Blossom recognized Rube through the footlights and stopped smack in the middle of a song. She angrily walked to the front of the stage and shouted before the startled audience, "Rube, what have you done with our son?"[7] Rube was naturally embarrassed and left the theater. The matter was quickly and easily straightened out but strained an already tense relationship between the former spouses. By the mid–1920s they had ceased talking altogether.

Rube's major league career had about run its course. Bancroft used him mainly in relief in 1925, preferring to experiment with younger, unproven pitchers who might eventually lead the Braves out of the baseball wilderness. Rube threw only 79 innings and won two games, pushing his career total to 201 victories. In 18 big league seasons, he had appeared in 536 ballgames, had thrown 3,307 innings, and had accumulated an earned run average of 3.13. When he announced his retirement at the end of the season, it surprised no one, although it was hardly the biggest news story of the time — Christy Mathewson was near death.

Matty breathed his last at 11 P.M. on October 7, 1925, in Saranac Lake, roughly six hours after Walter Johnson and his Washington Senators had beaten the Pirates in the first game of the World Series. For the rest of the Series, players from both teams wore black armbands in memory of Matty, the man who, according to Tom Meany of the New York *World-Telegram*, "had altered turn-of-the-century conceptions about men who played the game. Through him, the public learned that a professional ballplayer need be neither a hayseed nor a tough-talking, tobacco-chewing, whiskey-guzzling refugee from the poolrooms of the teeming cities.... He was the greatest sportsman the game has ever produced."[8] Three days later Matty was buried at Lewisburg, Pennsylvania, near the campus of his alma mater Bucknell. Rube and Naomi attended the funeral, as did John McGraw, Judge Landis, Wilbert Robinson, and many other baseball notables.

Casey Stengel had retired from major league baseball just 12 games into the 1925 season, and he spent the rest of the year as player/manager of the Worcester Panthers of the Eastern League, a franchise controlled in large part by the Boston Braves. In the fall he received a better offer to perform the same duties for Toledo of the American Association, and he recommended to club owner A. H. Powell that Rube replace him. Rube was happy for the opportunity, and his enthusiasm was not dampened when it was announced that the Panthers would move to Providence for the 1926 season and be renamed the Grays. Just before Christmas, Rube was officially installed as manager and part-time pitcher, and eventually he was named club president as well.

The Eastern League had been in existence for 10 years, and was composed of eight teams, including the Springfield Ponies, the Hartford Senators, and the Waterbury Brasscos, the two-time defending league champs. Rube had an advantage because of his club's working relationship with the Braves: He could choose from a crop of players just a notch below big league standards, or those who were not quite ready to move up, such as pitchers Art Mills and Bill Vargus and outfielder Dave Harris. He boldly predicted his team would contend for the championship. Rube pitched the opening game of the season but lost to Pittsfield and then restricted his appearances for the rest of the season to Sunday home games, when crowds would be larger. He contributed three wins but was generally content to work with the young players and pass on what he had learned in over 20 years of baseball. The Grays clinched the league title in September, finishing five games ahead of New Haven with a record of 97–55. The *Sporting News* commented: "Manager Marquard has demonstrated that he is a real leader. He is well liked by the players, who helped him put it over, by the fans who have gone to the games in goodly numbers, and the club owners."[9]

On September 15 the Grays celebrated Rube Marquard Day. Over 2,500 fans came out to see the game and honor the manager. Grays groundskeeper Malloy laid out in chalk a huge baseball, complete with seams and stitches, with a greeting to Rube inscribed therein. State Senator Metcalf presented Rube with a silver service, and the mayor of Providence read a proclamation. Then a brand new automobile was driven out onto the grass and given to Rube; this time, unlike back in 1912 at the Polo Grounds, the gift was genuine.

As a further show of appreciation, Rube was tendered a five-year contract to remain as manager. Strangely enough, he turned it down. Following the example set by so many men who had made the sport their life, Rube embarked on a sort of minor league odyssey, sojourning through a series of cities and ballclubs, moving on after a year or two and constantly keeping one eye out for the chance to return to the majors in some capacity. In 1928 Rube took the reins of the Birmingham, Alabama, club of the Southern League. He took the next year off from baseball, spending the summer and fall traveling with Naomi, visiting family and friends scattered throughout the country. But the game he loved lured him back. He spent two happy years with Jacksonville of the Southeastern League, for not only did the climate appeal to him, but the presence, for a month, of the big league clubs in spring training gave him the chance to renew old friendships and trade stories with many former teammates and adversaries. Rube and Naomi spent at least one winter there, and Rube found employment at the pari-mutuel window of a local racetrack, selling $6 tickets, a situation that suited him.

In 1931, Rube landed a job as baseball coach at Assumption College in Worcester, Massachusetts. The collegiate experience was fun, but the season was done when school adjourned in late spring. Too late to catch on as coach with one of the professional clubs, Rube took a job as umpire back in the Eastern League. It was not a totally unheard-of proposition; several former big leaguers had done the same thing. (A couple of pitchers, Bill Dinneen and Charlie Moran,

Kenesaw Mountain Landis, with a typically sour expression, and Naomi Marquard, Florida, circa 1933. Photo courtesy Charles Guggenheimer collection.

made it all the way to the majors as arbiters.) But one season spent calling balls and strikes was enough for Rube, and he looked for other opportunities. Once again his old friend Wilbert Robinson entered his life.

Robbie had weathered numerous storms in the decade following the 1920 NL championship. Always beloved by the Brooklyn fans, he hung on as manager despite mediocre records. In 1926, Charles Ebbetts died, and two weeks later one of the McKeever brothers, Edwin, passed away as well (supposedly from pneumonia caught while standing in the rain during Ebbetts' funeral). The surviving brother, Stephen, seemed the logical choice to take over as president of the franchise. But the Ebbetts heirs objected, and in a compromise Robbie took over front-office duties while continuing as manager. His tenure was undistinguished: The club finished in sixth place four years in a row, despite the presence of such stars as Babe Herman, Johnny Frederick, and pitching sensation Dazzy Vance. Robbie gave up the presidency but was retained as manager for two more years, guiding the Robins to two fourth-place finishes before he was replaced by former Pittsburgh standout Max Carey.

Dejected, Robbie retired to Dover Hall in Georgia, the former plantation-turned–hunting lodge he owned with former Yankee magnate Tillinghast Huston. It was Huston who had tried, unsuccessfully, to lure Robbie into accepting the Yankee managerial job back in 1918 (the job went to Miller Huggins), and now he tried to find another place for his friend. Huston purchased a controlling interest in the Atlanta team of the Southern Association League and promised to install Robbie as president and manager in 1933. Robbie agreed, provided he also hire Rube as coach and scout for the club in the meantime. Thus the deal was made, and Rube spent the season in Georgia, the first of what he hoped would be many years of working for his old mentor.

Rube spent a portion of the off-season writing a 15-page book entitled *How to Pitch*. The book was targeted for youngsters and would be used as a promotional item by the Atlanta club, sold for a quarter or sometimes given away on kids' days at the ballpark. Each chapter was devoted to a particular pitching topic such as "Change of Pace and the Curve Ball" and "How to Hold a Runner on First." Rube took the job of writing very seriously; there was to be no ghostwriter for this project. He recalled very clearly the way he had admired the older ballplayers back in Cleveland, how he had hung on their every word and tried to imitate their styles of play. Now was a good chance to be a role model for members of a new younger generation, and he produced something that he was proud of.

But the planned joint venture in Atlanta did not turn out well at all because Robbie's health deteriorated. He was bothered by a variety of ailments, and while attending Sally League meetings, he suffered a stroke, fell and broke an arm. He was unable to recover and died on August 8, 1934, at the age of 70. Rube and Naomi attended the funeral and stood beside Robbie's wife, still called "Ma" by all who knew her, as he was buried under some oak trees at Dover Hall.

There was yet more sad news in February when John McGraw died in New York at the age of 61. He had managed the Giants until June of 1932, when he abruptly retired to make way for Bill Terry. Rube attended the memorial service at St. Patrick's Cathedral and offered his condolences to McGraw's widow, Blanche. "There never will be another man like John McGraw in baseball," he said. "Color, glamour and romantic chapters connected with baseball passed out of the sport to a great extent with his death. He was rough and ready, to be sure, but he was always fighting for his men, his team, and for his club."[10] Rube never forgot how McGraw had stuck with him during the "lemon" years of 1909 and 1910, and as the years passed he had never missed a chance to express his admiration and gratitude. He was particularly pleased to learn that, before he died, McGraw had ranked Rube and Chief Meyers as the ninth-greatest battery combination of all time.[11]

Finally Rube left baseball, although he and Naomi continued to travel. He found fulltime employment at something he had learned to love almost as much as baseball: the racetracks. He worked at the betting windows at tracks along the coast, including Pimlico, Belmont, Tropical Park and Hialeah Park, among many others. He gradually worked his way up to the $50 and then the $100 windows. "It's as exciting as throwing curves and speed balls at batters," he told one reporter in Miami. "What I like about it, however, is that it keeps one out of doors. Don't think I'd ever be able to work indoors at this late stage."[12] Eventually Rube and Naomi bought a house in Coral Gables and spent every winter season there.

Every few years a columnist would mention Rube, always adding that he was healthy and happy and looking a good 15 years younger than his age (a neat trick considering he never let on that he was three years older than everyone thought). The stories usually centered around the 19-game winning streak, and included Rube's thoughts on the particular baseball phenom of the moment. On December 19, 1937, he pitched two innings in an old-timers' game in Miami Beach, breaking off curve balls against Josh Devore and Max Carey with Bill Klem behind the plate; coverage of the event was sent out nationwide through the Associated Press.

For several years, organized baseball sought a way to commemorate the 100th anniversary of baseball, an occasion grounded in the tenuous belief that Abner Doubleday had invented the game in Cooperstown, New York, in 1839. A Centennial Commission was established and given the task of recognizing an initial group of baseball immortals to be enshrined in a Hall of Fame. The Commission asked the 226 members of the Baseball Writers' Association of America and a special 78-member veterans' committee to hold elections. On January 29, 1936, the first set of five inductees was announced: Ty Cobb, Babe Ruth, Honus Wagner, Christy Mathewson, and Walter Johnson. In June of 1939 this group was formally inducted at the new museum and Hall of Fame in Cooperstown, along with 21 other greats.

World War II interrupted everyone's life, and Rube was no exception. On

A somber Rube reflects for the photographer on the sad occasion of Babe Ruth's death, August 1948. Photo courtesy National Baseball Library.

July 18, 1942, he was commissioned 1st lieutenant, junior grade, in the Coast Guard Reserve. He was assigned to the Coast Guard station at Curtis Bay, Maryland, not far from Baltimore. Rube was particularly proud to learn that his father Fred came out of retirement in Cleveland to assist in the war effort, putting his engineering experience to work at the Fawick Airflex Company, an armament manufacturing plant. Fred died after a 12-day stay at Cleveland's City Hospital on December 16, 1945, at the age of 81. (Rube's younger brother Frank had passed away three years before.) Fred's obituary in the Cleveland *Press*, besides detailing his personal and employment history, noted that "Mr. Marquard was an enthusiastic baseball fan and an ardent follower of the exploits of his famous son, 'Rube.' The latter pitched for Cincinnati and Boston but his greatest record was with the New York Giants."[13]

Occasionally there were other noteworthy events. In September 1947 a strange incident occurred in Baltimore which captured the attention of much of the national media. Eighteen men were arrested in the bowery section of town and charged with disorderly conduct, public intoxication, and loitering. Each appeared in front of night court magistrate Murphy and one of them gave his name as Rube Marquard before pleading guilty. "Aren't you the famous Rube?" asked Murphy.

"Yes, your Honor," the man said, staring at the floor. He told the judge he had been down on his luck since John McGraw died, that he had once been married to Blossom Seeley, and that he didn't have a cent to his name. Murphy handed the man a five-dollar bill, noting that he had always heard that Rube was known to have never turned a needy person down back in his golden era in New York.[14]

Reporters questioned the whole episode and began an investigation. It quickly came out, of course, that Rube was far from down on his luck, was in fact doing quite well, was living in his home in Haddonfield, New Jersey, and was employed at the pari-mutuel department at the Camden race track. The "bowery imposter" had pulled a fast one on the judge. A few days later the same man, whose name was really James Meehan, was arrested again on similar charges. He appeared in front of police recorder Robert McAlevy and offered the same story, but McAlevy didn't buy it. Meehan then told the truth before he received 10 days in jail. "It's all very ridiculous to me," Rube said when asked about the incident. You'd think a Judge would be more careful." Neither was Naomi impressed. "We can't understand how such a terrible mistake could be made," she said. "My husband never drinks."[15]

As Rube carried on with his life and post-baseball career, Blossom stayed in show business. She married Benny Fields in 1922, and together they toured the country with a very popular song-and-dance routine. Her renditions of "You Left Me Out in the Rain" and "A New Kind of Man with a New Kind of Love for Me" were popular hits, and George Gershwin composed a 25-minute jazz opera for her entitled *Blue Monday* (later renamed *135th Street*) which played at Carnegie Hall. Blossom's flair for the spectacular continued. In Chicago, for example, she was Al Capone's favorite nightclub performer; he almost never failed to attend her show and routinely sent flowers backstage.

Rube's sister Hattie passed away in 1931 at the young age of 38, and her death was a difficult loss for 17-year-old Richard, or Dick, as he was called. He went to live with Blossom and Benny in New York and remained forever grateful for the love and kindness Benny showed him. He began to tour with the famous duo, working as a stage hand or director's assistant. When in Los Angeles they stayed in a suite at the luxurious Chateau Maumont, and soon Dick's childhood pals included Jackie Cooper and Mickey Rooney. He attended private schools with the children of entertainment's brightest stars, including Jack Benny, Bob Hope, and the Marx Brothers, among many others.

In 1936, Dick was on tour back in New York as Benny and Blossom played the Palace. He watched, from the wings, an act called Helen Reynolds and the Famous Skaters. One lovely young lady in particular caught his eye. Her name was Kay Warner, and for Dick it was love at first sight. He vowed he would someday marry her, and in October 1937 his prediction came true. He and Kay eloped to Yuma, Arizona, and began their long and happy life together. The couple lived for three years in California and then settled in Milwaukee, Dick forging a successful career as a haberdasher. Dick was always appreciative of the love and support he received from Benny and Blossom and the many advantages their success gave him. He remained very proud, as well, of his father's fame.

Gradually the touring slowed down, and Blossom turned her talents to the screen. She starred in two feature films in the mid–1930s, *Blood Money* and *Broadway Thru a Keyhole*, and appeared in supporting roles in several more. In 1936 she unofficially retired from show business and watched contentedly as Benny's solo career took off. In 1952, Paramount Studios made a movie of Blossom's life and career called *Somebody Loves Me*. Betty Hutton played Blossom, and Ralph Meeker portrayed Benny Fields. (There was no mention of Rube in the film.) Blossom served as technical adviser for the production, and it opened to good reviews in Chicago. Benny and Blossom, along with the stars of the movie, attended the premiere, as did Dick and Kay.

The film served to revive Blossom's career, and in her trademark style she returned in spectacular fashion. She recorded albums for Mercury, MGM, and Decca, reprising all of the sensational numbers of her vaudeville days and putting her inimitable style on new standards, as well. In November 1952 she and Benny played the Cocoanut Grove in Los Angeles to great acclaim, and they continued to be regular performers on the Ed Sullivan Show in New York. Blossom was widely loved and admired in the entertainment world; Marilyn Monroe, for one, sought out her friendship and advice. In 1959, Blossom performed at the Sands in Las Vegas, again to terrific reviews. Unfortunately, Benny's health gradually faded, and "that special, wonderful man," as Dick and Kay (and of course, Blossom) remembered him, passed away later that year.

Chapter 16

Finally Cooperstown

On July 21, 1954, Naomi died at the age of 61 at the home she and Rube shared on Liberty Heights Avenue. She and Rube had been together for over 30 years, and her passing naturally was a cause of great sorrow. Rube was comforted by Naomi's mother and sister as Naomi was buried in Baltimore. But Rube was not one to close himself off from the rest of the world. He was no loner; he enjoyed the company of old friends and he had no objection to making new ones. He needed to broaden his horizons.

In the fall of 1955, Rube took a vacation to the Mediterranean on a cruise sponsored by Baltimore's First Church of Christ Scientist. Also an board was a woman named Jane Hecht Guggenheimer. Jane was 60 years old, twice widowed, a member of the family that had founded the Hecht department store chain. A friend introduced her to Rube, asking her, "You know who Rube Marquard is, don't you?"[1] Jane had to admit that she had never heard of the famous ballplayer. Rube got a kick out of that, and the friendship, and courtship, began. Back in Baltimore, Rube gave her a beautiful eight-carat diamond ring and matching set of earrings, and on October 21, just three weeks after they had met, Rube and Jane were married.

Despite Jane's lack of baseball expertise, the couple had much in common. Like Rube, Jane was an active, vibrant person. She played golf and tennis and was a regular bowler. She was particularly fond of ballroom dancing, and Rube happily agreed to take lessons so that they could enjoy that activity together. Jane was well off financially, and they traveled around the world, sailing on cruises once or twice each year. After their marriage they lived at Jane's prestigious Esplanade apartment in downtown Baltimore, near Druid Hill Lake Park. In 1960 they moved to a brand new cooperative apartment at 11 Slade Avenue in Pikesville, a northwest suburb, directly across the street from the Suburban Country Club.

Founded in 1901, the Suburban was (and is) an exclusive social hub for some

Rube married Jane Hecht Guggenheimer in 1955, a union that would last nearly 25 happy years. Photo courtesy Charles Guggenheimer collection.

of Baltimore's oldest and finest families. Predominantly Jewish, the Suburban was the setting for dinner, dancing, golf, and a variety of functions, and soon became the center of Rube and Jane's life. Most days they went there for lunch, a game of cards, or round of golf, and they habitually attended the Saturday night dinner and dance. They were one of the Suburban's more popular couples, outgoing and friendly and well-liked by all who knew them. Don Beach was the club's golf pro, as was his father before him, and he remembers the Marquards well.

"They were a couple of truly nice people," Beach says, "always pleasant, very happy together. I think that, on the golf course at least, Jane was more competitive than Rube was. He was a reasonably good (and right-handed) golfer, shooting 48–50 generally for nine holes, but Jane was tough to beat for her age group. And that was one of the things he loved about her. She probably had as many golf trophies displayed at their home as Rube had baseball awards."[2]

To the delight of other Suburban Club members, Rube often talked of his old baseball days, telling stories about the World Series, Mathewson, McGraw, and Babe Ruth. He called Honus Wagner the toughest hitter he ever faced; he said there wasn't a pitch Honus couldn't hit. "I waved my outfielders back, pitched low and inside and hoped the ball would not land on the elevated tracks."[3] The Suburban was very family oriented, and Rube was particularly fond of the kids who were around much of the time. He loved to demonstrate how he threw certain pitches and how he fooled certain hitters. He never failed to oblige requests for autographs and was always happy to pose for photographs. He liked to watch baseball on TV, and he enjoyed watching football as well. Like many old-timers, however, he was not always impressed with some aspects of the modern game. He was appalled when the American League installed the designated hitter rule. "I hate to see the rules altered in any way because the true beauty of baseball is the tradition it has."[4] It particularly disturbed him that starting pitchers seemed almost incapable of lasting past five or six innings; in his day, he rightly insisted, a starter was expected to go the distance.

Mary Hevey operated the switchboard at the Pikesville apartment and came to know Rube and Jane very well. "He was a classy gentleman, a good man," Mary recalls. "He always answered his fan mail and always had time for the Little Leaguers who admired him. To my son, Barry, he was a hero. Jane was not a big baseball fan, although she would often go to old-timers games with him. Rube liked to follow the Orioles, as I did, and together we would dissect the team and talk about the players. 'My manager,' he would call me. I have some nice memories of both of them."[5] Over the years Rube gave Mary autographed baseballs, newspaper articles, and other memorabilia, items which she eventually donated to the Babe Ruth Museum in Baltimore. A neighborhood boy named Edward Schechter developed a friendship with Rube in those years. "He was a generous and warm individual who fascinated me with stories of his New York Giants," wrote Schechter many years later. "Perhaps his most generous gesture was to give me — then a 15-year-old boy — the pitcher's glove he used during the 1912 season when he set his first record of 19 straight victories."[6]

For a few years, Rube continued to follow an abbreviated racetrack circuit. He generally worked three seasons, at Pimlico in Baltimore, Monmouth in New Jersey, and Tropical Park in Florida. At this stage he only worked the $100 windows, though he had long since given up gambling himself. He had seen too many people lose control and wager and lose far beyond their means. Often Jane would accompany Rube to the track, and for the first year of their marriage she went with him to Miami, where they lived at the Raven Hotel on Edgewater Beach. That season at Tropical Park Rube shared mutuels duties with Bullet Joe Bush, his old adversary with the Phillies, and former Yankee trainer Doc Woods. With Fred Merkle retired in the area, there were some pleasant reunions spent talking about the old days. But Jane grew tired of the routine after a while, and eventually Rube decided that he too had enough and retired for good.

Rube was always available for appearances at the ballpark, even if the occasions were bittersweet. On September 24, 1957, he attended the final game at Ebbetts Field in Brooklyn and watched along with 6,702 others as the Dodgers beat Pittsburgh 2–0. Five days later the Giants played their final game at the Polo Ground, losing to the Pirates 9–1. It was hard for Rube to believe that after 60 colorful and tumultuous years both franchises were deserting New York, the Giants for San Francisco and the Dodgers for Los Angeles. He believed, like many others, that California's gain was baseball's loss. For this final game, Rube sat in the front-row box seat next to Blanche McGraw, and alongside of Red Burns, Moose McCormick, Hans Lobert, and Larry Doyle. "It is great to be young and a Giant," Doyle had proclaimed 45 years earlier. It was still something to be proud of, even on this day.

Rube loved to attend old-timers celebrations and would appear whenever requested. On July 14, 1962, he was a special guest at one such New York Mets celebration at the Polo Grounds, where they played. Rube was featured for a special reason: the 50th anniversary of his 19-game winning streak. Still trim and energetic, he proudly donned a Giant uniform and was photographed with Dodger star Don Drysdale, demonstrating his grip on a fastball. His arm felt strong, he joked for the reporters. If he could trust his legs to hold out, he wouldn't mind throwing a few innings. He was asked to throw out the first ball of the sixth game of the 1971 World Series between the Orioles and Pirates. Catcher Elrod Hendricks took a position about 30 feet from the pitcher's mound, but Rube, now 84 years old, waved him back behind the plate and tossed it all the way, to the delight of the crowd.

In February of 1964, Rube was honored by the New York Baseball Writers with the fourth Retroactive Player of the Year Award for "outstanding contributions to the National Pastime." Rube was in select company; previous winners were Ty Cobb, Rogers Hornsby, and Max Carey. He attended the black tie affair and graciously accepted his award, sharing the podium with Stan Musial, Whitey

Ford, and Sandy Koufax. He was not shy about expressing his opinions about the state of the current game or its players. No doubt speaking from experience, he warned pitching sensations and notorious rebels Bo Belinsky and Dean Chance of the Angels that they would do better to curtail their wild lifestyle. "When they can't win regularly — and it always happens to those who follow the night life crowd — they'll find that these associates will drop them like a hot potato. Later, they'll wonder why their salaries were cut. There's so much money to be made in baseball these days that it's surprising pitchers with talent like theirs can't seem to realize it."[7]

The years with Jane were happy ones. Her son Charles Guggenheimer and his daughter Barbara have many fond memories of Rube and Jane and their life together. "He was a gracious man, a wonderful gentleman," says Charles. "He made my mother very happy and we were all happy for them." Barbara agrees and recalls that "they were just so devoted to one another, really made for each other. They were very much in love."[8]

And it was Jane who encouraged Rube to contact Blossom again, after all the years of bitterness and anger. "My mother's philosophy was live and let live," says Charles. "There was no reason to be enemies."[9] Rube was initially reluctant but came around to the idea, and he telephoned Blossom in New York, where she lived. Blossom was pleased to hear from him and was just as pleased to meet Jane when they eventually visited in person. In August of 1959, Blossom's beloved Benny had died, and she took up residence at the Warwick Hotel. When Jane's son Bob moved to New York to work for General Electric, Rube and Jane insisted that he go and see her. Blossom and Bob became good friends, and he visited her weekly, taking her to the Lambs Club or dining at Sardi's. Blossom was still a regular performer on television programs in the 1960s, and Bob recalls that "she was a great trouper.... When she would sing she would immediately look at least 20 years younger." Among the "hordes of friends" who regularly called on Blossom were Jack Benny, George Burns, and Sophie Tucker, and Bob remains appreciative for the time he spent with that "lovely little lady."[10] Blossom passed away in April 1979.

Rube was also able, on a more limited basis, to reestablish ties with his own son. Dick had embarked on a successful career as a haberdasher, living mainly in Wisconsin and Michigan with his wife, Kay. He had known Benny Fields as his father figure and loved him immensely, and while he and Rube had not been close, he was proud of Rube's fame. Kay suggested that they contact Rube and he agreed, and Kay wrote the letter. To their delight Rube responded right away, thanking them and adding that he was pleased with the fine manner in which their lives had turned out. For the rest of his life, Rube and Jane exchanged Christmas cards and other holiday greetings with Dick and Kay. Rube's late-life experiences with Blossom and their son proved that Jane's and Kay's instincts had been right on the mark: it was never too late to heal old wounds.

So as Rube reached and then surpassed his 75th year, he had much to be thankful for. He and his wife loved each other dearly. They were surrounded by caring family and friends, enjoyed a fulfilling social life, and traveled extensively. Rube could look back with great satisfaction on a marvelous baseball career, revel in his many accomplishments, and dismiss with a laugh some of the low spots he had endured along the way. He had connected again with the first love of his life and had forged some new ties with his only child. It seemed that only one thing was missing in his life. He believed that he deserved a place in baseball's Hall of Fame.

It was not an original idea. Rube had received a vote in the initial balloting in 1936 — a noteworthy accomplishment considering the competition — and had garnered consistent, if not overwhelming, support over the years. Every few years a sportswriter such as Joe Williams or Dan Daniel would produce a column reciting the highlights of Rube's career, invariably describing the stunning $11,000 purchase, the three dominant pennant-winning years with the Giants, the reemergence with Brooklyn, and, of course, the 19-game winning streak which had never been broken. Daniel once wrote that he received more letters of support for Rube's election to Cooperstown than for any other player.

Rube had watched as many of his contemporaries had been selected for the Hall, generally through the Veterans' Committee, which had evolved from the original Old-Timers' Committee. Mathewson, of course, had been one of the first five inductees in 1936, followed by John McGraw the next year. Tris Speaker and Pete Alexander went in soon after, all deserving figures and logical choices. Then came another group of greats in the 1940s, including Joe McGinnity and Three Finger Brown and his infield mates on the Cubs — Tinkers, Evers, and Chance. Judge Landis was selected, as was Wilbert Robinson. Then Chief Bender, Home Run Baker, Zack Wheat, and famed umpires Bill Klem and Tom Connolly. In the early years of the 1960s, Edd Roush, Eppa Rixey and Burleigh Grimes all were chosen. Rube was pleased for all his old friends, foes, and teammates and unfailingly sent telegrams of congratulations. But he worried that perhaps the ticket-scalping controversy of 1920 might be acting as an unofficial bar to his election, and he began to doubt that his time would never come. He needed a boost, perhaps, to remind voters of his prominence, and he got it from an unexpected source.

In 1964, Lawrence Ritter was in the middle of a distinguished career in economics. Born in New York in 1922 and educated at Indiana University and the University of Wisconsin, Ritter served as a professor at Michigan State University for several years before joining New York's Federal Reserve Bank. In 1960 he began to teach finance at New York University, and four years later he was chairman of the department at NYU's Graduate School of Business Administration. He was also a lifelong baseball fan.

When Ty Cobb died in 1961, it occurred to Ritter that the stories of the men who had played with and against Cobb during baseball's early days should be recorded, quickly and thoroughly, before they were lost forever. Those men, after all, had helped shape the game that had helped shape the nation. They were pioneers, Ritter knew, in every sense of the word, and their reminiscences of that wondrous time could illuminate and re-create the vigor of the era. They could tell us how it felt "to be a big leaguer in a high-spirited country a long time ago."[11]

And while Ritter's "strange crusade" had its particular social goal — to record and preserve, for posterity, the role baseball players had played in the country's development in those years from the turn of the century through World War I — he later realized that his deeper motives were more personal in nature. His own father, himself an educator, had passed away at roughly the same time as Cobb. Perhaps in uncovering the stories of yesterday's heroes, he might recapture the connection between father, son, and baseball that had become such a common experience for so many Americans who loved and lived the game. Through baseball, thought Ritter, he might recapture the "unforgettable ritual of childhood and draw closer to a father I would never see again."[12]

And so in 1962, Ritter set out to collect his narratives. For the next four years, he traveled over 75,000 miles in his search for old-time ballplayers. In locating his subjects, he tracked down their hometowns, consulted telephone books, inquired of often-distant relatives. More often than not his diligence paid off. He found the men, sometimes surprised that he would be interested but always eager to share with him their recollections. They talked in "modest, middle-class homes, in elegantly furnished mansions, and in run-down shacks ... on farms and in cities ... in 100° heat and in 10° below zero cold."[13] Ritter turned on the tape recorder, asked the questions, and was consistently amazed by the players' intelligence, their articulation, and their memories. He was also impressed by the warm and compassionate way they remembered the game they played and the men with whom they played it.

Fairly early in Ritter's odyssey, while he was visiting friends in Washington, D.C., he learned that Rube lived in nearby Pikesville. He called and explained his mission and asked if Rube would be willing to sit for an interview. Rube was always happy to talk baseball of course, and soon a meeting was arranged. In the summer of 1963, Ritter, accompanied by his son Stephen, arrived at Rube and Jane's apartment on Slade Avenue and asked Rube about his life and career.

The men quickly became friends, their relationship fueled, naturally, by the passion for baseball they shared (and also, perhaps, by their common military experience; Ritter had been a lieutenant in the navy during World War II). In the initial interview, Rube reminisced on tape for several hours. He told Ritter of his childhood in Cleveland, his father's disapproval of baseball, and the ugly arguments they had had over the game. He described in great detail his success on the sandlots, the hobo-style train trip to Waterloo while he was still a teenager, and the friendship with Bill Bradley and Charlie Carr that led to the start of a professional career at Canton. He told Ritter about the circumstances surrounding the spectacular $11,000 purchase from Indianapolis, the transformation from Lemon to Beauty, and the 19-game winning streak, still insisting that he should have been credited with 20 victories. Rube spoke glowingly of McGraw and Matty, of Fred Merkle, Smoky Joe Wood, and Robbie. His memory of those distant days, to be sure, was sometimes spotty. He gave no hint of the ill-fated jump to the Federal League of 1915, the public bickering between him and Mathewson in the wake of Frank Baker's 1911 World Series heroics, or the ticket-scalping fiasco that nearly ruined his career. He glossed over the stormy romance with Blossom and exaggerated his adherence to the straight and narrow. "I always said you can't burn the candle at both ends," he said. "You want to be a ballplayer, be a ballplayer. If you want to go out and carouse and chase around, do that. But you can't do them both at once."[14] He had, of course, done exactly that, and done it pretty well.

For all his reminiscences, whether perfectly accurate or fudged around the edges, what came across most clearly were the elements of a remarkable, and classically American, story. Rube really had run away from home, hopped the rails cross-country, overcome the odds, and found success in the big city. He had rubbed shoulders with the greatest ballplayers of all time and had more than held his own. He set out to pursue his dream — baseball — and the dream had come true. Lawrence Ritter had discovered something truly special.

When Ritter later played back the tape he discovered, to his dismay, that parts of the story Rube had related were nearly inaudible. The tape recorder, it seemed, had been placed too close to the air conditioner and the hum of the motor had frequently muffled the sound of Rube's voice. A second interview was arranged, under better conditions. Much of the same material was covered, and some of Rube's story was so similar to that of the earlier interview that Ritter wondered whether parts of it had been crafted, or scripted. But Ritter was interested mainly in the ballplayers themselves and their recollections, not the precise historical accuracy of events that had transpired half a century earlier and the details of which had, naturally enough, perhaps faded or blurred with the passage of time. "Ballgame scores and statistics were easy enough to verify," he said later, "but items more personal in nature were not. Besides, this was his story, not mine."[15]

In all Ritter collected the oral histories of 22 men, including many who had played with or against Rube, such as Chief Meyers, Harry Hooper, Stan Coveleski and Smoky Joe Wood.[16] Once the interviews were completed, he set about editing his material, arranging the stories into chapters (one player per chapter), selecting photographs and writing introductory commentaries to accompany each one. He gave each player the opportunity to review his story, but Rube made no suggestions, additions or corrections. Rube's story, because of its classically American feel (and particularly the father/son conflict) was placed as the lead-off chapter of the proposed book, which was entitled *The Glory of Their Times: The Story of the Early Days of Baseball Told by the Men Who Played It*. The final package, once assembled, now had to be accepted by a publisher. Surprisingly, three companies turned the project down before one, Macmillan, accepted it. It was a decision those three companies would come to regret very much.

The Glory of Their Times came out to great acclaim in 1966. While hopeful, Ritter did not know that it would be successful until it was enthusiastically reviewed on the cover of the September 18, 1966, *New York Times Book Review*. Critic Wilfrid Sheed called *Glory* "quite simply the best sports book in recent memory.... The average sports memoir is a prodigy of simpering modesty and high-minded platitude.... This one tells it right."[17] Excerpts of the book, always including Rube's chapter, appeared in *Life*, *Saturday Evening Post*, and the *Sporting News*. (If Rube remembered the criticism that particular publication had leveled against him many years ago, he must now have enjoyed some measure of satisfaction.)

As *Glory* climbed to the top of the best-seller lists, many of the players assisted in its marketing and promotion, appearing on television talk shows and at bookstore signings. This made good economic sense because the players shared equally with Ritter, in the royalties. Rube was a tireless and enthusiastic promoter of the book, even appearing on NBC's "Today" program, which was hosted by former ballplayer Joe Garagiola. Eventually a record album was produced which contained portions of the players' actual voices as recorded; Rube can be heard three times on the album, in segments labeled "A 16-Year-Old in Waterloo, Iowa," "Remember Me, Lieutenant?" and "You'll Be Proud of Me, Dad." Rube's photograph, taken as he warms up before either the 1911 or 1913 World Series against the Athletics, adorns the jacket cover on one of the record's issues. Finally a videocassette emerged, the voices of Ritter, Alexander Scourby, and the players narrating over beautiful and rare film footage of Matty throwing, Cobb running the bases, and Babe Ruth clouting mammoth home runs.

Now in its twelfth printing, *The Glory of Their Times* remains an immensely popular and often-imitated work. It has received, without exception, the highest of praise from the critics, who have regularly called it "wonderful," "almost perfect," and "a classic of Americana." In his review Ted Williams wrote of the "great feeling I got as I read it. The day after I finished it I started reading it all over again."[18] *Glory* is quite simply the best baseball book of all time, and in the over 30 years since its initial publication, it has sold over 350,000 copies and counting.

The impact the book had in baseball circles was immediate. "Everyone in baseball read it," statistician/historian Bill James has written. "There was a very significant 'attention effect' directed towards the players who were interviewed for that book, and several of them wound up in the Hall of Fame."[19] Goose Goslin, for example, a fine hitter who had played for Washington, St. Louis, and Detroit, was elected in 1966, almost immediately after *Glory* was released. Three years later Stan Coveleski was also inducted.

Rube's friends at the Suburban Club took notice of their again-famous fellow member and waged a minor assault on the Veterans' Committee, urging them to look more closely at Rube's record. The Committee comprised 11 men in 1971, including former league presidents Joe Cronin, William Harridge, and

Warren Giles; sportswriters Dan Daniel, Fred Lieb, Charles Segar and Roy Stockton; ballplayers Frankie Frisch, Charlie Gehringer and Waite Hoyt; and Hall of Fame President Paul Kerr. Just how much influence *The Glory of Their Times*, or the urging of Suburban Club members, had on the Veterans' Committee is impossible to determine. (Discussion and voting is not made public, and as of this writing the only member of the Committee still living is Segar, who declined to comment.) But on January 30, 1971, the Committee members, meeting in person in Florida, announced that Rube was at last selected for enshrinement at Cooperstown.

Ironically, one of the last people to hear about his election was Rube, for he and Jane were on board the *Queen Elizabeth 2* on one of their many cruises. The Hall of Fame contacted Barbara, who contacted Charles, who had the trip itinerary. Finally the shore-to-ship connection was made, and Lawrence Ritter was given the honor of informing Rube of his selection. Rube described the reaction the next day in a letter he wrote to Ritter:

> Dear Larry:
> I was the happiest and most surprised man in the world when I heard your voice yesterday telling me that I was voted into the Hall of Fame. The reason I didn't say anything for so long was that I couldn't. I was all choked up and tears were running down my cheeks.
> Yesterday evening, a few hours after you called, everybody was dancing and having a good time and suddenly the Captain of the ship stopped the music and said he wanted to make an important announcement. He said they had a very prominent man on board who had just been elected to the Baseball Hall of Fame. His name is Rube Marquard and he is right here dancing with his wife.
> Well, all hell broke loose, people yelling and clapping and the band played "Take Me Out To The Ball Game." I was so happy and Jane just loved it too. When we go to Cooperstown this summer, please come with us and be my guest.[20]

Back in Baltimore the celebration continued. The Suburban Club threw a special party to honor Rube, an old photograph of him in his Robins uniform gracing the event's brochure. Rube remained "stunned" at the news of his election, according to Charles, and "ecstatic."[21] He had thought that the honor of induction might never come, or if it did, that he would not be around to enjoy it. Cards and letters of congratulations arrived from many friends, both in and out of baseball, and he graciously responded to every one. His election was featured in columns in the *Sporting News*, as well as all the New York, Baltimore, and Cleveland newspapers. Even the Waterloo *Daily Courier* took notice of it, sportswriter Russ L. Smith recounting Rube's 1906 train trip and two-game tryout. Rube was then destined "to become one of baseball's greats," wrote Smith, and is "one of Waterloo's most prominent baseball alumni."[22]

HALL OF FAMER RUBE MARQUARD

The Suburban Club was the social center of Rube and Jane's life in Baltimore. Photo courtesy of Marie Hooper Strain.

The year 1971 was a busy one for the Hall of Fame, for along with Rube seven other men were chosen for enshrinement, tying 1953 for the most ever. Also elected by the Veterans' Committee were Charles "Chick" Hafey, a career .317 hitter for the Cardinals and Reds in the 1920s and 1930s; Joe Kelley, who had played and managed with John McGraw before the turn of the century; first baseman Jake Beckley, who also starred in those early years; Yankee executive George Weiss, whose leadership brought 10 pennants in 13 years to the Bronx; and second baseman Dave Bancroft, who had been traded to the Braves back in 1924 with Casey Stengel and then served as Rube's manager for the last two years of his career.

And much to Rube's delight, the Veterans' Committee also elected one of his great friends from the old days, outfielder Harry Hooper. After 12 outstanding seasons in Boston, where his superb defensive play and clutch hitting led the Red Sox to four world championships, Harry was traded to the Chicago White Sox just before the 1921 season. Charles Comiskey acquired him because he needed a man of unquestioned virtue and honesty to win back fans after the stain of the Black Sox scandal. Chicago fans, and the club's manager Kid Gleason, raved about the deal; Boston faithful, however, saw it as yet another in a long line of Harry Frazee's moves to dismantle a once-great team for the sake of cash. Harry played for Chicago for five years, three times hitting over .300, exceeding Comiskey's expectations in every way. He retired contentedly to his California home after 17 big league seasons, with nearly 2500 hits and a career .281 average.

In March of 1969, Harry's beloved wife Esther died of cancer, and Harry was inconsolable with grief. His children, Harry, Jr., John, and Marie, slowly lifted him from his depression by coaxing him to recall the playing days of his youth and by renewing their efforts to bring Harry's career to the attention of the Veterans' Committee. John, in particular, spearheaded the cause, asking for "clarification on Harry's play, slowly engaging the old man in the research and restoring some purpose to his life."[23] With the assistance of Harry's fellow alumni of St. Mary's College, the "Campaign for Cooperstown" paid off, and Harry's election represented a well-earned lesson in the shrine's "electoral reality."

The final Hall of Fame selection of 1971 was shrouded in controversy. The legendary pitcher Satchel Paige was the greatest of all the Negro Leaguers and constantly toured the country with his barnstorming troupes, but his race kept him out of the big leagues when he was in his prime. He was excluded from the majors until 1948, when he was on the downside of a dominant and turbulent career, and he had only enough time to record 28 wins with Cleveland and St. Louis. He continued to pitch sporadically for a number of minor league clubs, finally wrapping it up with Peninsula of the Carolinas League in 1966. He became technically eligible for Hall of Fame induction five years after that, although he did not have the required 10 years of big league service. The question was how, or even if, enshrinement could be accomplished, giving Satchel the justice he richly deserved while appeasing hard-liners like former commissioner Ford Frick and Hall of Fame president Paul Kerr, who firmly opposed the idea that Negro Leaguers deserved, or qualified for, Cooperstown recognition.

Among the many supporters of Paige's election were Ted Williams and Bob Feller, New York *Post* columnist Dick Young, and author Robert Peterson, whose book *Only the Ball Was White* included a thoughtful and persuasive argument that many great Negro League players ought to be voted into the Hall of Fame. Into the fray stepped Commissioner Bowie Kuhn, who in 1970 presided over a raucous meeting that included Frick, Kerr, Negro League and New York Giant star Monte Irvin (who worked in Kuhn's office), and BBWAA chief Jack Lang. A compromise was reached: Kuhn would empower a committee of experts to select a group of the most outstanding Negro League players, Paige among them, to be honored in a separate wing of the Hall of Fame or, as Bill James has put it, in a "separate-and-almost-sort-of equal" display.[24] In the aftermath of widespread criticism of the plan, common sense prevailed; it was eventually scrapped, and in 1971 Satchel Paige was the first of many great and deserving Negro Leaguers to be inducted into the Hall of Fame, on a full and equal basis.

Induction weekend in Cooperstown was August 7, 8, and 9, 1971. Charles and his son drove Rube and Jane up from Baltimore, and they checked into the beautiful Otesega Hotel. The Hall of Fame hosted a banquet and dance, and Charles recalls that Rube proudly introduced his family to many famous ballplayers, including Jackie Robinson, Casey Stengel, and Harry Hooper. Harry's children were also there for their father's induction, and Marie remembers that she was impressed that Rube took the time to chat with her. "He was very friendly, especially pleasant and down-to-earth," Marie says. "He made us all feel comfortable. It seemed as if we had been friends for a long time." Marie's husband Ed Strain thought that next to Harry Hooper, Rube was "the greatest man there."[25] Many fans attended the event as well, and Rube happily received all who came to him, signing baseballs and photographs. As always, he especially enjoyed being around children, and he loved it when one of them would say, "My dad told me you were a great ballplayer."[26]

Monday, August 9, was the big day. Rube and the other inductees were seated on the library porch, in front of several thousand baseball fans spread out before them in the hot sun. Hall of Fame secretary Ed Stack introduced Bob Stevens, sportswriter for the San Francisco *Chronicle* and president of the BBWAA, who was to act as master of ceremonies. Stevens introduced Harold Hollis, the mayor of Cooperstown, and then presented the J.G. Taylor Spink Award (Spink was the longtime publisher of the *Sporting News*) to the late Heywood Broun, a colorful and controversial sportswriter who had begun his career during the dead-ball era and had traveled to Marlin Springs with the Giants for many years. Then a number of introductions were made, each person standing to acknowledge the crowd's applause. Many of them had a special meaning for Rube. Mrs. Babe Ruth was there, as was the Babe's daughter Julia and sister Mamie. Christy Mathewson's niece, Mrs. William Van Lengen, was present, as was Honus Wagner's daughter, Mrs. Leslie Blair. Several members of the Veterans' Committee were in attendance, as were various league officials and executives. Twenty members of the Hall of Fame were also on hand, among them Zack Wheat, Edd Roush, Casey Stengel, and Stan Coveleski, and they were loudly cheered when they were introduced by Bowie Kuhn. Now with preliminary matters taken care of, it was time for the seven newest members to receive, as Kuhn put it, "the ultimate glory of baseball."[27]

Dave Bancroft was the first inductee. Because he was too ill to attend the ceremony, his old teammate with the Giants, Frankie Frisch, accepted the plaque on his behalf. Jake Beckley had died in 1918, and another teammate, Pie Traynor, gladly accepted the award for "Old Eagle Eye." Chick Hafey was next, and in his brief remarks he told the crowd that "this was the greatest thing that ever happened to me in baseball."[28]

Harry Hooper was the fourth inductee, and it was an emotional time for

Rube and Jane with Charles Guggenheimer and son Stephen, Hall of Fame induction day, August 9, 1971. Photo courtesy Charles Guggenheimer collection.

him. "It is very hard to explain the feelings, my feelings of being on the stand today," he said. "This is a culmination of many years of dreams and hopes, often very faint." He thanked the fans of Boston — the Royal Rooters of 60 years ago — and those of Chicago as well, who had once voted him the greatest right fielder in White Sox history. He had kind words for his teammates and the writers, coaches, and college instructors who had helped shape his life. He thanked his parents, saying that if they had not encouraged him to attend college and play baseball, he would probably have turned out a "farmer in the San Jacquin Valley, and nobody would have heard of me." As his children listened joyfully, Harry closed with a heartfelt "God bless you all."[29]

After Joe Kelley's son accepted his father's award, it came time for Rube. Commissioner Kuhn recited Rube's record as it appeared on the plaque which would hang in the great hall: "He was a three-time 20-game winner with the Giant champions of 1911, 1912 and 1913. He tied all-time records with 19 victories in a row while winning 26 and losing 11 in 1912. He led the National League in winning percentage and strikeouts in 1911. He tied for the most victories in 1912. He hurled a no-hit game against the Dodgers in 1915." As Rube rose to receive his plaque, Kuhn concluded, "This is the record of Richard William 'Rube' Marquard."[30]

Rube stood at the microphone, smiling, and looked out into the crowd. He thanked Kuhn for the introduction and said: "This is my day. I've been waiting

Charles, Jane, and Rube (now in a wheelchair) on one of their visits back to Cooperstown. Photo courtesy Charles Guggenheimer collection.

for this for the past 10 or 12 years. I'm going to make the best of it right now." The crowd laughed and applauded, and Rube continued, "I'm going to tell you when I first started to play baseball in Cleveland, Ohio..."

He recounted again the sandlots beginnings, the arguments with his father, the Telling Ice Cream company ballclub. He mentioned Charlie Carr and Bill Bradley, and to the delight of the audience he told how he beat the Indians in an exhibition game, showing up club president Somers who had refused to pay him what he was worth. He reminded the crowd that he had been purchased for the record sum of $11,000, and then he spoke of John McGraw. He was "the grandest, greatest manager in baseball.... He loved his players, and his players loved him."

Rube acknowledged his family from Baltimore and made special mention of "my beautiful wife. She's sitting over there, come on, Mrs. Marquard." Jane stood as the crowd applauded, and then Rube concluded his remarks. "I want to thank the world for this day," he said, "because it is mine."[31]

The next inductee was Satchel Paige, who entertained the crowd with a trademark humorous and rambling speech, quoting himself by saying, "Don't ever look back; something may be gaining on you," and, telling why he never ran out to the pitcher's mound: "I knew they couldn't play till I got there." He singled out from the audience Bill Veeck, the club owner who had first brought Satchel to the big leagues in 1948. Veeck was "fixin' to get run out of Cleveland

Rube's final resting place in Baltimore. Photo courtesy David D'Antonio.

if I didn't do good.... Well, Mr. Veeck, I got you off the hook today."[32] Finally, Ford Frick accepted a plaque for George Weiss, and the ceremony concluded.

Rube made the trip back to Cooperstown several times in the next few years. He greatly looked forward to the festivities and enjoyed reminiscing with old friends. One year Chief Meyers showed up, and the old battery mates swapped stories and made appearances at Doubleday Field at the annual exhibition game. Each year all attending Hall of Famers were photographed in front of Lake Otesega, and Rube proudly smiled for the camera, usually sitting next to Harry Hooper. (Harry was, until his death in 1974, regarded as the Hall's oldest living member; Rube never revealed his true birthdate or claimed the honor for himself.) As with most Hall of Famers, who gladly spent time with the fans (there were always a very few exceptions who did not feel they could be bothered), Rube never turned anyone away, and his sense of humor shone through clearly. Charles remembers how Rube roared with laughter once when a young boy, perhaps six or seven years of age, hesitatingly approached him with a baseball to be signed. "Are you anybody?" the boy asked.[33] In August of 1976 he received a letter from New York governor Hugh Carey, who had not been able to attend that summer's inductions at Cooperstown but had sent his children instead. "I write to express a father's appreciation," wrote Carey, "for your taking time and being so nice to my Little League sons.... They were still bubbling with enthusiasm upon their return home to tell me that they had met you and of your expressions of interest."[34] The letter meant enough to Rube that he kept it among his important papers for the rest of his life.

Cooperstown was glad to have Rube back every year on induction weekend. "Al Jolson, George M. Cohan and Christy Mathewson still come swinging down the lane in pictures, books and phonograph records," wrote Hall of Fame director Ken Smith in 1972, "but here is their pal Rube still charming the public in person. Glamorous favorite in the first two decades of the century, by his presence he is giving fans today an in-person taste of the days he shared rotogravure space with Mary Pickford, John McGraw, Victor Herbert and Caruso."[35]

Rube was immensely proud of his Hall of Fame membership, a fact made clear by a congratulatory birthday letter he sent to Harry Hooper in 1972:

> Dear Harry:
> I want to congratulate you on your 85th birthday and have many more with good health.
> Harry I am happy we are friends and in the same profession, baseball. You were loved by all your teammates and players you played against, and the baseball world.
> Now you are in the baseball Hall of Fame with all the great players. I am in it with you at Cooperstown.
> Have a good birthday and God be with you.[36]

Over the many years since 1912, Rube had seen several pitchers challenge his 19-game winning streak; all had fallen short. Pittsburgh's Roy Face had come the closest with 17 straight in 1959, and Carl Hubbell, Ewell Blackwell and Bob Gibson, among others, had reached 15 or 16. In 1978 the Yankees' Ron Guidry began his season with 13 wins in a row, and once again the media brought Rube's record back into the spotlight. Sportswriter Maury Allen interviewed Rube in Pikesville as Guidry's streak mounted. "I've followed the boy," said Rube. "He must be a pretty good pitcher to win all those games. Give him my best, and wish him well."[37] Rube's endorsement did Guidry little good, however; Milwaukee beat him in his next outing.

Inevitably Rube's health declined. He went for a check-up, and cancer of the prostate was discovered. The disease had spread so significantly, however, that Rube was beyond effective treatment. He started to experience trouble with his legs and began to use a cane, and then a wheelchair. On at least one occasion Charles drove him to Cooperstown, Rube's wheelchair folded in the back seat. Rube spent much of his time there sitting on the porch of the Otesega, contentedly greeting all who came by to say hello. In Baltimore he continued to attend social functions with Jane, sitting patiently at their table at the Suburban Club while she danced or bowled. He remained mentally alert and kept his sense of humor, slapping his thighs and telling friends that "these old legs of mine just don't seem to want to hold me up."[38] But there was no hope he would get better.

As a Christian Scientist, Rube refused to go to hospitals. Two nurses were hired to tend to him round the clock; it was particularly difficult for Rube to get in and out of bed, or the bathtub, and the fact that he needed such assistance wounded his pride. Finally the end came on Sunday night, June 1, 1980. Rube passed away in his sleep at the Pikesville apartment at the age of 93. He was cremated at the Louden Park Crematorium and then interred at Baltimore's Hebrew Cemetery, in Jane's family plot. She would join him there ten years later.

Appendix A: Playing Record of Richard W. (Rube) Marquard

Year	Club	League	G	IP	W	L	Pct	H	R	ER	SO	BB	ERA
1907	Canton	Cent	40	—	23	13	.639	—	—	—	—	—	—
1908	Indpls	AA	47	367	28	19	.596	234	—	—	250	135	—
1908	NY	NL	1	5	0	1	.000	6	5	—	2	2	—
1909	NY	NL	29	173	5	13	.278	155	81	—	109	72	—
1910	NY	NL	13	69	4	4	.500	65	35	—	52	40	—
1911	NY	NL	45	278	24	7	.774	221	98	—	237	106	—
1912	NY	NL	43	295	26	11	.703	286	112	84	175	80	2.56
1913	NY	NL	42	288	23	10	.697	248	100	80	151	49	2.50
1914	NY	NL	39	268	12	22	.353	261	117	91	92	47	3.06
1915	NY-BKN	NL	33	194	11	10	.524	207	102	87	92	38	4.04
1916	BKN	NL	36	205	13	6	.684	169	54	36	107	38	1.58
1917	BKN	NL	37	233	19	12	.613	200	84	66	117	60	2.55
1918	BKN	NL	34	239	9	18	.333	231	97	70	89	59	2.64
1919	BKN	NL	8	59	3	3	.500	54	17	15	29	10	2.29
1920	BKN	NL	28	190	10	7	.588	181	83	68	89	35	3.22
1921	CIN	NL	39	266	17	14	.548	291	123	100	88	50	3.38
1922	BOS	NL	39	198	11	15	.423	255	131	112	57	66	5.09
1923	BOS	NL	38	239	11	14	.440	265	127	99	78	65	3.73
1924	BOS	NL	6	36	1	2	.333	33	17	12	10	13	3.00
1925	BOS	NL	26	72	2	8	.200	105	60	46	19	27	5.75
1926	PROV	EAST	7	44	3	1	.750	49	19	18	22	17	3.68
1927	BALT	INTL	6	30	1	2	.333	38	—	—	5	6	—
1927	BIRM	SOU	3	11	0	1	.000	10	—	—	1	5	—
1928				(Out of organized baseball)									

Year	Club	League	G	IP	W	L	Pct	H	R	ER	SO	BB	ERA
1929	JACK	SE	3	3	0	0	.000	2	—	—	4	2	—
1930	JACK	SE	15	114	5	4	.556	106	36	27	47	21	2.13
1931				(Umpire, Eastern League)									
1932	ATL	SOU	6	42	1	3	.250	61	—	—	13	14	—
Major League			536	3307	201	177	.532	3233	1443	966	1593	858	3.13

WORLD SERIES RECORD

Year	Club	League	G	IP	W	L	Pct	H	R	ER	SO	BB	ERA
1911	NY	NL	3	11.2	0	1	.000	9	6	2	8	1	1.54
1912	NY	NL	2	18	2	0	1.000	14	3	1	9	2	0.50
1913	NY	NL	2	9	0	1	.000	10	7	7	3	4	7.00
1916	BKN	NL	2	11	0	2	.000	12	9	8	9	6	6.55
1920	BKN	NL	2	9	0	1	.000	7	3	1	6	3	1.00
Totals			11	58.2	2	5	.286	52	28	19	35	16	2.91

Appendix B: Rube Marquard's Nineteen Straight Victories in 1912

	Date	Opponent	H/A	Score	Opposing Pitcher	Hits	Walks	SO
1.	4-11	Brooklyn	A	18–3	Nap Rucker	7	3	3[a]
2.	4-16	Boston	A	8–2	George Tyler	6	1	3
	4-20	Brooklyn	H	4–3		0	0	0[b]
3.	4-24	Philadelphia	A	11–4	Grover Alexander	7	5	5
4.	5-01	Philadelphia	A	11–4	Tom Seaton	10	1	9
5.	5-07	St. Louis	A	6–2	Bill Steele	6	3	5
6.	5-11	Chicago	A	10–3	Lew Richie	8	3	5
7.	5-16	Pittsburgh	A	4–1	Marty O'Toole	4	1	3
8.	5-20	Cincinnati	A	3–0	Art Fromme	6	2	2
9.	5-24	Brooklyn	A	6–3	Pat Ragan	8	4	4
10.	5-30	Philadelphia	A	7–1	Tom Seaton	9	3	7
11.	6-03	St. Louis	H	8–3	Slim Sallee	9	3	6
12.	6-08	Cincinnati	H	6–2	Rube Benton	4	3	9
13.	6-13	Chicago	H	3–2	Three Finger Brown	8	0	5
14.	6-17	Pittsburgh	H	5–4	Marty O'Toole	12	3	8
15.	6-19	Boston	A	6–5	Otto Hess	2	0	3[c]
16.	6-21	Boston	A	5–2	Hub Perdue	10	1	5
17.	6-25	Philadelphia	H	2–1	Grover Alexander	6	0	5
18.	6-29	Boston	H	8–6	Buster Brown	11	0	5
19.	7-03	Brooklyn	H	2–1	Nap Rucker	9	5	3
Totals						142	41	95

[a] *Game called after six innings because of darkness.*
[b] *Relieved Jeff Tesreau in ninth inning with Giants trailing 3–2. Allowed no runs or hits. Giants scored two runs in the bottom of the ninth to win. Under modern scoring rules, credit for the victory would go to Marquard.*
[c] *Relieved Red Ames in the eighth inning, and NY won in the 10th.*

Notes

CHAPTER 1: THE SANDLOT CAPITAL OF THE WORLD

1. Cleveland *Daily Herald*, February 16, 1861.
2. David D. Van Tassel and John J. Grabowski, eds., *The Encyclopedia of Cleveland History* (Bloomington: Indiana University Press, 1987), p. 5,6.
3. *Ibid.*, p. 191.
4. *Ibid.*, p. 190.
5. *Ibid.*, xxix.
6. *Ibid.*, p. 541.
7. Credit for this discovery goes to Fred Schuld of Cleveland, Ohio.
8. Cleveland *Press*, July 6, 1912.
9. Van Tassel and Grabowski, *Encyclopedia of Cleveland History*, pp. 32, 33.
10. *Ibid.*
11. Harold Seymour, *Baseball: The Early Years* (New York: Oxford University Press, 1960), p. 26.
12. Lawrence S. Ritter, *The Glory of Their Times: The Story of the Early Days of Baseball Told by the Men Who Played It*, new enlarged edition (New York: William Morrow, 1984), p. 1.
13. Van Tassel and Grabowski, editors, *The Encyclopedia of Cleveland History*, p. 79.
14. Cleveland *Plain Dealer*, September 16, 1905.
15. *Ibid.*, September 17, 1905.
16. *Ibid.*, September 25, 1905.
17. *Ibid.*, October 16, 1905.
18. *Ibid.*, February 3, 1913.
19. Ritter, *Glory of Their Times*, p. 10.
20. Cleveland *Plain Dealer*, March 9, 1906.
21. Ritter, *Glory of Their Times*, p. 3,4.
22. Waterloo *Daily Courier*, June 16, 1906.

23. Ritter, *Glory of Their Times*, pp. 6, 7.
24. *Ibid.*, p. 8.
25. Cleveland *Plain Dealer*, June 23, 1906.

CHAPTER 2: THE ONE BEST BET

1. Lawrence S. Ritter, *The Glory of Their Times: The Story of the Early Days of Baseball Told by the Men Who Played It*, new enlarged edition (New York: William Morrow, 1984), p. 8.
2. Cleveland *Plain Dealer*, July 21, 1905.
3. For the best discussion of state baseball federations and the initial National Association, see Harold Seymour, *Baseball: The Early Years* (New York: Oxford University Press, 1960), Chapter Three.
4. Seymour, *Baseball: The Early Years*, p. 57.
5. Cleveland *Plain Dealer*, October 2, 1920.
6. Ritter, *Glory of Their Times*, p. 10.
7. Canton *Repository*, April 15, 1907.
8. *Ibid.*, April 19, 1907.
9. *Ibid.*, June 9, 1907.
10. *Ibid.*, June 15, 1907.
11. *Ibid.*, July 1, 1907.
12. *Ibid.*, July 22, 1907.
13. Ritter, *Glory of Their Times*, pp. 10, 13.
14. Indianapolis *Star*, April 14, 1908.
15. *Ibid.*, April 18, 1908.
16. *Ibid.*, April 25 and May 10, 1908.

CHAPTER 3: "I CAN BEAT ANYBODY"

1. Charles C. Alexander, *Ty Cobb* (New York: Oxford University Press, 1984), pp. 46, 47.
2. Lawrence S. Ritter, *The Glory of Their Times: The Story of the Early Days of Baseball Told by the Men Who Played It*, new enlarged edition (New York: William Morrow, 1984), pp. 12, 13.
3. Indianapolis *Star*, July 1, 1908.
4. Ritter, *Glory of Their Times*, p. 13; Indianapolis *Star*, September 3, 1908.
5. Ritter, *Glory of Their Times*, p. 13.
6. *Ibid.*, p. 11.
7. Cleveland *Plain Dealer*, July 2, 1908.
8. *Ibid.*, October 20, 1920.
9. *Sporting News*, July 2, 1908.
10. *Ibid.*, July 16, 1908.
11. Cleveland *Leader*, July 5, 1908.

12. Cleveland *Press*, July 5, 1908.
13. New York *Globe*, July 1, 1908.
14. *Sporting News*, June 18, 1908.
15. *Ibid.*, July 16, 1908.
16. *New York Times*, July 9, 1908.
17. *Ibid.*, July 12, 1908.
18. *Sporting News*, July 16, 1908.
19. Cleveland *Star*, July 5, 1908.
20. New York *Globe*, July 9, 1908.
21. New York *World*, August 2, 1908.
22. *Sporting Life*, quoted in *The Unforgettable Season* by G. H. Fleming (New York: Holt, Rinehart and Winston, 1981), p. 282.
23. *Sporting News*, August 12, 1908.
24. New York *Globe*, August 20, 1908.
25. Cleveland *Plain Dealer*, August 16, 1908.
26. Indianapolis *Star*, September 16, 1908.
27. *Sporting News*, November 5, 1908.
28. Indianapolis *Star*, September 16, 1908.

CHAPTER 4: MCGRAW, MERKLE, AND MAYHEM

1. New York *World*, September 17, 1908.
2. *Sporting News*, October 1, 1908.
3. New York *American*, quoted in Geoffrey C. Ward and Ken Burns, *Baseball: An Illustrated History* (New York: Alfred A. Knopf, 1994), p. 98.
4. Lawrence S. Ritter, *The Glory of Their Times: The Story of the Early Days of Baseball Told by the Man Who Played It*, new enlarged edition (New York: William Morrow, 1984), p. 23.
5. Charles C. Alexander, *John McGraw* (New York: Viking, 1988), p. 4.
6. *Ibid.*
7. *Ibid.*, p. 11.
8. *Ibid.*, pp. 7, 8.
9. *New York Times*, September 18, 1908.
10. New York *American*, September 18, 1908.
11. *Chicago Tribune*, September 23, 1908.
12. Carroll R. Tenney to the author, July 25, 1996.
13. Ritter, *Glory of Their Times*, p. 133.
14. John P. Carmichael, *My Greatest Day in Baseball* (New York: Grosset & Dunlap, 1955), p. 69.
15. *Sporting News*, September 17, 1908.
16. Ritter, *Glory of Their Times*, p. 137.
17. New York *Evening Mail*, September 24, 1908.
18. New York *Sun*, undated article, Rube Marquard file, National Baseball Library, Cooperstown, New York.
19. New York *American*, September 26, 1908.

20. *New York Times*, September 26, 1908.
21. New York *Morning Telegraph*, September 26, 1908.
22. *New York Times*, September 26, 1908.
23. Indianapolis *Star*, September 28, 1908.
24. Carmichael, *My Greatest Day in Baseball*, p. 24.
25. New York *Times*, October 9, 1908.
26. Carmichael, *My Greatest Day in Baseball*, pp. 25, 26, 28.
27. *Ibid.*, p. 26.
28. Ritter, *The Glory of Their Times*, p. 108.
29. Carmichael, *My Greatest Day in Baseball*, p. 24.
30. *Ibid.*, pp. 23, 24, 27.
31. *Ibid.*, p. 28.
32. *New York Times*, October 9, 1908.
33. Ray Robinson, *Matty: An American Hero* (New York: Oxford University Press, 1993), p. 109.

CHAPTER 5: THE $11,000 LEMON

1. Ray Robinson, *Matty: An American Hero* (New York: Oxford University Press, 1993), p. 85.
2. *New York Times*, April 11, 1909.
3. *Ibid.*, March 16, 1909.
4. Transcribed interview of Chief Meyers by Lawrence Ritter, National Baseball Library, Cooperstown, New York.
5. *New York Times*, March 17, 1909.
6. *Ibid.*, March 13, 1909.
7. *Ibid.*, April 7, 1909.
8. *Ibid.*, March 24, 1909.
9. *Ibid.*, April 18, 1909.
10. *Ibid.*
11. *Ibid.*, May 25, 1909.
12. *Ibid.*, June 6, 1909.
13. *Ibid.*, July 10, 1909.
14. *Ibid.*
15. *Ibid.*, July 11, 1909.
16. Lawrence S. Ritter, *The Glory of Their Times: The Story of the Early Days of Baseball Told by the Men Who Played It*, new enlarged edition (New York: William Morrow, 1984), p. 94.
17. *Sporting Life*, undated article.
18. *New York Times*, September 21, 1909.
19. *Ibid.*, September 24, 1909.
20. *Ibid.*, March 11, 1910.
21. *Ibid.*
22. *Ibid.*, March 17, 1910.
23. *Ibid.*, March 5, 1910.

24. *Ibid.*, March 19, 1910.
25. *Ibid.*
26. *New York Times*, April 21, 1910.
27. *Ibid.*, April 22, 1910.
28. *Sporting News*, June 2, 1910.
29. *Ibid.*, July 7, 1910.
30. *New York Times*, September 16, 1910.
31. *Ibid.*, September 18, 1910.
32. Unidentified article, Rube Marquard file, National Baseball Library, Cooperstown, New York.
33. Rube Marquard, "I Was a Big-League Failure," *Baseball* magazine, April 1912.
34. *Sporting News*, October 13, 1910.

CHAPTER 6: BEAUTY

1. Lawrence S. Ritter, *The Glory of Their Times: The Story of the Early Days of Baseball Told by the Men Who Played It*, new enlarged edition (New York: William Morrow, 1984), p. 176.
2. *Ibid.*, p. 96.
3. *Ibid.*, p. 16.
4. *New York Times*, March 17, 1911.
5. Unidentified article, Rube Marquard file, National Baseball Library, Cooperstown, New York.
6. *New York Times*, March 7, 13, 27, 1911.
7. *Sporting Life*, March 25, 1911.
8. *New York Times*, April 5, 1911.
9. *Ibid.*, April 8, 1911.
10. *Ibid.*, April 14, 1911.
11. *Ibid.*, April 15, 1911.
12. *Ibid.*
13. Fred Lieb, *Baseball As I Have Known It* (New York: Coward, McCann & Geoghegan, 1977), p. 35.
14. *New York Times*, April 15, 1911.
15. *Ibid.*, April 18, 1911.
16. *Ibid.*
17. New York *Globe*, April 19, 1911.
18. Rube Marquard, "I Was a Big-League Failure," *Baseball* magazine (April 1912).
19. *New York Times*, July 9, 1911.
20. *Sporting Life*, October 21, 1911.
21. *Sporting News*, July 12, 1911.
22. *Ibid.*, August 17, August 31, 1911.
23. *Sporting Life*, October 21, 1911.
24. Cleveland *Leader*, September 8, 1911.

25. *New York Times,* July 30, 1911.
26. *Ibid.,* August 15, 1911.
27. New York *Tribune,* August 15, 1911.
28. New York *American,* August 15, 1911.
29. Cleveland *Press,* September 18, 1911.
30. Thomas S. Busch, "In Search of Victory: The Story of Charles Victor 'Victory' Faust," *Kansas History: A Journal of the Great Plains* (summer 1983): 96.
31. Ritter, *Glory of Their Times,* p. 103.
32. Busch, "In Search of Victory," p. 101.
33. "Rube Marquard's Lucky Charm," unpublished manuscript researched and prepared by Gabriel Schecter, Los Gatos, California.
34. *Ibid.*
35. Tommy Holmes, "Remember Your Uncle Wilbert?" *Sport Life* (February 1949): 95.
36. *Sporting News,* October 9, 1911.

Chapter 7: Dangerous Men

1. *New York Times,* October 15, 1911.
2. New York *Herald,* October 17, 1911.
3. *Ibid.*
4. Bruce Kublick, *To Every Thing a Season: Shibe Park and Urban Philadelphia* (Princeton: Princeton University Press, 1991), p. 33.
5. *New York Times,* October 17, 1911.
6. New York *Herald,* October 17, 1911.
7. Lawrence S. Ritter, *The Glory of Their Times: The Story of the Early Days of Baseball Told by the Men Who Played It,* new enlarged edition (New York: William Morrow, 1984), p. 181.
8. Cleveland *Plain Dealer,* October 17, 1911.
9. *New York Times,* October 18, 1911.
10. Fred Lieb, *Baseball As I Have Known It* (New York: Coward, McCann & Geoghegan, 1977), p. 80.
11. *New York Times,* October 18, 1911.
12. Charles C. Alexander, *John McGraw* (New York: Viking, 1988), p. 158.
13. *New York Times,* October 18, 1911.
14. *Ibid.*
15. New York *American,* October 18, 1911.
16. Lieb, *Baseball As I Have Known It,* p. 81.
17. Cleveland *News,* October 21, 1911.
18. John J. McGraw, *My Thirty Years in Baseball* (New York: Boni and Liveright, 1923), p. 200.
19. *New York Times,* October 20, 1911.
20. *Ibid.,* October 19, 1911.
21. *Ibid.,* October 26, 1911.

22. Daniel Okrent and Harris Lewine, eds., *The Ultimate Baseball Book* (Boston: Houghton Mifflin, 1984), p. 84.
23. *New York Times*, October 27, 1911.

CHAPTER 8: A POPULAR YOUNG MAN

1. "Rube Marquard's Lucky Charm," unpublished manuscript researched and prepared by Gabriel Schecter, Los Gatos, California.
2. *Variety*, December 16, 1911.
3. *Ibid.*, January 13, 1912.
4. Cleveland *Plain Dealer*, January 7, 1912.
5. *Ibid.*
6. New York *Globe*, undated article by Sid Mercer, Rube Marquard file, National Baseball Library, Cooperstown, New York.
7. *Variety*, October 14, 1911.
8. New York *Globe*, undated article by Sid Mercer, Rube Marquard file, National Baseball Library, Cooperstown, New York.
9. *Ibid.*

CHAPTER 9: CLIMBING THE LADDER OF FAME

1. *New York Times*, April 21, 1912.
2. *Ibid.*
3. Cleveland *Leader*, May 26, 1912.
4. *New York Times*, May 25, 1912.
5. *Ibid.*, June 4, 1912.
6. *Ibid.*, June 13, 1912.
7. *Sporting Life*, June 22, 1912.
8. *New York Times*, June 18, 1912.
9. *Ibid.*
10. *Ibid.*
11. *Ibid.*
12. *Ibid.*
13. *Ibid.*, June 22, 1912.
14. *Ibid.*, June 26, 1912.
15. Cleveland *News*, July 2, 1912.
16. *Ibid.*
17. *New York Times*, July 8, 1912.
18. *Ibid.*, July 9, 1912.
19. *Sporting Life*, July 20, 1912.
20. *Ibid.*
21. *Ibid.*, July 27, 1912.
22. *New York Times*, July 22, 1912.
23. *Ibid.*, September 9, 1912.

24. *Moving Picture World* (August 1912).
25. *New York Times*, May 10, 1912.
26. *Sporting Life*, September 3, 1912.
27. Joseph Durso, *The Days of Mr. McGraw* (New York: Prentice-Hall, 1969), p. 89.
28. Lawrence S. Ritter, *The Glory of Their Times: The Story of the Early Days of Baseball Told by the Men Who Played It*, new enlarged edition (New York: William Morrow, 1984), p. 164.
29. Boston *Post*, October 10, 1912.
30. *Ibid.*, October 11, 1912.
31. *New York Times*, October 11, 1912.
32. *Ibid.*
33. *Ibid.*
34. *Ibid.*
35. *Ibid.*, October 15, 1912.
36. *Ibid.*, October 16, 1912.
37. Ritter, *Glory of Their Times*, p. 165.
38. Transcribed interview, Rube Marquard to Lawrence Ritter, National Baseball Library, Cooperstown, New York.
39. Ritter, *Glory of Their Times*, p. 149.
40. *Ibid.*, p. 150.
41. *New York Times*, October 17, 1912.
42. Article by Jeff Tesreau, New York *Herald*, October 17, 1912.
43. *New York Times*, October 17, 1912.
44. *Ibid.*

CHAPTER 10: SCANDAL

1. *Variety*, 1911, quoted in Anthony Slide, *The Encyclopedia of Vaudeville* (Westport, Conn.: Greenwood, 1994).
2. *Variety*, October 11, 1912.
3. "The Marquard Glide," lyrics by Rube Marquard and Thomas J. Gray, music by Blossom Seeley and W. Ray Walker, Jerome H. Remick & Company.
4. *Variety*, November 1, 1912.
5. Unidentified article dated November 23, 1912, Rube Marquard file, National Baseball Library, Cooperstown, New York.
6. Unidentified newspaper article dated December 12, 1912, Rube Marquard file, National Baseball Library, Cooperstown, New York.
7. *Ibid.*
8. *Sporting News*, February 6, 1913.
9. *Ibid.*, February 13, 1913.
10. Unidentified newspaper article, Rube Marquard file, National Baseball Library, Cooperstown, New York.
11. Cleveland *Press*, March 25, 1913.
12. *Sporting News*, March 13, 1913.

CHAPTER 11: THE BEST LEFT-HANDED PITCHER IN BASEBALL

1. *New York Times*, May 10, 1913.
2. *Ibid.*, June 31, 1913.
3. *Ibid.*, July 2, 1913.
4. *Ibid.*
5. *Ibid.*, July 5, 1913.
6. *Ibid.*, July 10, 1913.
7. *Ibid.*, August 6, 1913.
8. *Ibid.*, August 21, 1913.
9. *Ibid.*, October 6, 1913.
10. *Ibid.*
11. Cleveland *Leader*, October 6, 1913.
12. Cleveland *Plain Dealer*, October 8, 1913.
13. *New York Times*, October 8, 1913.
14. Cleveland *Plain Dealer*, October 8, 1913.
15. *Ibid.*
16. *New York Times*, October 8, 1913.
17. Cleveland *Plain Dealer*, October 8, 1913.
18. *Ibid.*
19. *New York Times*, October 12, 1913.
20. *Variety*, November 7, 1913.
21. *Ibid.*

CHAPTER 12: "WE WERE BOTH PRETTY MAD"

1. *New York Times*, March 7, 1914.
2. Charles C. Alexander, *John McGraw* (New York: Viking, 1988), p. 171.
3. *New York Times*, July 18, 1914.
4. *Ibid.*, July 21, 1914.
5. *Ibid.*
6. *Ibid.*, July 22, 1914.
7. *Ibid.*
8. *Ibid.*
9. *Ibid.*, August 29, 1914.
10. Daniel Okrent and Harris Lewine, eds., *The Ultimate Baseball Book* (Boston: Houghton Mifflin, 1984), p. 90.
11. Lowell Reidenbaugh, *The Sporting News: The First Hundred Years 1885–1986* (St. Louis: Sporting News Publishing, 1986), p. 62.
12. Lawrence S. Ritter, *The Glory of Their Times: The Story of the Early Days of Baseball Told by the Men Who Played It*, new enlarged edition (New York: William Morrow, 1984), p. 115.
13. *Ibid.*, p. 116.
14. *New York Times*, September 9, 1914.
15. *Ibid.*, September 22, 1914.

16. *Ibid.*, October 2, 1914.
17. Joe Tinker, "Putting Across the Federal League," *Everybody's Magazine* (May 1914).
18. *Sporting Life*, December 12, 1914.
19. *Sporting News*, December 10, 1914.
20. New York *Press*, undated article, Rube Marquard file, National Baseball Library, Cooperstown, New York.
21. *Ibid.*
22. New York *Press*, February 20, 1915.
23. *Sporting Life*, December 7, 1914.
24. New York *Press*, undated article, Rube Marquard file, National Baseball Library, Cooperstown, New York.
25. Unidentified article dated February 6, 1915, Rube Marquard file, National Baseball Library, Cooperstown, New York.
26. *Ibid.*
27. *Ibid.*
28. *Sporting News*, January 14, 1915.
29. *Sporting Life*, March 6, 1915.
30. *Sporting News*, March 4, 1915.
31. *New York Times*, April 13, 1915.
32. *Ibid.*, April 16, 1915.
33. *Ibid.*
34. *Ibid.*, June 31, 1915.
35. Transcribed interview of Chief Meyers by Lawrence Ritter, National Baseball Library, Cooperstown, New York.
36. *New York Times*, August 22, 1915.
37. Ritter, *Glory of Their Times*, pp. 16, 17.
38. *Sporting Life*, September 4, 1915.

CHAPTER 13: THE BOYS FROM ACROSS THE BIG BRIDGE

1. Geoffry C. Ward and Ken Burns, *Baseball: An Illustrated History* (New York: Alfred A. Knopf, 1994), p. 123.
2. Peter Golenbeck, *Bums: An Informal History of the Brooklyn Dodgers* (New York: G. P. Putnam's Sons, 1984), p. 19.
3. *New York Times*, April 30, 1916.
4. Cleveland *Press*, May 19, 1916.
5. *New York Times*, September 31, 1916.
6. *Ibid.*, September 26, 1916.
7. *Ibid.*, October 4, 1916.
8. *Ibid.*
9. *Ibid.*, October 14, 1916.
10. Burt Solomon, *The Baseball Timeline* (New York: Stonesong Press, 1997), p. 206.

11. *New York Times*, October 7, 1916.
12. *Ibid.*
13. Boston *Post*, October 7, 1916.
14. *Ibid.*
15. *Ibid.*
16. San Francisco *Chronicle*, October 8, 1916.
17. Lawrence S. Ritter, *The Glory of Their Times: The Story of the Early Days of Baseball Told by the Men Who Played It*, enlarged edition (New York: William Morrow, 1984), p. 165.
18. Boston *Post*, October 8, 1916.
19. Boston *Herald*, October 8, 1916.
20. Cleveland *Press*, October 8, 1916.
21. Boston *Post*, October 7, 1916.
22. *Ibid.*, October 10, 1916.
23. *New York Times*, October 12, 1916.
24. *Ibid.*, October 13, 1916.
25. Boston *Herald*, October 13, 1916.
26. *Variety*, December 23, 1916.
27. *New York Times*, July 2, 1916.
28. *Ibid.*, August 14, 1916.
29. *Sporting News*, January 17, 1918.
30. *New York Times*, June 19, 1918.
31. Maury Allen, *You Could Look It Up: The Life of Casey Stengel* (New York: Times Books, 1979), pp. 65, 66.

CHAPTER 14: "I GUESS I'M THE FALL GUY"

1. *New York Times*, May 5, 1919.
2. Lawrence S. Ritter, *The Glory of Their Times: The Story of the Early Days of Baseball Told by the Men Who Played It*, (New York: William Morrow, 1984), p. 16.
3. *Sporting News*, September 24, 1943.
4. Cleveland *Plain Dealer*, October 10, 1920.
5. *Ibid.*, October 6, 1920.
6. Cleveland *Press*, October 6, 1920.
7. Cleveland *Plain Dealer*, October 6, 1920.
8. Cleveland *Press*, October 6, 1920.
9. *Ibid.*, October 10, 1920.
10. Cleveland *Plain Dealer*, October 10, 1920.
11. *Ibid.*
12. Cleveland *Press*, October 11, 1920.
13. John Holway, "All in One Day," *Timeline* (September-October 1995): 20.
14. Ritter, *Glory of Their Times*, p. 239.
15. Cleveland *Plain Dealer*, October 11, 1920.
16. Cleveland *Press*, October 12, 1920.

17. *Ibid.*
18. *Ibid.*, October 13, 1920.
19. *Ibid.*, October 12, 1920.
20. *Ibid.*, October 13, 1920.
21. Cleveland *Plain Dealer*, October 12, 1920.

CHAPTER 15: BASEBALL'S MOST PICTURESQUE FIGURE

1. *Baseball* magazine, February 7, 1921.
2. *Sporting News*, December 23 and December 30, 1920.
3. Baltimore *Sun*, April 23, 1921.
4. Howard County *News*, October 11, 1979.
5. Ray Robinson, *Matty: An American Hero* (New York: Oxford University Press, 1993), p. 211.
6. Captioned photograph dated April 1, 1925, National Baseball Library and Archives, Cooperstown, New York.
7. Kay Marquard to the author, May 21, 1997.
8. New York *World-Telegram*, October 8, 1925.
9. *Sporting News*, September 23, 1926.
10. Unidentified article dated December 18, 1934, Rube Marquard file, National Baseball Library, Cooperstown, New York.
11. *Sporting News*, 1934. McGraw ranked the greatest batteries as follows: Christy Mathewson/Roger Bresnahan, Lefty Grove/Mickey Cochrane, Walter Johnson/Gabby Street, Three Finger Brown/Johnny Kling, Sadie McMahon/Wilbert Robinson, Rube Waddell/Ossie Schreckengost, Addie Joss/Harry Bemis, Joe McGinnity/Roger Bresnahan, Rube Marquard/Chief Meyers, Carl Hubbell/Gus Mancuso, Tim Keefe/Buck Ewing, Amos Rusie/Buck Ewing.
12. Unidentified article dated December 18, 1934, Rube Marquard file, National Baseball Library, Cooperstown, New York.
13. Cleveland *Press*, December 17, 1945.
14. Baltimore *Herald-Tribune*, *New York Times*, Cleveland *News*, September 4 and 5, 1947.
15. Baltimore *Herald-Tribune*, September 5, 1947.

CHAPTER 16: FINALLY COOPERSTOWN

1. Charles Guggenheimer to the author, September 16, 1996.
2. Don Beach to the author, April 3, 1996.
3. New York *World Telegraph*, April 29, 1932.
4. Undated newspaper article by John F. Steadman, National Baseball Library, Cooperstown, New York.
5. Mary Hevey to the author, March 26, 1997.
6. Letter to the editor of the Baltimore *Sun* from Edward Schechter, July 13, 1986.

7. Article dated April 13, 1963, Rube Marquard file, National Baseball Library, Cooperstown, New York.
8. Charles Guggenheimer and Barbara Guggenheimer Rock to the author, September 16, 1996.
9. Charles Guggenheimer to the author, September 16, 1996.
10. Bob Guggenheimer letter to the author, April 22, 1997.
11. Lawrence S. Ritter, *The Glory of Their Times: The Story of the Early Days of Baseball Told by the Men Who Played It*, new enlarged edition (New York: William Morrow, 1984), Original Preface, xvi.
12. *Ibid.*, Preface to the new enlarged edition, xiii.
13. *Ibid.*, Original Preface, xvii.
14. *Ibid.*, p. 15.
15. Lawrence Ritter to the author, May 6, 1995; published in Larry Mansch, "Rube Marquard Revisited," *National Pastime* (spring 1996).
16. An enlarged edition of *The Glory of Their Times* published in 1984 included additional chapters containing the stories of George Gibson, Babe Herman, Specs Toporcer, and Hank Greenberg.
17. *New York Times*, September 18, 1966.
18. Ted Williams' review of Ritter, *The Glory of Their Times*, 1966.
19. Bill James, *The Politics of Glory: How Baseball's Hall of Fame Really Works* (New York: Macmillan, 1994), p. 170.
20. Ritter, *Glory of Their Times*, Preface to the new enlarged edition, x.
21. Charles Guggenheimer to the author, September 16, 1996.
22. Waterloo *Daily Courier*, April 27, 1971.
23. Paul J. Zingg, *Harry Hooper: An American Baseball Life* (Urbana: University of Illinois Press, 1993), p. 221.
24. James, *Politics of Glory*, p. 187.
25. Marie Hooper Strain letter to the author, October 2, 1996.
26. Charles Guggenheimer letter to the author, September 16, 1996.
27. Transcript, induction ceremony, August 9, 1971, National Baseball Hall of Fame Library and Archive, Cooperstown, New York.
28. *Ibid.*
29. *Ibid.*
30. *Ibid.*
31. *Ibid.*
32. *Ibid.*
33. Charles Guggenheimer letter to the author, September 16, 1996.
34. Governor Hugh Carey letter to Rube Marquard, August 16, 1976, in the possession of Charles Guggenheimer.
35. Unidentified article dated July 21, 1972, by Ken Smith, director, National Baseball Hall of Fame and Museum, Cooperstown, New York.
36. Rube Marquard letter to Harry Hooper dated August 24, 1972, in the possession of John Hooper.
37. Unidentified newspaper article, July 1978, Rube Marquard file, National Baseball Library, Cooperstown, New York.
38. Bob Guggenheimer letter to the author, November 1996.

Bibliography

ARCHIVAL RESOURCES

John J. McGraw Collection, National Baseball Library, Cooperstown, New York.
Rube Marquard Collection, National Baseball Library, Cooperstown, New York.
Rube Marquard personal scrapbook and miscellaneous clippings, Guggenheimer family archives, Rockville, Maryland.
Christy Mathewson Collection, National Baseball Library, Cooperstown, New York.
Wilbert Robinson Collection, National Baseball Library, Cooperstown, New York.
Blossom Seeley sound recordings, Library of Congress Collection, Washington, D.C.

NEWSPAPERS

Baltimore *Sun*, 1921–22, 1986.
Boston *Herald*, 1912, 1916.
Boston *Post*, 1912, 1916.
Canton *Repository*, 1907–1908.
Chicago Tribune, 1908.
Cleveland *Leader*, 1908–1920.
Cleveland *Plain Dealer*, 1886–1980.
Des Moines *Register*, 1906.
Indianapolis *Star*, 1907–1908.
New York *Clipper*, 1908.
New York Times, 1908–1980.
New York *World*, 1908.
San Francisco *Chronicle*, 1916.
Sporting Life, 1911–1917.
Sporting News, 1908–1971.
Variety, 1908–1915.
Waterloo *Daily Courier*, 1906, 1971.

PERSONAL COMMUNICATIONS

Telephone conversation, Vince Bagley, Baltimore, Maryland, April 2, 1997, and correspondence.
Telephone conversation, Don Beach, Orlando, Florida, April 3, 1997.

Telephone conversation, Jim Breatty, Baltimore, Maryland, March 27, 1997, and correspondence.
Telephone conversation, Bucky Brush, Milwaukee, Wisconsin, June 16, 1996, and correspondence.
Telephone conversations, Charles Guggenheimer, Rockville, Maryland, March 22, April 11, June 8, August 23, 1996. Personal interview, September 16, 1996.
Interview, Barbara Guggenheimer Rock, Rockville, Maryland, September 15, 1996.
Telephone conversation, Mary Hevey, Reisters Town, Maryland, March 26, 1997, and correspondence.
Telephone conversation, John Hooper, Baytown, Texas, September 5, 1996, and correspondence.
Telephone conversation, Dave Kelly, Washington, D.C., July 9, 1996; personal interview, September 13, 1996.
Telephone conversation, Bob Maisel, Ellicott City, Maryland, May 7, 1997.
Telephone conversations, Kay Marquard, Shelby Township, Michigan, January–June 1997, and correspondence.
Interview, Lawrence S. Ritter, New York, New York, May 6, 1995, and correspondence.
Interview, Ray Robinson, New York, New York, May 5, 1995, and correspondence.
Telephone conversation, Gabriel Schecter, Los Gatos, California, February 22, 1997, and correspondence.
Correspondence, Marie Hooper Strain, Capilita, California, September 1996–June 1997.
Telephone conversation and correspondence, Carroll Tenney, winter, 1996–97.
Telephone interview, Frank Youngwerth, Hudson, Ohio, July 7, 1996.

BOOKS

Alexander, Charles C. *John McGraw*. New York: Viking, 1988.
_____. *Rogers Hornsby*. New York: Henry Holt, 1995.
_____. *Ty Cobb*. New York: Oxford University Press, 1984.
Allen, Frederick Lewis. *Only Yesterday*. New York: Harper & Brothers, 1931.
Allen, Maury. *You Could Look It Up*. New York: Times Books, 1979.
Asinof, Elliot. *Eight Men Out: The Black Sox and the 1919 World Series*. New York: Holt, Rinehart, and Winston, 1963.
Astor, Gerald. *The Baseball Hall of Fame 50th Anniversary Book*. New York: Prentice-Hall, 1988.
Blake, Mike. *Baseball Chronicles*. Cincinnati: Betterway Books, 1994.
Brown, Warren. *The Chicago Cubs*. New York: G.P. Putnam's Sons, 1946.
Carmichael, John P. *My Greatest Day in Baseball*. New York: Grosset & Dunlap, 1951.
Cobb, Ty, with Al Stump. *My Life in Baseball: The True Record*. New York: Doubleday, 1961.
Creamer, Robert. *Babe: The Legend Comes to Life*. New York: Simon and Schuster, 1974.
Donald, David Herbert. *Lincoln*. New York: Simon and Schuster, 1995.

_____. *Stengel: His Life and Times.* New York: Simon and Schuster, 1984.
Ehrenberg, Lewis. *Steppin' Out: New York Nightlife and the Transformation of American Culture, 1890–1930.* Chicago: University of Chicago Press, 1981.
Evers, John J., and Hugh S. Fullerton. *Touching Second: The Science of Baseball.* Chicago: Reilly and Britton, 1910.
Farrell, James T. *My Baseball Diary.* New York: Vanguard Press, 1959.
Fleming, G.H., ed. *The Unforgettable Season.* New York: Penguin Books, 1982.
Fowler, Gene. *Spalding's Official Base Ball Record.* New York: American Sports Publishing, 1907–32.
Frommer, Harvey. *Baseball's Greatest Managers.* New York: Franklin Watts, 1985.
_____. *Shoeless Joe and Ragtime Baseball.* Dallas: Taylor Publishing, 1992.
Golenbock, Peter. *Bums.* New York: G.P. Putnam's Sons, 1984.
Graham, Frank. *The Brooklyn Dodgers: An Informal History.* New York: G.P. Putnam's Sons, 1945.
Greenberg, Eric Rolfe. *The Celebrant.* Lincoln: University of Nebraska Press, 1993.
Gropman, Donald. *Say It Ain't So, Joe!* New York: Lynx Books, 1979.
Hageman, William. *Honus: The Life and Times of a Baseball Hero.* Champaign: Sagamore, 1996.
Honig, Donald. *Baseball Between the Lines.* New York: Coward, McCann & Geoghegan, 1976.
_____. *Baseball When the Grass Was Real.* New York: Coward, McCann & Geoghegan, 1975.
Humphries, Rolfe. *Collected Poems of Rolfe Humphries.* Bloomington: Indiana University Press, 1965.
James, Bill. *The Politics of Glory.* New York: Macmillan, 1994.
Kunhardt, Dorothy Meserve, and Philip B. Kunhardt, Jr. *Twenty Days.* New York: Castle Books, 1965.
Lewis, Franklin. *The Cleveland Indians.* New York: G.P. Putnam and Sons, 1949.
Lieb, Fred. *Baseball As I Have Known It.* New York: Coward, McCann & Geoghegan, 1977).
_____. *The Story of the World Series.* New York: G.P. Putnam's Sons, 1965.
McGraw, John J. *My Thirty Years in Baseball.* New York: Boni and Liveright, 1923.
McGraw, Mrs. John J. *The Real McGraw.* Edited by Arthur Mann. New York: David McKay, 1953.
Mack, Connie. *My 66 Years in the Big Leagues.* New York: John C. Winston, 1950.
Mathewson, Christy. *Pitching in a Pinch.* Reprint. New York: Stein and Day, 1977.
Okkonen, Marc. *The Federal League of 1914–1915: Baseball's Third Major League.* Garrett Park, Md.: Society for American Baseball Research, 1989.
Okrent, Daniel, and Harris Lewine, eds. *The Ultimate Baseball Book.* Boston: Houghton Mifflin, 1984.
Reichler, Joseph L. *The Great All-Time Baseball Record Book.* New York: Macmillan, 1981.
Ribowsky, Mark. *Don't Look Back: Satchel Paige in the Shadows of Baseball.* New York: Simon and Schuster, 1994.
Rice, Damon. *Seasons Past.* New York: Praeger, 1976.
Rice, Grantland. *The Tumult and the Shouting: My Life in Sport.* New York: Dell, 1954.

Riess, Steven. *Touching Base: Professional Baseball and the American Culture in the Progressive Era.* Westport, Conn.: Greenwood, 1980.
Ritter, Lawrence S. *The Glory of Their Times: The Story of the Early Days of Baseball Told by the Men Who Played It,* new enlarged edition. New York: William Morrow, 1984.
_____. *Lost Ballparks.* New York: Viking, 1992.
_____, and Donald Honig. *The Image of Their Greatness.* New York: Crown, 1979.
Robinson, Ray. *Matty: An American Hero.* New York: Oxford University Press, 1993.
Ruth, George Herman (Babe), and Bob Consodine. *The Babe Ruth Story.* New York: E.P. Dutton, 1948.
Seymour, Harold. *Baseball: The Early Years.* New York: Oxford University Press, 1960.
Smelser, Marshall. *The Life That Ruth Built.* New York: Quadrangle, 1975.
Sobol, Ken. *Babe Ruth and the American Dream.* New York: Ballantine Books, 1974.
Soloman, Burt. *The Baseball Timeline.* New York: Avon Books, 1996.
Sowell, Mike. *The Pitch That Killed.* New York: Macmillan, 1989.
Spritzer, Marian. *The Palace.* New York: Atheneum, 1969.
Suehsdorf, A.D. *The Great American Baseball Scrapbook.* New York: Rutledge, 1978.
Thomas, Henry W. *Walter Johnson: Baseball's Big Train.* Washington D.C.: Phenom Press, 1995.
Thorn, John, ed. *The National Pastime.* New York: Warner, 1987.
_____. *Total Baseball.* New York: HarperCollins, 1993.
Van Tassel, David D., and John J. Grabowski, eds. *The Encyclopedia of Cleveland History.* Bloomington: Indiana University Press, 1987.
Voight, David Quentin. *American Baseball.* Norman: University of Oklahoma Press, 1970.
Ward, Geoffrey C., and Ken Burns. *Baseball: An Illustrated History.* New York: Alfred A. Knopf, 1994.
Weinberg, Robert L. *The Suburban Club of Baltimore County: 1900–1995.* Baltimore: Suburban Club, 1995.
Yardley, Jonathan. *Ring: A Biography of Ring Lardner.* New York: Atheneum, 1984.
Zingg, Paul J. *Harry Hooper: An American Baseball Life.* Urbana: University of Illinois Press, 1993.

ARTICLES

Busch, Thomas S. "In Search of Victory: The Story of Charles Victor 'Victory' Faust." *Kansas History: A Journal of the Great Plains* (summer 1983): 96–106.
Chambers, Bill. "Young and a Giant." *National Pastime* 13 (1993): 43–44.
Holway, John. "All in One Game." *Timeline* (September-October 1995): 16–23.
Keetz, Frank. "The Board." *National Pastime* 13 (1993): 3–4.
Mansch, Larry D. "Rube Marquard Revisited." *National Pastime* (1996): 16–20.
Ritter, Lawrence S. "Ladies and Gentlemen, Presenting Marty McHale." *National Pastime* (Premiere Issue, fall 1982): 16–21.
Williams, Franklin J. "All the Record Books Are Wrong." *National Pastime* (Premiere Issue, fall 1982): 50–62.

Index

Adams, Babe 63, 144, 145, 174
Adams, Franklin P. 41
Alexander, Grover Cleveland 79, 103, 106, 108, 110, 130, 131, 147, 160, 166, 168, 172, 174, 209
Allen, Maury 220
Ames, Leon "Red" 34, 55, 59, 67, 73, 81, 92, 93, 108, 130
Anklam, Ernest 15, 16
Archer, Jimmy 106
Aulick, W.W. 44, 48, 75, 130, 155
Austin, George 97
Austin, Jimmy 22

Bagby, Jim 181, 184, 185
Bailey, Bill 171
Baker, Frank "Home Run" 84, 85, 86, 88, 89, 90, 91, 92, 96, 111, 136, 137, 139, 140, 142, 159, 209, 211
Baker, Newton 176
Bancroft, Dave 193, 196, 214, 216
Bang, Ed 109
Barnes, Gertrude 183
Barry, Jack 84, 92, 93, 137, 168
Barrymore, Ethel 141
Bates, John 130
Beach, Don 206

Becherman, Nate 184
Beck, Martin 141
Becker, Beals 108, 115
Beckley, Jake 214, 216
Bedient, Hugh 113, 116, 117, 151
Belinsky, Bo 208
Bender, Charles "Chief" 85, 86, 92, 93, 96, 111, 137, 138, 139, 140, 151, 209
Bennett, Eddie 180, 183
Benny, Jack 203, 208
Benton, Rube 106, 110, 138
Berlin, Irving 97
Bernhardt, Sarah 141
Bescher, Bob 47, 143, 145
Bishop, Paul 78
Blackwell, Ewell 220
Blair, Leslie 216
Bradley, Bill 19, 22, 23, 26, 99, 151, 210, 218
Brannan, Addison "Eddie" 131, 167
Bresnahan, Phil 53
Bresnahan, Roger 42, 43, 47, 48, 51, 53, 60, 76, 79, 145
Bressler, Rube 178, 191
Brice, Fannie 121
Bridwell, Al 42, 45, 47, 58, 59, 62, 68, 77, 94, 150
Britton, Schuyler 152
Broun, Heywood 75, 182, 216

Brown, Buster 65
Brown, Charley 97
Brown, "Three Finger" 41, 44, 47, 50, 51, 54, 63, 106, 209
Brush, John T. 30, 31, 34, 44, 50, 57, 58, 61, 65, 75, 77, 86, 150
Bryce, T.J. 35
Bugler, Bozeman 78, 96
Burns, George (ballplayer) 129, 130, 138, 139, 164, 191, 207
Burns, George (entertainer) 208
Burns, "Tioga George" 181, 184, 186
Bush, Bullet Joe 140, 142
Bush, Donie 93
Bush, Ted 102
Byrne, Bobby 68, 107
Byron, Bill 144

Cadore, Leon 176, 179, 184
Cady, Forrest 116, 169
Caldwell, Ray 181
Camnitz, Howie 130
Capone, Al 202
Carey, Hugh 219
Carey, Max 199, 200, 207
Carr, Charlie 23, 24, 25, 26, 27, 29, 30, 36, 37, 38, 39, 54, 210, 218
Carrigan, Bill 114, 168, 171

245

246 Index

Cartwright, Alexander 19
Chadwick, Henry 20
Chalmers, George 156
Chance, Dean 208
Chance, Frank 44, 45, 46, 47, 50, 51, 77, 209
Chandler, Happy 178
Chapman, Ray 180
Chase, Hal 150
Cheney, Larry 110, 112, 159, 160, 163, 165, 171, 173, 175
Chesbro, Jack 107
Cigranz, Fred 113
Clarke, Fred 41, 42, 76, 77, 107
Cliff, Laddie 98
Clymer, Jim 158
Cobb, Ty 26, 28, 31, 41, 53, 63, 82, 93, 96, 111, 113, 115, 145, 168, 200, 207, 209, 210, 212
Cohan, George M. 137, 220
Cole, Harry Dix 152, 160
Collins, Eddie 84, 87, 88, 136, 137, 138, 139, 140
Collins, Ray 113, 115
Comiskey, Charles 22, 137, 214
Conner, William 121
Connolly, Tom 139, 169, 209
Cook, Nate 169
Coombs, Jack 85, 89, 93, 137, 160, 164, 165, 170
Cooper, Jackie 203
Corbett, Gentleman Jim 70
Corbett, Joe 77
Courthope, Jane 98
Coveleski, Harry 49, 167
Coveleski, Stan 181, 182, 184, 186, 211, 212, 216
Cowan, Lynn 171
Cox, Rae 97
Crandall, Doc 67, 75, 76, 79, 92, 106, 115, 134, 140
Crandall, Otis 44, 62
Crane, Sam 149
Cravath, Gavvy 130, 145, 160
Creamer, Dr. William 50
Cronin, Joe 50
Cross, Harry 89, 90
Cullen, James 127
Cuppy, George "Nig" 21
Curley, James M. 148
Cutshaw, George 136, 159, 169, 170, 173, 174, 175

Dahlen, Bill 103
Daniel, Dan 209, 213
Daniels, Bert 146
Daubert, Jake 103, 145, 159, 169, 170, 173, 174, 175
Davis, Harry 84, 86, 89, 92, 93, 134
Day, John B. 58
Delahanty, "Big Ed" 22, 99, 151, 191
Delahanty, Joe 62
Dell, Wheezer 164, 172
Demaree, Al 132, 136, 140
Devery, William 75
Devlin, Art 51, 53, 55, 73
Devore, Josh 64, 77, 78, 79, 85, 89, 92, 197, 109, 113, 114, 116, 117, 118, 123, 130, 132, 200
Dillingham, Charles 121
Dinneen, Bill 197
Doak, "Spittin' Bill" 191
Donlin, Mike 42, 51, 53, 54, 61, 64, 78, 79, 83, 96, 97, 121, 125, 150
Dooin, Charles 96, 131
Dooley, William 172
Doubleday, Abner 200
Douglas, "Shufflin' Phil" 146
Dowling, Frank 177
Doyle, Larry 42, 49, 53, 59, 60, 77, 87, 92, 107, 108, 114, 115, 123, 129, 138, 139, 140, 143, 145, 154, 173, 177, 207
Dreyfuss, Barney 41, 63, 79
Drucke, Lou 105
Drysdale, Don 207
Duncan, Pat 191
Durham, Lou 27, 33, 39, 40, 48, 55, 63, 65

Ebbetts, Charles 78, 85, 146, 159, 161, 162, 168, 174, 180, 183, 186, 189, 199
Edwards, Henry P. 99, 183
Egan, Dick 47
Emslie, Bob 45
Engle, Clyde 114, 118
Ervin, Tex 75, 103
Eubanks, Doc 27
Evans, Billy 82
Evans, Joe 181
Evans, Steve 68
Evers, Johnny 45, 46, 47, 50, 77, 146, 209

Fabrique, Albert 172
Face, Roy 220
Farrell, Frank 75, 76
Faust, Charles Victor 81, 82, 83, 86, 87, 99, 103
Feix, Henry S. 127
Feller, Bob 215
Fields, Benny 188, 202, 203, 208
Fields, Lew 79, 120
Fitzgerald, F. Scott 195
FitzGerald, John J. 114
Fletcher, Art 19, 64, 77, 90, 91, 92, 105, 115, 123, 135, 139, 144, 155
Flick, Elmer 99
Flynn, Marie 121
Ford, Whitey 207, 208
Fox, William 97
Frazee, Harry 172, 215
Frederick, Johnny 199
Frefield, George 172
Frick, Ford 215, 219
Frisch, Frankie 180, 213, 216
Fromme, Art 130, 133, 155
Fuchs, Emil 193
Fullerton, Hugh 115, 168
Fultz, David 146, 152

Gainor, Del 170
Gardner, Larry 113, 114, 118, 168, 170, 171, 180
Gehringer, Charlie 213
Gershwin, George 202
Gibson, Bob 220
Giles, Warren 213
Gilmore, "Fighting Jim" 151
Gleason, Kid 215
Gonzalez, Mike 191
Gordon, David 96
Gowdy, Hank 149
Grant, Eddie 139, 149
Grant, George W. 192
Gray, Thomas J. 121, 137, 141
Griffith, Tommy 177, 179
Grimes, Burleigh 174, 175, 179, 182, 184, 185, 209
Groh, Heinie 130, 177
Guggenheimer, Bob 208
Guggenheimer, Charles 208, 213, 216, 219, 220
Guidry, Ron 220

Hafey, Charles "Chick" 214, 216
Hall, Al 21

Index

Hammanoto, Togo 73
Hammerstein, Willie 97
Hanlon, Ned 21, 70, 161
Harper, John 189
Harridge, William 212
Harris, Dave 197
Hartley, Grover "Slick" 83, 131
Hartnett, Gabby 163
Hawkins, Tommy 14
Hawley, E.F. 97
Hazelton, Clara 52
Heiser, Lena 8, 9, 10
Hempstead, Harry 132, 151, 153
Hendricks, Elrod 207
Hendrix, Claude 133, 150
Henriksen, Olaf 115, 117
Herbert, Fred 158, 159
Herbert, Victor 220
Herman, Babe 199
Herrmann, August "Garry" 30, 34, 145
Herz, Ralph 121
Herzog, Buck 47, 77, 83, 86, 87, 89, 90, 108, 115, 123, 129, 131, 139, 146, 147
Hevey, Barry 206
Hevey, Mary 206
Heydler, John 107, 131, 183, 184, 186, 187
Higgins, John F. 73
Hite, Mabel 42, 53, 66, 64, 79, 96, 99, 121
Hoblitzell, Dick 168, 169, 170
Hofman, Artie 45
Hollis, Harold 216
Hooper, Esther 215
Hooper, Harry 113, 114, 115, 117, 118, 168, 169, 170, 172, 211, 214, 216, 217, 219, 220
Hooper, Harry, Jr. 215
Hooper, John 215
Hooper, Marie 215, 216
Hope, Bob 203
Hornsby, Rogers 207
Houdini, Harry 97
Howard, Eddy 127
Hoyt, Waite 213
Hubbell, Carl 220
Huff, George 28
Huggins, Miller 146, 199
Huston, Tillinghast 199
Hutton, Betty 203

Irvin, Monte 215
Isman, Felix 61

Jackson, Joe 98
Jackson, Shoeless Joe 134, 159
James, Bill 147, 212, 215
Jamieson, Charlie 181, 184, 185
Janvrin, Harold 168, 169, 170
Jefferson, Joseph 141
Jennings, Hughie 30, 159
Johnson, Ban 21, 90, 137, 145, 146
Johnson, Walter 82, 110, 113, 151, 165, 196, 200
Johnston, Doc 185
Johnston, Jimmy 59, 62, 170, 185
Jolson, Al 121, 137, 220
Joyce, Alice 112
Judge, Joe 179

Kane, Johnny 47
Kane, Joseph 100, 121, 124, 126
Kauff, Benny 151, 188
Keefe, Bobby 78
Keefe, Tim 106
Keeler, Wee Willie 70
Kelley, Joe 214, 217
Kellogg, Shirley 120
Kelly, Bill 107
Kelly, Mike "King" 31
Kenetchy, Ed 165, 177, 181, 184
Kent, Annie 97, 98, 99
Kerr, C.H. 98
Kerr, Paul 213, 215
Kilduff, Pete 179, 181, 185
Kilfoyle, John 22, 23
Killifer, Bill 108
Kinsella, Dick 127
Kirk, William 48, 97
Kitchenor, Lord 65
Klass, Charlie 97
Klem, Bill 50, 92, 100, 130, 138, 143, 148, 209
Kling, Johnny 42, 51, 61, 96
Koph, Bill 192
Koufax, Sandy 208
Kraft, Clarence "Big Boy" 145, 146
Kroh, Floyd 45
Kuhn, Bowie 215, 216, 217

LaCroix, Paul 97
Lajoie, Napoleon 19, 22, 23, 26

Lampton, W.J. 50
Landis, Kenesaw Mountain 30, 151, 152, 161, 183, 188, 189, 196, 209
Lang, Jack 215
Lanigan, Ernest 67
Lapp, Jack 87, 90
Lardner, Ring 168
Lashwood, George 98
Latham, Arlie 57, 62
Lavender, Jimmy 110, 111
Law, Ruth 163
Leach, Tommy 22, 41, 42, 68, 77, 99, 145, 191
Lederer, George 121
Leonard, Dutch 168, 170
Levine, Charles 193
Lewis, Duffy 113, 114, 115, 118, 168, 170, 171
Lewis, Katie 52
Lewis, Tom 96
Lieb, Fred 75, 89, 91, 106, 151
Lincoln, Abraham 5, 7
Lincoln, Mary 5
Lincoln, Robert 5
Livingston, Arthur "Paddy" 25, 26, 27
Lobert, Hans 47, 155, 157, 207
Lord, Bristol 85, 87, 88
Luby, John 106
Lumley, Harry 59
Lunte, Harry 180
Luque, Dolf 191
Lynch, Thomas 137

Mack, Charles 97
Mack, Connie 26, 83, 84, 85, 91, 92, 93, 134, 136, 137, 141, 159
Magee, Lee 151
Magee, Sherwood 61, 130, 165
Mails, Walter 186
Mamaux, Al 174, 175, 179, 184
Maranville, Rabbit 147, 150
Marquard, Frank 8, 200
Marquard, Fred 8, 9, 12, 14, 15, 17, 18, 23, 25, 52, 99, 191, 200, 202, 210
Marquard, Hattie 8, 10, 188, 195, 202
Marquard, Herbert 8, 183, 186

Index

Marquard, Jane Hecht Guggenheimer 204, 206, 208, 209, 210, 213, 216, 218, 220, 221
Marquard, Naomi Malone 181, 188, 189, 190, 191, 192, 195, 197, 200, 202, 204
Marquard, Richard "Dick" William, Jr. 134, 142, 150, 171, 188, 195, 196, 202, 203, 208
Marquardt, Charles 8
Marquardt, Christina 8, 10, 155
Marquardt, Ferdinand 8, 14
Marquardt, Paul 8
Marsans, Armando 78
Mathewson, Christy 33, 42, 50–55, 59, 60, 62, 63, 65, 67, 68, 71, 72, 76, 78, 79, 81, 83, 86–92, 96, 100, 102, 105, 113–115, 117–119, 123, 129–132, 134, 136, 137, 139, 140, 143, 147, 149, 150, 154–157, 165, 166, 190, 192, 193, 196, 200, 209, 210, 212, 220
Mathewson, Nicholas 53
Mays, Carl 168, 169, 170, 180
McAlvey, Robert 202
McBeth, William 125
McConnell, Lulu 98
McCormick, "Moose" 45, 105, 139, 207
McDonough, James 193
McGinnity, Joe 33, 34, 42, 43, 44, 45, 49, 53, 71, 209
McGraw, Blanche 143, 207
McGraw, John J. 21, 30, 31, 33–34, 37, 38, 42–45, 47–49, 51–55, 57–73, 76–78, 81–94, 96, 100, 102, 103, 105, 108, 111, 112, 114–116, 118, 119, 123–127, 129–132, 134, 136–141, 144, 146, 147, 149, 151–159, 162, 166, 167, 179, 180, 191, 193, 196, 200, 202, 206, 209, 211, 218, 220
McGreevey, Mike "Nuf Sed" 114, 117
McGregory, F.E. 73
McHale, Marty 150
McInnis, Stuffy 84, 137, 138, 140

McIntire, Harry 77
McKean, Ed 99
McKeever, Edwin 162, 199
McKeever, Stephen 162, 199
McKinley, Mrs. William 24
McLean, Larry 134, 139, 140
McNally, Mike 170
Meany, Tom 196
Medicus, Henry 162
Meehan, James 202
Meeker, Ralph 203
Menke, Fred 86, 91
Mensor, Eddie 144
Mercer, Sid 36, 75, 100
Merkle, Fred 42, 45–47, 51, 55, 58, 60, 63, 64, 68, 73, 77, 82, 86, 88–90, 92, 115, 117–119, 134, 138–140, 143, 149, 155, 164, 166, 167, 173, 211
Meyers, Chief 33, 49, 54, 55, 58, 60, 65, 71, 77, 82, 86–89, 93, 96, 106–108, 113, 115, 118, 123, 132, 135–139, 156, 157, 163, 164, 166, 169, 171, 200, 211, 219
Miljus, Johnny 176
Miller, Dots 68, 107
Miller, Gump 106
Miller, Hack 170
Mills, Art 197
Mitchell, Clarence 185
Mitchell, Fred 192
Monroe, Marilyn 203
Moran, Charlie 197
Moran, Herbie 136
Moran, Pat 189
Moren, Lew 61
Morgan, Cy 96, 97
Mowrey, Mike 143, 172
Murphy, Charles Webb 33, 81
Murphy, Dan 85, 89, 90, 92, 136, 137, 138
Murray, Jack 156
Murray, Red 55, 60, 77, 90, 93, 107, 114, 117, 118, 123, 134, 137, 156, 158
Musial, Stan 207
Myers, Bade 22, 24, 25
Myers, Hy 155, 170, 173, 179

Navin, Frank 30
Neale, Greasy 178
Nichols, Kid 193

O'Day, Hank 46, 62
Oldring, Rueben 85, 87, 88, 90, 92, 137, 138, 140
Olson, Ivan 169, 173, 178, 181
O'Neill, Steve 181, 182, 185
O'Toole, Marty 79, 82, 103, 107, 108, 110, 147
Overall, Orval 41, 44

Paige, Satchel 215, 216, 218
Paskert, Dode 73
Paulette, Eugene 188
Pearl, Kathryn 96
Pearl, Violet 96
Perritt, Bill "Pol" 155, 156, 165, 166
Peterson, Robert 215
Pfeffer, "Big Ed"Schauer, Alex 156, 164–166, 170, 174, 176, 179
Pfeister, Jack 41, 44, 51
Phalon, W.A. 127
Phillippe, Deacon 41
Pickford, Mary 220
Pius X, Pope 143
Plank, Eddie 85, 87, 92, 93, 136, 139, 140, 151
Porter, Mary 110
Pounds, L.H. 167
Powell, A.H. 196
Powers, Mike "Doc" 60
Primrose, George 97
Pulliam, Harry 47, 51

Rath, Morris 177
Raymond, Arthur "Bugs" 55, 59, 62, 112, 113
Reisner, James 136
Reulbach, Ed 41, 107, 151
Reynolds, Helen 203
Rice, Grantland 153, 165
Richmond, John Lee 20
Rigler, Charles 103, 107
Rigler, John 60
Ritter, Lawrence 209–213
Ritter, Stephen 210
Rixey, Eppa Jeptha 166, 173, 191, 209
Robertson, Dave 156
Robinson, Frank 21
Robinson, Jackie 216
Robinson, John 96
Robinson, Stanley 96
Robinson, Wilbert 21, 54, 70–72, 81, 82, 92, 94, 100, 103, 130, 144, 155, 158–160, 162, 163, 165–168,

Index

171–175, 179, 180, 182, 186, 190, 196, 209, 211
Rock, Barbara Guggenheimer 208
Rockefeller, John D. 7
Rogers, Will 97
Rooney, Mickey 203
Roosevelt, Theodore 116
Ross, Rita 150
Rothstein, Arnold 179
Roush, Edd 150, 178, 191, 209, 216
Rucker, Nap 60, 108, 110, 136, 147, 155, 156, 164, 171, 175
Rudolph, Dick 147, 149, 150, 165, 173
Ruether, Walter "Dutch" 189
Runyon, Damon 79, 163, 181
Russell, John Armstrong 175
Ruth, Babe 165, 169, 170, 172, 182, 190–192, 200, 206, 212
Ruth, Clare 216
Ruth, Julia 216
Ruth, Mamie 216

Sallee, Slim 105
Schaefer, Germany 96
Schafer, Art 106, 115, 117
Schang, Wally 138, 140, 142
Schauer, Alex 157
Schechter, Edward 206
Schlei, George 57
Schleman, Herman 13
Schulte, Wildfire 77
Schultz, Joe 157
Schumacher, Harry 105
Schupp, Ferdie 174
Scott, Everett 170
Scott, Jack 192
Scourby, Alexander 212
Seeley, Blossom 79, 100, 121–127, 129, 132, 133, 137, 141, 142, 148–151, 162, 169–172, 178, 188, 189, 195, 196, 202, 203, 208
Segar, Charles 213
Sewell, Joe 180, 181, 185
Seymour, Cy 51, 57, 60
Shafer, Tilly 138–140
Shakespeare, William 167
Shaw, Lillian 97, 98
Sheed, Wilfrid 212

Sheehan, Jack 177
Sheldon, Staley 15
Sherman, Sadie 96
Shibe, Ben 87
Shore, Ernie 168, 169, 171
Shorten, Chick 170
Siever, Ed 28, 30, 31
Simpson, Nate 98
Sinclair, Harry 161
Smith, Elmer 181, 184, 185
Smith, Frank W. 183
Smith, H.C. 53
Smith, Harry 164
Smith, Ken 220
Smith, Russ L. 213
Smith, Sherrod 164, 169, 172, 176, 182
Snodgrass, Fred 50, 60, 62, 64, 71, 73, 78, 81, 82, 86, 89–92, 105–108, 114, 115, 118, 119, 123, 129, 130, 133, 136, 138, 139, 147, 148, 156, 158
Sockalexis, Louis 21, 22
Somers, Charles 22, 23, 159, 218
Spade, Robert 34
Spaulding, Albert 137
Speaker, Tris 113–115, 118, 119, 168, 180, 181, 185, 186, 209
Spink, J.G. Taylor 216
Stack, Ed 216
Stahl, Jake 113, 114, 117, 119, 168
Stallings, George 147
Stearns, Ed 13
Steinfeldt, Harry 45
Stengel, Casey 159, 160, 163, 164, 166, 173–176, 193, 196, 214, 216
Stevens, Bob 216
Stevens, Harry M. 73
Stock, Milt 144
Stockton, Roy 213
Stone, Louis 97
Strain, Ed 216
Strunk, Amos 138
Sullivan, Cornelius J. 152
Sullivan, Ed 203
Sullivan, Joe 98
Sump, Bill 15
Sunday, Billy 136

Taft, William Howard 63, 65
Taylor, "Dummy" 42–44

TeBeau, Pat 21
Tener, John 148
Tenney, Fred 42, 45, 55, 57–59, 64, 77
Terry, Bill 200
Tesreau, Jeff 103, 105, 108, 113, 114, 116, 129–131, 137, 139, 140, 147, 154, 155, 157, 164, 174
Thomas, Ira 93
Thorpe, Jim 129, 134, 136, 143, 155, 156
Tinker, Joe 50, 51, 77, 83, 96, 150, 161, 209
Titus, John 59
Traynor, Pie 216
Tucker, Sophie 120, 208
Tulley, May 96
Twitchell, Larry 99
Tyler, Lefty 83, 147–149

Vance, Dazzy 199
Van Lengen, Mrs. William 216
VanZelst, Luis 86, 89
Vargus, Bill 197
Vaughn, Jim "Hippo" 173
Veeck, Bill 218, 219
Villa, Pancho 86
Voix, Jim 143
Vonder Horst, Harry 161

Waddell, Rube 14, 36
Wagner, Heinie 113–115
Wagner, Honus 41, 42, 53, 63, 68, 77, 78, 81, 82, 107, 111, 134, 143, 166, 173, 200, 206
Walker, Otto 168, 170
Wambsganss, Bill 181, 184, 185
Ward, Chuck 174, 176
Ward, John Montgomery 60, 152, 154
Ward, Robert B. 150, 151
Warner, Jack 105
Warner, Kay 203, 208
Washington, George 131, 162
Watkins, W.H. 27, 29–31
Weimer, Jake 34
Weiss, George 214, 219
West, Mae 120
Whalen, John 108
Wheat, Zack 155, 156, 159, 169, 170, 179, 181, 209, 216

Wheegman, Charles 161
Wheeler, John 86
White, Doc 96
Whitted, Possom 132
Wilhelm, Irvin "Kaiser" 59
Williams, Joe 178, 209
William, Ted 212, 215
Wilson, Alf 96
Wilson, Art 103, 115, 131
Wilson, John 107
Wilson, Pete 33
Wilson, Woodrow 176
Wiltse, George "Hooks" 33, 34, 47, 53, 60, 62, 65, 67, 76, 92, 93, 139, 140, 151
Wood, Smoky Joe 110, 114–118, 168, 169, 181, 211
Woods, Doc 207
Yerkes, Steve 113, 115, 118
Young, Denton True "Cy" 21, 191, 193
Young, Dick 215
Youngs, Ross 180

Zimmerman, Henry "Heinie" 77, 146, 174

www.ingramcontent.com/pod-product-compliance
Ingram Content Group UK Ltd.
Pitfield, Milton Keynes, MK11 3LW, UK
UKHW041935140426
5217IPUK00014B/486